Pornography, the Theory

Pornography, the Theory   **What Utilitarianism Did to Action**

Frances Ferguson

The University of Chicago Press

Chicago and London

Frances Ferguson is the Mary Elizabeth Garrett Professor of Arts and Sciences at The Johns Hopkins University. She is the author of *Wordsworth: Language as Counter-Spirit* and *Solitude and the Sublime: Romanticism and the Aesthetics of Individuation* and coeditor of *Misogyny, Misandry, and Misanthropy*.

The University of Chicago Press, Chicago 60637
The University of Chicago Press, Ltd., London
© 2004 by The University of Chicago
All rights reserved. Published 2004
Printed in the United States of America

13 12 11 10 09 08 07 06 05 04   1 2 3 4 5
ISBN: 0-226-24320-6 (cloth)
ISBN: 0-226-24321-4 (paper)

Library of Congress Cataloging-in-Publication Data

Ferguson, Frances, 1947–
   Pornography, the theory : what utilitarianism did to action / Frances Ferguson.
      p. cm.
Includes bibliographical references and index.
   ISBN 0-226-24320-6 (alk. paper) — ISBN 0-226-24321-4 (pbk. : alk. paper)
   1. Sex in literature.   2. Fiction—History and criticism.   I. Title.
PN3352.S48 F47 2004
809′.933538—dc22

                                          2003014560

∞ The paper used in this publication meets the minimum requirements of the American National Standard for Information Sciences—Permanence of Paper for Printed Library Materials, ANSI Z39.48-1992.

For Ruth Leys

Contents

	Preface	ix
	Acknowledgments	xix
	Introduction	1
1	Pornography, the Theory	34
2	Justine, or The Law of the Road	57
3	Eugénie, or Sade and the Pornographic Legacy	75
4	Emma, or Happiness (or Sex Work)	96
5	Connie, or The Lawrentian Woman	125
	Patrick: An Epilogue	146
	Notes	157
	Index	179

Preface

As a general rule, I am leery of writing the sort of preface that traces out the experience of thinking the various thoughts that combined to make up the book. The reader does not, I think, need or want to know where I was when a particular observation dawned on me, much less the sequence of thoughts. In this particular case, however, it seems useful to give some account of the specific situation that led me to write a book about pornography, because that process has a very material bearing on the substance of the discussions that follow. It will help to explain what might sometimes be mistaken for an absurd agnosticism on a controversial subject and indicate why, despite my general preference for a pro-pornography position, I see limitations in both the pro-pornography and anti-pornography positions. The discussions that follow do not, as most books that discuss pornography do, lay out a position that is unequivocally pro-pornography or anti-pornography, defend it to the death, and heap scorn on those who hold the opposing view. My principal motive for wanting to write about pornography was dissatisfaction with the polarization of the debate and the conviction that pornography raised issues for modernity that were not being addressed. The discussion had, I thought, become as formulaic as the so-called exchanges on political news shows in which "conservatives" and "liberals" "debate" along lines as ritualized as the wrestling matches broadcast on television. As I tried to think my way out of that impasse, I came to realize that I was talking not just about pornography but about basic techniques developed by utilitarian philosophers and practitioners that were designed to capture actions and give them extreme perceptibility.

The book's genesis was a practical situation—my colleague Ruth Leys and I had decided to teach a course on pornography that would enable us to address feminist theory, psychoanalysis, and various English and continental novels. As we were planning the course, I understood myself to be making the plans that one would make as what Catharine MacKinnon has characterized as a pro-pornography feminist: I planned to move efficiently to an account of the weaknesses of MacKinnon's position, to deride Lawrence's *Lady Chatterley's Lover* as both misogynistic and sentimental about sex. In practice, however, the teaching that I did in those particular weeks was decisive for me, because I had the experience of thinking that I saw more in these texts than I had seen before, that my opinions were changed by rereading them and trying to present them to a group of students.

Indeed, the experience of teaching that course was perhaps the most startling intellectual experience of my adult life. It was the occasion for Ruth Leys and me to have intense and productive disagreements that helped me to refine my own thinking and see how little refinement hers needed; it gave me the opportunity to be grateful for a genuine intellectual comradeship with someone from whom I was differing on many substantive points. The course also prompted me to recognize how the teaching situation itself creates the possibility of questioning even the stands that I had held—or thought that I had held. Hearing some students argue on behalf of the beneficent alchemy of literature that could convert the pain Sade describes into pleasure, hearing others worry about the relationship between domestic privacy and domestic abuse, made me aware of how much the classroom is an often-misrecognized instance of the impact of the mass media. Although students talk to their teachers and to one another, they are, in relation to the texts, reading words of mechanical manufacture and impersonal distribution, and they encounter a situation in which they cannot interact with the authors whose words they read. (Not least because most of those authors are dead.) This basic problem helped me to appreciate the ways in which pornography relies on features of literary production that have characterized the dissemination of texts from at least the time of the rise of the novel, the ways in which it intensifies what Niklas Luhmann has called the "body-to-body analogy" that enables readers to orient themselves by constant references to the bodies of persons and their movements in specific contexts while also limiting the authority of the responses of the individual reader.[1] For the power of the analogy between the bodies of readers and viewers and of fictitious or actual persons is that it triggers readers' and viewers' experiences of their own bodies in such a way as to make personal memories look like recognitions of hypothetical or fictitious experiences.

We, especially when we are literary critics, frame the problems of the classroom as problems of interpretation, but they might more productively be thought of as problems of the limitations of interpretation. Even if one were to "win" a debate with one's students about the meaning of a text, it's not clear what that victory would secure, apart from the pleasures of temporary and local agreement, temporary and local success. The agreement about the particular text would be an island of agreement in the larger circulation of competing and unexplicitated views in the mass media, in which we continually come up against our own limitations to engage thought as thought and to resolve our actions and perceptions into statements of belief. The very fact of my changing my views about at least parts of MacKinnon's argument and all of Lawrence's most famous novel prompted me to rethink what it means to have a position, take a stand, and urge that on other people. One model for changes in the ideas we think we live by is the Pauline one of conversion: I was once blind but now I see. The conversion model aims to argue people into changing what they think and, as a consequence, what they see. Catharine MacKinnon and Andrea Dworkin's work on pornography is work of that kind. It imagines that now that they have produced arguments that ought to have cleansed our avenues of perception, we will walk around the world seeing everything in the light of our new clarity. MacKinnon and Dworkin's ambition is revolutionary in this sense, because it tries to assemble a historical narrative that will provide leverage on perception. Another, significantly contrasting model for altered perception, however, is Wittgenstein's account of Jastrow's famous duck-rabbit—the drawing that someone can plausibly see as a duck or a rabbit. Seeing the drawing as an image of a duck and then as a rabbit does not involve anything approaching a conversion—only a subtle shift of attention. Moreover, one implication of Wittgenstein's discussion of his example is that it would be more than a little absurd to act as though we could settle the question by deciding that it ought to be seen as a duck or a rabbit. Even if most people saw the image as a drawing of a duck, the matter would still not be resolved. It provides a simple, merely perceptual example of the kinds of insights that both Marx and Freud marshaled to lead us to suspect the sufficiency of our characterizations of our experience.

With twentieth-century accounts of pornography, the kind of modest but significant instability in perception and characterization that the duck-rabbit bespeaks has played itself out in the testimony of individuals about the nature of their own life experiences. Even without resorting to psychological explanation, we are all familiar with the ways in which people produce contradictory testimony about the experiences that they participate in. At one moment in her life, Linda Lovelace achieved a certain fame as a pornographic actress whom viewers might have imagined to be a happy and enthusiastic participant in *Deep Throat* and other films. At another she completely reevaluated her life during the period in which she was making pornographic films and came to see herself as having been coerced into those performances. Her view of her own experience, however, did not settle there. If we are to believe the obituary that the *New York Times* published in 2002, she subsequently went on to bask in the light of her former fame, to take great pleasure in being recognized for her earlier pornographic work. The Linda Lovelace problem helped me to see how far the problems of testimony and confession that Foucault identified (in, for instance, *I, Pierre Rivière . . .*) extend and to understand Flaubert's searching account of the difference between taking the measure of one's happiness and having reliable testimony to give about one's satisfaction in one's own experience.

What I came to see in teaching the course on pornography was not that I wanted to promote what is usually dismissively called abstract tolerance for other people's views, but that I believed the conjunction between the rise of modern democracies and the rise of pornography was significant and believed that this conjunction betokened something even more radical about modern democracies than is usually addressed—namely, the importance of what Raymond Williams called culture and what someone like John Rawls has called inevitable dissensus. In the name of cultural regulation, people characteristically treat the notion of culture as if it entails ideas and proceed to make guesses about what other people's ideas will allow them to do and to devise plans for outlawing various things that their ideas apparently now allow them to do. Williams, by contrast, looked at culture (notably in *Culture and Society, 1780–1950*)[2] as a notion that enabled one to see a larger process than that of individual arguments in salient examples of linguistic change in the nineteenth century. If words like "imagination" could come to mean something very nearly the opposite of what they had usually meant in the eighteenth century, such shifts were developing accretively, in a way that was captured—but only partially captured—by people's explicit definitions and expositions. For Williams, recognizing culture meant acknowledging paired and contrasted figures, not to capture difference as such, but to indicate the extent to which culture does not produce unequivocal winners. While a conservative like Edmund Burke might seem to have virtually cornered the market on effective political rhetoric, Williams observed, the less obviously talented William Cobbett continued to exert an influence because of the force of his intuitive sense of social injustice. Williams's account of culture could even be seen as a tolerance that people did not need to choose. Tolerance was not, for him, a matter of insisting upon a principle that would tie the hands of one's own belief; it was instead always implicit in what Williams took as an inevitability—that the very project of perfecting individual beliefs may blind one to other views but is not likely to eradicate them.

Moreover, the kind of point that Williams was trying to capture about culture is illustrated on the individual level. What poststructuralism identified as the demise of the unitary subject represents the societal analogue for individuals. Culture, on the social level, represents a notion of society and its representational resources that exceeds the various different representations that people provide for it. (It is, in that sense, democracy conceived not as a form of state government but rather as the voice of the people, a remainder that continually puts pressure on forms and apparatuses of governments.) Culture, on the individual level, is the whole that exceeds the various positions and representations that individuals take on their own experience. Individual culture, as I am describing it, is not just a term to identify self-cultivation and the self-reinforcing features of behavior in which we continually forward ourselves the way we are going. It also involves projecting something like a heuristic whole or a capacity to do more than simply take our past experience as a new rule; it is the capacity at stake in the possibility of an individual's continually changing his or her view of which particular animal appears in the duck-rabbit drawing.

From my standpoint, the political importance of Williams's notion of culture is that it suggests that democratic politics gestured toward a liberalism deeper than liberal doctrine. Implicit in the modern democratic notion of culture is not just an insight into the inadequacy of a particular view but the inadequacy of particular views as such to achieve dominance and effectively silence the views they contravene. If Mill's discussion of liberalism includes the recommendation that we had best tolerate the doctrines and inconsistencies of other people, the modern unpacking of that notion shifts that view considerably. The modern democratic notion of culture involves freeing all of us from the requirement that we describe ourselves in terms of our beliefs and doctrines, and from the illusion that we can successfully drive out opposed beliefs and perfect the view of the world or of ourselves. As Jacques Rancière has argued, modern democracy suggests that there are more people in any society than our institutional representations can acknowledge. And as both Lacanian and deconstructive criticism have argued, there is more to all of us than our self-representations can acknowledge.

The revival of pornography in the late eighteenth century, I began to see, involved biopolitics in a fuller sense than that we have usually appreciated in adopting Foucault's use of the term, because pornography was not routing its claims through beliefs—however affectively intense—but rather through descriptions of actions. Catharine MacKinnon defines pornography as "the graphic sexually explicit subordination of women, whether in pictures or in words," and goes on to specify some examples in the ordinances that she and Andrea Dworkin drafted for Minneapolis, Indianapolis, and other cities.[3] Yet critics have repeatedly faulted her account of pornography as a civil harm and have argued that, even while she distinguishes her position from the obscenity approach (which would attack socially unacceptable images), the objects under attack in the ordinances cannot really be distinguished from the socially unacceptable. She goes on to provide comfort for their views by referring to our culture as a culture made by pornography. For her, that assertion makes it possible to see why people are not alert to the harms that they ought to be seeing: the culture of pornography effectively brainwashes individuals, she thinks, leaving them inured to the forms of injustice that pornography generates and sustains. MacKinnon's view returns us to the model of interpretation of beliefs, so that the harm of pornography is ultimately in its disseminating views—albeit through intensely corporeal appeals.

This study represents my earnest effort to describe the profound importance of utilitarian thinking, as epitomized in the work of Jeremy Bentham, for moving away from the interpretative model and offering ways of capturing the importance of actions that are not always resolvable into statements of belief. Pornography, I argue, works in the same way that many other features of modern organized social life do. It, like lists of the ten or twenty or one hundred "best of . . . ," like scores of athletic games, intensively uses comparison and displays relative value to create extreme perceptibility. In the process, it sets aside or minimizes the place of individual beliefs and emotions as explanations for what we have done and what we will do. The action that a sports team performs in winning a game is not, in the utilitarian view, a matter of their spirit or heart, because attitude disappears in the score, which makes their victory as much a matter of their opponents as themselves. The action that I undertake in going to one of the "ten best restaurants" in New York is not one that has an oblique relationship to beliefs and opinions. That aspect of the utilitarianism of everyday life and the perception of Sadean pornography's interconnection with it is what led me to doubt MacKinnon's account of pornography as an expression and producer of beliefs about women.

The question that I have tried to take seriously in the chapters that follow is, what do specific texts from various periods say about the conditions of cultural production that enabled pornography to reemerge in modern Western societies in the late eighteenth century? Where MacKinnon imagines that we can retire certain texts or images because they have been used for discrimination against identifiable persons, I take the central problem of pornography to revolve around its participation in the larger cultural project of trying to identify the increased importance of action in modernity. Pornography, in my view, did not develop and flourish as the private practice of libertines who sought to create a world of private despotism. Instead, it directly participated in various highly public social systems that gave a shape to what might otherwise be the impalpability of action itself. Pornography is not, I argue, by any means unique in pointing to individuals in terms of use. It is part of an array of systematic social practices that have made it possible for us to evaluate individuals by making their actions look as though they could plausibly be described in terms of their perceptibility and value in public. The most general of these was the rise of wages based on work. The most specific was the kind of utilitarian social device of providing artificial social systems for education and work that Bentham outlined in his Chrestomathic and Panopticon writings, with their effort continually to compare individual actions with one another and to create hierarchies of value in the process. Pornography, like Bentham's Panopticon, was central in moving politics from a way of representing property rights to a way of capturing the importance of actions, and of using the social group as a way of establishing a relative value for individual actions. The utilitarian perspective of both Sade and Bentham moved discussion from individual identities to actions and highlighted the uses that even fictitious representations came to have in encouraging people to feel that they can *see* actions, which are by their very nature less conspicuous than persons themselves. In utilitarian systems, power does not simply, as Foucault puts it, come from everywhere as a contribution of all the participants in a social group.[4] It is also continually being redistributed. If this insight made me suspicious of MacKinnon's tendency to use the language of utilitarianism to point out (rightly) that pornography might consist in actions rather than ideas and then (wrongly) to convert that insight into an identity claim (pornography is always action), I also came to see that questions of justice and truth, intractable as a series of statements about how the world is, had some purchase in relation to utilitarian social structures that both Sade and Bentham, to very different effect, treated as necessary devices for capturing the value of individuals. Sade imagined that his pornographic hierarchies would provide continuing grounds for acknowledging the eliteness of the elite. Bentham thought that his highly articulated ways of capturing actions by displaying them and their relative value in and to a group would make it possible to identify otherwise imperceptible merit and to thereby create a new meritocratic elite. Both minimized the place of worldviews and individual character, and instead tried to give palpable form to the ways in which actions regularly gave groups techniques for valuing individuals that did not rest on the abstract awarding of theoretical rights.

Once I appreciated the importance of the artificial social structures of Sadean pornography and the Benthamite Panopticon, I came to think that MacKinnon did have a point when she imagined that pornography might be used to deny an individual access to the value-enhancing activities of such artificial social structures as the workplace and the school. Both the social systems that Sade regularly convened and dismantled in the name of pornography and the social structures that Bentham and other reform-minded educators and legal thinkers developed recognized the force of modern social systems and that such systems did not simply produce and reproduce opinions, but also yielded perceptions and evaluations that were not completely guided by those opinions. For the crucial insight behind the modern utilitarian social systems that both Sade and Bentham devised was that it was inadequate to look to beliefs in order to explain and predict what people would do, and that it was also inadequate to try to derive people's beliefs from their actions. Instead, they focused on the contributions of social systems in enabling people to act without benefit of belief and without continually feeling compelled to regard their actions with the suspicion that Marx and Freud urged on us. These social systems, in their violent Sadean mode and in their seamlessly bureaucratic efficiency in Bentham, came to achieve their importance, I began to think, because they introduced information, as opposed to knowledge, into the social world. These social systems did nothing to fill in the void at the core of societies of the general will like those Rousseau identified, did not make it possible for individuals to locate large-scale truths about the world or where they stood in it. Yet the very limitations of these systems, their rigid constraint on the range of possible actions, enabled individuals and social groups to see value as more than just a matter of individual preference and election. They were social media. And like the mass media of print and broadcasting, they answered the question of knowledge in societies of the general will by sidestepping it, offering themselves as a substitute and supplement that would enable people to replace questions of the truthfulness of their knowledge of the world with the regular experience of information about where they stood here and now, in this or that particular group.

To appreciate this point is to begin to understand how far our most common understandings of Foucault's account of Bentham's Panopticism misstate the place of utilitarian social structures, which continually attach us to an evanescent but dynamic world by providing us with news, giving us information. For utilitarian social structures did not—do not—debar us from access to knowledge that we might, but for coercion, freely experience. Instead, they create an economy of experiential information, in which we bracket the question of the absolute truth or reality of our perceptions and see the importance of these social media in making information—not just news but news as repeated displays of value—render our experiences in terms of constant reports.

Acknowledgments

When I began writing this book on pornography, one of my friends told me in very matter-of-fact tones, "People will think you're strange." I was thus prepared for various forms of skepticism. What I was unprepared for was tolerance verging on generosity for some of my arguments about the deep links between the rise of pornography and aspects of modernity that are both uncensored and insistently public. I am especially grateful to a variety of audiences for having given me a hearing: the English Seminar of the University of Zurich; the Conference of Women Historians; the Townsend Center of the University of California, Berkeley; the Dickens Project of the University of California; the English department of Tel Aviv University; the University of Massachusetts, Amherst; the School for Criticism and Theory; the English department of the State University of New York at Buffalo; the English department of the University of California, Berkeley; the French department of Johns Hopkins; the English department of Duke University; the English department of the University of California, Santa Barbara; and the English department of Washington College. Mandy Merck, Linda Williams, Bernard Williams, and Robert Post all offered useful comments and challenges to various features of my argument at various stages of its development. My colleagues in the English department at Johns Hopkins—Amanda Anderson, Sharon Cameron, Jerome Christensen, Simon During, Avrom Fleishman, Jonathan Goldberg, Allen Grossman, John Guillory, Richard Halpern, Walter Benn Michaels, Michael Moon, Ronald Paulson, John Plotz, Mary Poovey, Robert Reid-Pharr, Sasha Torres, Irene Tucker, and Larzer Ziff—have been extraordinary interlocutors over many years. I am perhaps most grateful to have had a host of readers and friends who have given me the courage to be thought strange: Lauren Berlant, Leo Bersani, Bill Brown, Judith Butler, James Chandler, Carol Clover, Arnold Davidson,

Catherine Gallagher, Stephen Greenblatt, Bob Griffin, Miriam Hansen, Elizabeth Helsinger, Neil Hertz, Carla Hesse, Ian Hunter, Laura Kipnis, Tom Laqueur, Françoise Meltzer, Tom Mitchell, Stephen Nichols, Zephyra Porat, Giulia Sissa, Gabriel Spiegel, Susan Varney, and Hana Wirth-Nesher. Diane Knapp, Steven Knapp, Julia Strand, Michael Fried, and Ruth Leys know how instrumental they have been in the production of this book, and Barbara Packer and Geoffrey Hartman should be told that they have been sustaining presences in my thought. I am especially grateful to my stepdaughter, Becky Michaels, and my son, Sascha Michaels, for being exactly who they are. Alan Thomas has been as serious and helpful in his role as editor as any author could wish. He read the manuscript shrewdly and knew how to inspire similar shrewdness in acute and helpful readers for the University of Chicago Press. Erin DeWitt has repeatedly demonstrated how copyediting may be practiced as a fine art.

Randy Newman has a song in which the singer describes himself telling his girlfriend not to talk to strangers, only to be told in reply, "I'll talk to strangers if I want to, because I'm a stranger too." Sometimes one does not have to be a Russian formalist and to have a theory about the value of defamiliarization to experience the pleasure of recognizing that intellectual work enables us to be strangers too.

Introduction

In this study I advance the argument that pornography is one among an array of practices that developed with modern utilitarianism, which has accustomed us to evaluate actions in a relative way and to see them as the output of a system rather than of an individual intention or agent. Although Foucault suggested, several decades ago, that Bentham's Panoptic structures made relative values effective by assembling groups of persons and making their relative standings visible, the importance of this insight has, I argue, been largely unexplored. Instead, Foucauldian critics have largely adopted a now-familiar account of utilitarianism, namely, that it subordinates the interests of the individual to those of the social and collective, and have thus revived a notion of shadowy collective agency as an antagonist to individuals.

By contrast, I try to present utilitarianism (particularly as represented by the work of Jeremy Bentham) as significant for introducing an account of objectification and perceptibility that tries to capture the notion of use. Utilitarian social structures were crucial, I argue, in directing attention to actions and to lending a sense of perceptible value to acts that might otherwise seem impalpable. In modernity, utilitarianism has made it possible for us to imagine that persons can act, and act minutely, without seeing action only in the epic terms that recruited two nations to war in the *Iliad* so as to make anger over adultery look perceptible.

While Catharine MacKinnon represents pornography as reprehensible because it is an objectification of sex and an occasion in which some are subordinated to the uses of others, I try to represent utilitarian social structures from within and to take seriously Bentham's arguments for the importance of minimizing one's epistemological and metaphysical claims. Thus, while MacKinnon describes pornography in utilitarian terms when she claims that pornography is what it does, her account of utilitarianism is overwhelmingly negative. I argue, by contrast, that an appreciation for utilitarian perspectives provides the strongest argument for identifying the real but extremely limited situation in which pornography might be plausibly described as harmful: the case of sexual harassment. MacKinnon wrongly obliges herself to produce an account with heavy epistemic burdens and an entirely nonsensical claim on behalf of women's knowledge, when in fact the possibility of finding fault with pornography derives from the possibility that pornography might be used for purposes of sexual harassment and thus deprive individuals of access to the value-enhancing aspects of utilitarian social structures such as the school and the workplace. In other words, while MacKinnon wants to treat the notion of use as if it had existence, I argue that the importance of utilitarian social structures is that they bypass questions of what there actually is and how fully individuals need to be believed and acknowledged by others. Instead, utilitarianism, by emphasizing the importance of evaluating actions in relation to others and through others, makes the perception of value more significant than the perception of essences and identities. In so doing, utilitarianism has helped to restrict the reach of belief—since individuals operating within the orbit of their structures did not have to provide a strong doctrinal justification for their actions—and also to free individuals from both self-knowledge and self-advocacy. Persons did not need, within the context of these utilitarian social structures, to believe in themselves and require that others acknowledge the legitimacy of that belief. Instead, an objective procedure for analyzing the social group and redistributing the power of the social group, in serial fashion, to individuals created the possibility for a new form of social recognition, one that was not based in either property or a strong account of personal character. Bentham developed these social structures, I argue, to capture the possibility that the relative value of individuals' actions might be variable and open to display—to each and every participant in the artificial social groups that they temporarily occupied.

In the pages that follow, I will be addressing the question of pornography—or rather, the conditions of the possibility of pornography. When the use of the word "pornography" was revived in the late eighteenth century and pornography came to be distinguished from erotica, I will argue, the content of pornography became less and less important and the development of a context (or environment) that amounts to a representational technology assumed center stage. This process is largely a by-product of the rise of the utilitarian social structures developed by philosophers like Jeremy Bentham, educators like Andrew Bell in India and Joseph Lancaster in England and America, and social engineers like Charles Fourier in France.[1] These social structures, which mainly took the form of classrooms and workhouses, constituted a representational device for uniting members of a group in a common activity and evaluating their relative performance at that common activity—so that even words might become actions, and evaluations might be, for a brief time and in a limited space, objective. In the utilitarian perspective, what Bentham called publicity and what we call publicness was crucial to a modern objectification of learning and working: an action unseen was a contradiction in terms under the new dispensation of evaluating action by output and observable behavior. Facts were collapsed into values, or rather the most factual aspect of an action was its displayed value.

Utilitarianism prepared the way for pornography not merely by saying that it was less concerned with what things were than with what they were used for. Its practitioners articulated specific social structures that enabled them to identify the moments in which speech might count as action (which is not the same thing as an individual exertion of the will to make words be "performatives").[2] Utilitarian social structures tried to analyze an entire group in serial fashion, to coax action from individuals. Just as Bentham originated the concept of "sentence meaning" in his *Theory of Fictions* to capture the pressure that an ensemble of words puts on individual words, so he laid out plans for analyzing how social ensembles and the individuals who composed them interacted.[3] If he imagined that it was impossible to know the meaning of a word unless one used it in a sentence, he also imagined that it was impossible to know the value of actions without seeing how they related to the operation of a larger social group. In his Panopticon writings, he devised plans in which he treated the overall environment as if it were the equivalent of a sentence and the individual persons in it as if they were the equivalents of individual words. Just as the sentence as a whole made it possible to say if a word served as a noun or a verb, Bentham thought, these concrete transcendental structures would make it possible to see the value of individual actions in classrooms and workhouses and to reward them with public recognition.

Such utilitarian social structures powerfully abetted upward social mobility. Yet it is safe to say that they did so less by expressing personal ambition than by provoking it. Indeed, the remarkable aspect of these social structures was that their functioning was indifferent to the memories, anticipations, and beliefs that persons frequently define themselves by. Rigorously oriented to the immediate present, utilitarian social structures were developed to be environments that would elicit actions from individuals by making persons visible to one another, by creating artificial groupings that made individuals feel their "propinquity" in time and space. Coherence, such as it was, lay with the social structure, not the person. Persons might be assumed to have coherence or character outside of a particular situation, but for the purposes of the social structures, they were dissolved into actions. The value of a particular individual's action depended as much on which group they were participating in as on the exact nature of their performance. In the new utilitarian social structures, therefore, both the performance and the evaluation of individual acts could occur without benefit of doctrine, personal zeal, and favoritism. Instead, motivation could come to individuals nearly wordlessly—without traveling the route of homilies and injunctions. Motivations were, in Bentham's treatment, made physical; they were by-products of the environment, rather than independent expressions of a metaphysical notion like being or individual will.

In their positive aspect, the utilitarian social structures attempted to objectify even such customarily ineffable things as evaluations, because Bentham thought that evaluations themselves were not simply subjective. He took them to be objective insofar as they were shared and shareable, and thought that their usefulness lay in such objectivity and shareability. The palpable sense that someone had social regard made it possible for social regard to become a reward, an incentive. In creating techniques for objectification, he was developing a position that is not unrelated to Donald Davidson's—that objectivity involves claiming that external objects are the cause of our beliefs about them and that the human interaction between "at least two speaker-interpreters" is importantly bound up with an individual's "claiming that he could locate objects in an objective space and time."[4] In Bentham's view, utilitarian social structures made it possible to speak in even more narrowly particularized terms than Davidson employs of beliefs that were caused rather than merely chosen. Someone from one of his Chrestomathic schools would have been able to say that the cause of her belief that Susie was the best student at arithmetic was that the public and oral examination in arithmetic had shown Susie to be first in the class. Bentham imagined that the benefit of increasing the number of beliefs that were attached to objective causes was that the perceptibility of objectified actions, combined with the perceptibility of their evaluation in a perceptible social group, might have greater weight for people than beliefs that could never be objectified. Indeed, he thought that his objectifying structures might perform important work in getting people to see that they believed Susie was the best at arithmetic, even when they might, as "good" Englishmen, have said in advance of the examination that Susie, being Catholic, was unlikely to have the moral or mental capacity to do arithmetic well. From his standpoint, the way around prejudice did not involve arguing against the prejudice (and, for instance, explaining that Catholics are not really the way the "good" Englishman thought they were). Instead, prejudice would be combated simply by rendering it irrelevant by providing something more persuasive than argument: what one saw people do would replace what one might expect people to do. In the oral and public examination, Susie's performance was something one believed because one saw it. In addition, it cemented the social group by providing objectifications that everyone saw.

Yet if I have been arguing that Benthamite utilitarianism saw and tried to manifest the advantage of enabling persons to act without having to develop strong doctrines and motivations as solitary thinkers, I should also acknowledge that commentators from Mill and Marx onward have drawn out the negative implications of Benthamite utilitarianism: that individuals, in coming to have perceptible value within the action of a group, are fragmented, so that their biographies begin to look like the multiple entries for words in a dictionary. The individual whose value is confirmed by the objective evaluation of a particular social environment at a particular moment may be granted a perspicuous value then and there, but he or she has no existence independent of that environment. Being is not merely postponed. It ceases to be an available notion. What Mill called "character" is omitted (whether because it is assumed or dismissed), and what Marx gestured toward as a whole life in his rhapsodic conclusion to *The German Ideology* seems insufficiently acknowledged by Bentham's world-producing objectifications.

The chapters of this study use various literary examples—novels by Sade, Flaubert, Lawrence, and Bret Easton Ellis—to trace the history of the process of utilitarian objectification and to provide a genealogy for Catharine MacKinnon and Andrea Dworkin's contemporary critique of pornography. All of those examples, it is safe to say, participate in the utilitarian reexamination of actions and identities. They—like MacKinnon and Dworkin's view of pornography, which claims that "pornography is what pornography does"—describe persons and objects in terms of what they do.[5] Yet the point of including the literary examples is not simply to produce a history of objectification that will focus on action, only to recuperate the notion of existence by arguing that women's use comes to be their existence (as I think MacKinnon and Dworkin do). It is also to look at the types of critique that novels offer utilitarianism and their effectiveness in challenging it. (MacKinnon is, I argue, most effective in explaining the injury of pornography when she links pornography to the question of access to the modern spaces—classrooms and workplaces—that most nearly resemble Benthamite social structures in their claims to offer advantages to the individuals who participate in them.)

Sade, in the reading that I advance of him, is not only first to apply the epithet "pornographer" to himself in the modern era. He also helps to capture the utilitarian emphasis on restricting time and space in organizing groups of persons and having them both act and rank themselves simultaneously. His novels are the first to point to the strong links between utilitarian representational techniques and pornography. In *Justine* he treats tort law as the first formalization of utilitarian social structures, suggesting how even persons who may not know one another may become linked by action, how action may be seen in the objective terms of a law of consequences, and how personal ties may cease to be compelling. In *The Philosophy in the Bedroom* he treats sex between persons of different generations as if it made them contemporaries of one another, as if the confines of the bedroom emblematized the utilitarian device of simply collecting individuals and evaluating them in the context of the group while ignoring such personal attributes as age, height, weight, and the like.

Sade is an enthusiastic proponent of the utilitarian project of replacing metaphysical notions with physical environments, and he is thus content to write novels that are profoundly episodic, in which characters are delivered from one environment to another to be dealt with as the new context will. With Flaubert, however, the cost of the utilitarian approach to action becomes more apparent. Even as Flaubert presents utilitarian social structures without moralizing comment, he focuses on the dissolution of an individual character, Emma Bovary, into episodes—the adolescent with religious idealism, the adulteress, the exceptionally good wife, the ambitious wife of a surgeon. And he stresses the ways in which the objectification of action can make even one's own action seem as if it comes from elsewhere (which it in some sense does, in relying on other people to be completed in recognition). Action, in his presentation, is not synonymous with accomplishment, but with the alternation between longing and nostalgia—as if the really important version of something for a character to do could only arrive from afar, as if it were an unanticipated check or set of instructions that came in the mail.

Lawrence, in his *Lady Chatterley's Lover,* provides a contrasting example by presenting a character who seems designed to illustrate that sex has become as important as class. Although Lawrence revisits many of the accounts about property that loom large in Sade's *Justine* and *Philosophy in the Bedroom,* he depicts Connie's choice of Mellors and his sexuality over the heritable property that Clifford Chatterley represents to identify a moment in which sex counts as a motive stronger than the lure of property and class. The explicitness of the descriptions of particular sex acts may be scarcely greater than that of many classic novels, but Lawrence mounts an explicit defense of sex as a serious motive by enabling it to override the claims of class interest. And if Lawrence writes *Lady Chatterley's Lover* to demonstrate the power of sex, Bret Easton Ellis sets up *American Psycho* to represent its failure in a world that is so commodified and objectified that it can no longer retain a shape for its environments and a profile for its persons. For the story of the novel's protagonist Patrick Bateman is that of someone who responds so quickly to the slightest motivations that he becomes unrecognizable, invisible not because he isn't physically there but because most of the people who think they know him call him by the names of various other people. Bateman may go unpunished, since no one believes that he killed all the people he killed, but he is not in need of the conscience that he so conspicuously lacks. For he represents the moment at which the utilitarian conception of actions and recognition lose their capacity to benefit individuals.

Pornography, in our most common general understanding of the word, is a sexually explicit representation. It may be viewed in public, but it must, we think, be basically a private matter, because the responses to pornography vary widely. Some pornography may be arousing to some and may assist masturbation or serve as what is known as a "marital aid"—with or without the benefit of marriage. Other people may find that same pornography distasteful or boring. Many of our customary ways of dealing with this variety of responses involve saying that pornography is a matter of opinion. Sometimes we even register a certain amusement at the legal efforts to identify lines that pornography is said to have crossed—and quote Justice Potter Stewart's remark that he doesn't know what pornography is but knows it when he sees it, as if it represented an inexplicable and naive confidence in his—or anyone's—powers of discernment.[6] The effort of this study is to argue for the seriousness of Justice Stewart's famous observation and to say how one can *evaluate* instances of pornography with some confidence *even when one cannot produce a particularly good definition of it*. Stewart's remark is justly famous because it anticipates and confutes a view that many people are content to repeat endlessly, that the variability of the "meaning" of pornography is so great that one can never hazard any account of how it functions in a specific situation, that the variation in responses to pornography means that all responses are "opinions" on an equal footing. Some argue that there can be no regulation of pornography because we might find the Song of Songs or medical textbooks banned under those regulations and contend that they might conceivably be taken as sexually explicit appeals to prurient interest. There are, they say, always the weak-minded, the fundamentalist, and the provincial to worry about. Stewart, however, *assumes* that the difficulty with a definition of pornography is that many things that could exemplify the definition scarcely seem pornographic. He thus shifts the burden of his discussion from definitions that would enable us to pick out objects that we had never seen before to the issue of what it means to recognize something *less because of what it is than because of what it does in a particular situation.*

Stewart's remark makes it clear that we are likelier to learn something about "prevailing community standards" from seeing what counts as pornographic for those communities than we are to identify examples of pornography by announcing what "prevailing community standards" are. His view amounts, I think, to recognizing that judgments of objects like pornography are *not really descriptions of objects but descriptions of objects in context.* He thus shifts the question. No longer does one have to worry whether statements can be made about the value and use of pornography in the absence of universal agreement about it—any more than one has to worry about whether the use of a word is grammatical in a particular sentence even if it would not be grammatical in all possible sentences, or if it made sense in one phrase even while it wouldn't have in another.

In this study I follow Stewart's lead in advancing an argument against the view that the law should not try to regulate anything that produces less than universal agreement. Since it is difficult to think of anything—even an action like murder—that produces such agreement, proponents of the view that you can never tell what anyone might have done with pornography are left with a libertarianism that endorses privacy, and a privacy that is, ultimately, at the expense of the less powerful members of private communities (in particular, couples and families). In addition, I argue against one way of understanding the rationale for appealing to "prevailing community standards." To its detractors, reliance on "prevailing community standards" looks like an attempt to treat majoritarian views as if they were an adequate substitute for universal agreement. For them, the appeal to "prevailing community standards" thus looks like a simple recapitulation of the debate over the interpretation of pornography—only now ratcheted down, so that any forcibly advanced interpretation can be claimed as an authoritative representation of "community standards."[7] Stewart's remark, however, cuts another way. It calls attention to the notion that people actually respond to pornography as offensive or abusive or pleasurable or arousing not because they have a settled view about everything that someone might want to call pornography, but because they are responding to a particular case, to the way in which a representation works within a given social field. And this process does not revolve around generalizing about either pornographic objects or community standards. Stewart essentially says of pornography that "you have to be there," that this is a situation in which acquaintance—our actual experience—takes precedence over description—a report from someone else.

It is, of course, true that even descriptions rely on there being a social world in which they can be apprehended, so that it makes sense to speak of the "ductility" and "metallic properties" of gold to someone who can recognize gold in those terms. Pornographic representations, however, have an even greater reliance on a social field, because they are not oriented toward statements of existence that can be broken down into attributes capable of being described. Instead, pornographic representations foreground a process in which evaluation is as important as description; pornographic representations continually have an orientation toward society—even if only a virtual or imagined society. What is pornographic about pornography, I maintain, is less what it presents than the relative actions and relative assessments it offers of the various parties to it. Pornography offers more a social evaluation than an evaluation of an object.

Justice Stewart's position acknowledges the importance of thinking about representations, not as sets of words or images that might be displayed or uttered without any context, but as expressions that define and are defined by a social field. Like the ancient division of rhetoric into high, middle, and low styles directed at more and less learned audiences, his position includes the sense that "decorum" does not involve a simple appeal to propriety. Instead, it embraces the notion that one's words and one's meanings are crucially inflected by one's consciousness of their audience or addressee—so that it is not a sign of dishonesty to say different things to one's partner and to one's children, to strangers and to intimates. Those differences of diction and phrasing are, rather, a way of acknowledging that we are saying different things when we use the same words to different audiences. The classic device of ribald humor is to displace the responsibility for an utterance from the author or speaker to the audience, as if to suggest that hearers are equally complicit in the joke. That approach imagines that everyone who is party to the words is equally part of a community created by them. Yet the question Stewart's remark raises is one that engages me throughout this study: Are there representations that can be shown to have a differential impact on the various parties to them? Or is it less useful to complain of the oppressiveness of social opinion about propriety and impropriety than to identify the different relationships to power implicit in those representations? If both rich and poor have what Hugo derisively called a choice to sleep beneath the bridges of Paris, are there similar problems of choice that attach to the relative positions of participants in pornography (or "hate speech" or a host of similar linguistic activities)?

For many people, a statement about the importance of the difference in audiences will sound like a call for an age-coordinated television- and movie-rating system or censorship—or both. It may also sound like advocacy of paternalism toward children and, perhaps, women, or like political correctness that tries to police thought. Yet the discussions that appear in the succeeding pages should give no comfort to either paternalism or political correctness. The approach I am pursuing in this study addresses pornography by trying to understand the difficulties with identifying the meaning of pornographic texts as censorship law has historically tried to do. This difficulty stems, I think, from the fact that censorship laws end up describing images that don't really exist—representations without audiences, without social fields. In other words, censorship laws end up addressing content as if there could be meaningful content that were not addressed to persons. In addition, censorship laws compound their mistaken search for meaning without social fields by treating the audience itself as a version of content, since they imagine the audience as a simple generalization of a set of concepts—the susceptible young person, the mature adult.

In this study I proceed from the assumption that pornography must be addressed from the other way around—that pornography should not be seen as representations of context-free concepts being presented to persons who are themselves representatives of context-free categories and concepts. Indeed, I argue that it is a notable fact about pornography that it is hard to identify it with ideas that can be paraphrased or summarized. My view is not unfamiliar. Bernard Williams, in writing the *Report of the Committee on Obscenity and Film Censorship,* points to the difficulty of seeing pornography in terms of ideas, even as he provides an impressive reprise of John Stuart Mill's classic defense of the importance of the free circulation of thought in the marketplace of ideas: "Mill's notion was that the truth would emerge 'by a form of natural selection,'" he writes, and that coercion of thought is not appropriate because "human beings have no infallible source of knowledge about human nature or how human affairs may develop, and do not know in advance what arrangements of forms of life may make people happy or enable them to be . . . original, tolerant, and uncowed individuals."

Yet, Williams continues,

if the "survival of the true" notion applies to anything, it applies to publications which indeed contain *ideas,* which may be true or false. It can be extended more widely—to works of serious literature, for instance. . . . It is hard to see, however, how the argument can be extended to everything that is published. In particular it is hard to see how it applies to such things as standard photographic pornography, and we find it a rather ironical comment on the survival power of good ideas that some submissions to us have put forward in defense of the most vacant and inexpressive pornographic material the formulations which Mill hoped would assist in furthering ". . . the permanent interests of man as a progressive being."[8]

Pornography looks ill suited to defense in terms of free speech, as Williams says, because the notion of free speech was devised to create a space for ideas that could be debated and evaluated in terms of their truth. And it is an important feature of pornography that it is not particularly committed even to its own ideas. Whether pornography is as filled with thinking as Sade's works are or as empty of it as *Debbie Does Dallas,* it does not aim to reach its audience by getting the members of that audience to agree or disagree with its ideas. The judicial language of "redeeming" intellectual or artistic "content" makes it seem as if pornography can slough off its less seemly aspects if it enlists ideas or artistic accomplishment. Yet to demand ideas and artistic beauty of pornography is to miss its particular claim on our attention as part of a constellation of efforts to talk about actions that do not rest on propositions that can be stated or content that can be paraphrased.[9]

To ask not what pornography lacks but what it accomplishes is to begin to see that it makes an important contribution, which lies not in its occasional dalliance with ideas but in representing the impact of communication without entirely paraphrasable content, messages that constitute themselves *at least as much as expressions of evaluations as of ideas.* Ideas are, by their nature, things that can be expressed in the language that individuals use, and they communicate themselves from individual to individual. While fashion may add new dimensions to their power as statements and rhetoric may introduce deviations into the statements used to express them, ideas enter the public world through the mouths of individuals. But there is a whole class of communication that can scarcely be said to be defined exclusively by individual speakers. It is the kind of utterance that J. L. Austin described in the lectures that he published as *How to Do Things with Words* when he gave instances of the "speech acts" that he called "performatives." Performatives are not, Austin maintained, utterances that can be evaluated as true or false in the way that logical or descriptive statements (which he called "constatives") can be. Performatives are, rather, utterances that manifest themselves primarily in their effects—even though those effects would seem virtually inexplicable if you were simply to focus on the words that had been pronounced. Thus, to take one of Austin's classic examples, the "I do" that a bride or groom says in a wedding ceremony amounts, from one standpoint, to two very slight words. No dictionary search would enable you to understand what had been done with them if you didn't have an entire ceremony pivoting around them and if that ceremony were not itself an expression of an enormous reservoir of social practices that were communicated in a kind of social shorthand. The number of words that are used in performatives can be minimized, because the efficacy of those words relies to an unusual degree on such highly elaborated social fields. Indeed, Austin suggested, one can infer the existence of a strong social field from seeing how much such slight utterances accomplish and can develop a sense of a social field from looking at what is necessary for such slight words as "I do" to yield the consequences that they do in a host of acts that follow on from them.[10]

To recognize a statement like "I do" as a performative is to make explicit the ways in which a social field creates a structure that captures those words and enables them to register as actions. To understand them is to see how that field gives them the value of efficacy, and how they can be utterances that are what Austin (following Bentham) called "happy" or "successful" utterances. Even when they are uttered in irony or insincerity, their acceptance in the social context is a judgment that they "work," that questions of social trust and cooperation are being engaged rather than questions of the truthfulness or falsehood of statements. Performatives are, in that sense, different from the subjective statements that reviewers pass on aesthetic objects such as poems and sculptures when they express their approval by saying that they "work." For if aesthetic judgments cannot be gainsaid (since no one can plausibly tell you that you don't like or admire a particular painting, only that they think you shouldn't), performatives rely on some interpersonal recognition of a context (so that people start questioning the plausibility of someone's fulfilling the wedding vows that they have spoken, not whether the words that they have spoken have any sense). The abbreviation and telegraphic quality of performatives is inversely related to the depth of the social field that they betoken.

Yet if the grammar of performatives involves acknowledging how much work a social field is doing to underwrite individual utterances, pornography raises a question about the ways in which social groups divide themselves. Pierre Bourdieu has, in *Distinction,* maintained that if one were to take the Kantian view, one would see individuals as expressing their freedom when they evaluate aesthetic objects, but that this freedom is more than a little suspect. Individuals, he argues, also reflexively identify themselves and their social positions in the process. Their freedom to determine what they like is their freedom to express all the ways in which their choices are determined. Under the lens of Bourdieu's reflexive sociology, individuals' evaluations become evidence of how they can be evaluated and assigned to particular socioeconomic classes. The evaluators are evaluated, in keeping with an account of class that produces an aggregated description of the apparently individual and subjective aspects of social reproduction.[11]

Another type of social evaluation, however, particularly concerns me here. Such evaluation does not so much identify individuals as examples of a general class. Rather, it relies on competition among members of a group to specify relative values for individuals performing an action as a group activity. This is a mode of social evaluation that classic utilitarian thinkers (in particular, Jeremy Bentham and, I would argue, the Marquis de Sade) developed in the late eighteenth and nineteenth centuries. In addition to identifying the values that individuals attach to statements and social fields, the classic utilitarian tradition invented powerful artificial social structures in the classroom, workhouse, and prison on the Panoptic model of mutual visibility. Those structures treat values as things that can be precisely demonstrated within the confines of a specific social group. This meant, in the first place, applying the infamous "felicific calculus" to determine whether an action was good for a smaller or a larger number of people. In the second place, however, it meant tapping into the recognition that some public actions were more beneficial, more valuable to some of their participants than others. Utilitarian social structures aimed to analyze actions in the context of a group and to give recognition to various parties to an action by arranging them in evaluative sequence. Every individual in the group might equally participate in an activity such as running or spelling or doing sums, but utilitarian social structures aimed to identify the ways in which individuals garnered different degrees of reward from their participation in those activities. The view underwriting all these social structures was that the choices open to individuals were—and should be represented as—relative. Individuals did not make choices of absolute goods, because they were seldom presented with choices of absolutes. Instead, persons were continually choosing what looked best among a rather narrowly circumscribed array, and what it meant for a choice to look rational was for it to look like a plausible choice for other people presented with the same array.

One basic claim of this study is that those social structures did indeed capture abilities in a positive and progressive fashion, that they did mine various different social groups for individuals with specific abilities. Another claim is that those social structures raised the question of justice as a basic question not just of crime and punishment but as a matter of fair recognition for individuals in the social field. *Pornography is, I argue, one of the principal examples of essentially utilitarian social structures that aim to manifest the differential value of actions to individuals and that raise questions about the justice of social recognition.* It is not surprising that pornography frequently displays sexual activity in such a way as to assign different degrees of relative power to its participants: it indeed exaggerates such distinctions in the notion of sexual slavery and sexual sovereignty (to use Sade's term).

Most instances of pornographic hierarchization may seem as acceptable as the hierarchization of a spelling bee (with its pyramidal structure) or a baseball game (with its winning and losing teams). They may even seem like desirable affronts to our narcissistic desire always to win, always to be most highly regarded, because they involve our being able to learn from a social world of action—and even to develop the ambition to increase our skills.[12] Yet pornography, like these other hierarchizing social structures, also enables us to raise a question about when a collective action exacts too great a cost for an individual, and whether individuals should be required to continue a game or competition for the purpose of demonstrating the superiority of everyone else.

The term "pornography" was revived in the late eighteenth century (by Sade and Restif de la Bretonne), having fallen into disuse after late Roman antiquity. The etymological explanations of the term resolve it into "writing on the bodies of whores," and a writer like Andrea Dworkin associates it particularly with the actual branding of slaves. Yet even though there would be no pornography without actual bodies (if only those of its audience), actual branding is a minor subgenre in pornography. The main link between late Roman antiquity and Western modernity is that both epochs developed a full-blown account of the efficacy of social structures. Roman legions, like the organized classrooms, workhouses, and prisons that were planned in the late eighteenth century, aimed to augment the power of individuals by systematically harnessing their physical proximity to other individuals. And Roman legions, like the Prussian and Napoleonic legions modeled on them in the eighteenth and nineteenth centuries, undertook not just to collect numbers of soldiers but to strengthen them by putting them into formation. Such organized structures sought to influence the behavior of persons by relying on their individual capacities for reason—what would strike them as plausible to do in simply employing their own wits—and also by supplementing their individual reasonable judgments with a rationalized account of the group.

Social formations—in ancient Rome, as in Western modernity—are, in other words, importantly distinct from crowds. The insight that modern social systems capture from ancient Rome is the importance of an artificial representation of a group. Since social formations have no heart or brain of their own, the conception of a group as a group has the effect of manufacturing a perceptible body for an otherwise impalpable abstraction. (Along these lines, Bentham maintained that Rousseau's notion of the "social contract" could not be connected with a sensible meaning, and one can see his experiments with social structures as an effort to replace a metaphysical account of the general will with a physical account of how the preferences of a group might visit themselves on individuals.) What utilitarian thinkers like Bentham sought to do was not to produce a purely metaphorical body, but rather to *give social groups the means to make themselves felt by individuals.* Such representations, he thought, must present the artificial reason that they embody in strongly perceptible terms. They must promulgate order—but, more, visible order. They must create perceptibility for purely social productions—hierarchy, rank order, and social evaluation. It was the modern rediscovery of the force of such social formations that made pornography a newly available representational form in the eighteenth century and that converted talk about sex into the rationalized representations of pornography. From Sade's writings on, pornography is as distinct from sex as rationalized social structures are distinct from individual reason. Pornography does not merely recommend particular sexual experiences, as if to have its actors say, "Try this, you'll like it." It also, as is most intensely clear in Sade's writings, arranges its participants. It takes what is visible and gives it explicit value by ranking everything into good, better, best, or, in Sade's case, strong, stronger, strongest and sexy, sexier, sexiest.

The most famous twentieth-century account of social formations is that of Michel Foucault, in *Discipline and Punish.* There, Foucault coins the term "bio-power," to describe the operations of what he calls "disciplinary societies." Contrasting an older pre-Enlightenment regime of spectacular punishments with modern disciplinary structures, Foucault outlines the techniques of rationalized social formations in order to explain how they altered the movement of power. He begins his book with evocative descriptions of two strongly distinguished moments. The first is the bloody execution by drawing and quartering in 1757 of Damiens the regicide, in which torture was protracted partially by the ad hoc decisions of the various executioners. (Everything was more complicated than the executioners had anticipated. The four horses initially secured for the job of quartering Damiens were unaccustomed to drawing and needed the assistance of two more horses and a surgeon, who cut off the regicide's thighs.) The second moment, the moment of the emergence of discipline, is represented in a transcript of the rules "for the House of young prisoners in Paris" drawn up by Léon Faucher eighty years later. The rules not only described what kinds of activities the inmates had to follow—dressing, making beds, forming into work teams, praying—but also when they applied, at "six in the morning in winter and at five in summer," and what time frames they involved: "There is a five-minute interval between each drum-roll." As Foucault summarizes this contrasting pair, "We have, then, a public execution and a time-table."[13]

The first example deployed all the spectacular effects of a kind of anti-celebration to make punishment appear to follow directly and obviously on crime. It sought to put crime and punishment into a cause-and-effect relationship. Yet, as the ad hoc nature of the arrangements suggests, the parties to the execution were concerned with achieving a certain fixed goal: the death of the condemned man. The second example, less histrionic, aimed at a new kind of visibility that Foucault characterizes as constituting a new disciplinary regime. Here, the total institution preceded the individual elements of the system. Nothing could, from its perspective, be genuinely ad hoc—not so much because every outcome was planned as because the institution had no very specific aims. The timetable specified that individuals would perform certain actions at a certain time, but the point of the institution was not simply—or even primarily—to have these actions performed. Instead, the institution synchronized individual actions, so that individuals were constantly reading from the same page or eating from the same table. The importance of such techniques was that they did not require that individuals have the same, or even similar, apprehensions of the world of objects and actions. Instead, remarkably enough, the institution was aimed at distinguishing individuals from one another. The institution synchronized activities so as to create a host of occasions for comparing individuals and their actions with one another, so that it could display them in terms of their relative values. (You might know that you were trying to run a fifty-yard dash, but only the competition with the others in your heat would enable you to know your actual goal, running fifty yards faster than those others.)

Foucault's account of the rise of disciplinary societies in the late eighteenth and early nineteenth centuries gave Jeremy Bentham's Panopticon writings new celebrity. Foucault captured Bentham's interest in creating social structures that displayed the actions individuals performed and that systematized this display to make it possible to see the relative values of those actions instantaneously. Class rank showed in the seating arrangements, which were adjusted with each new instance of an exercise. A Panoptic classroom or prison made it easy for even nonperformance to become perceptible and have a value: if an entire group of persons was being commanded to display their supper dishes or their writing slates simultaneously, inaction was not merely nothing but rather became a gap or interruption in the larger action. It was delinquency, a marked failure to produce something; as such, nonparticipation became an action within the context of the larger collective action. (To put this another way, delinquency did not register as a mere decision to do something else in that moment, because the group action defined the parameters of the competitive evaluation.) As Foucault recognized, a Panoptic classroom or prison or workhouse circulated narrowly defined actions—such as spelling, adding, and dividing—through a series of persons in order to produce rank orders. In Bentham's utilitarianism, the general usefulness of learning—learning for learning's sake—was not an aim. Rather, Benthamite utilitarianism was committed to identifying who was good, who was better, and who was best at various specific and comparatively small activities. It regularly relied on a model of public examination that we retain in modern spelling bees, where a right answer enables one to continue to compete, and the rightness of one's answer is necessary but not sufficient for success. The Panoptic examination displayed not just correctness but the value of that correctness, as a person's rank in the class depended on its relation to other people's answers. The examination captured both accuracy and its relative value, its value as a relatively rare capacity. As with spelling bees today, the examination aimed to make individuals distinguishable from one another and to award one person's mistake or omission as a windfall profit to the person who had not committed any mistakes or omissions. Disciplinary social structures, in other words, provided a perceptible and justifiable hierarchy; they gave people good reasons for going to Joe to ask for the spelling of a word or for asking Mary to do sums. They were self-analyzing evaluative systems that aimed to make individuals distinctive and to reward them with what Bentham called "proportionable shares of general respect."[14]

Moreover, because these disciplinary social structures collected individuals into a group formation that was simultaneously present to all of them, their results were *available to individual perception* as statistical information about the distribution of health or disease, wealth or poverty, was not. Statistical studies require application. Indeed, they have no need to identify specific individuals as individuals, so that blind trials of drugs or diet or exercise regimens can proceed without their participants knowing what categories they fall into. By contrast, the Panoptic techniques assemble their participants into an inclusive social group and arrange them so as to eliminate the need for any question of application. You may inquire if you are part of the statistical group that might develop cancer, but you need not ask if you are second or twenty-third in your math class, because you are always being told. Students in Bentham's classic Panoptic classrooms were supposed to change seats with every academic exercise and to take their places in the seats that indicated how well they had done in the previous trial. In this way, Panoptic disciplinary systems aimed to display both fact and values, or, rather, to display the value of facts.

There is so much that is deeply and importantly true in Foucault's account of disciplinary regimes in *Discipline and Punish* that it may seem perverse to draw attention to its limitations. Yet there is a real limitation in Foucault's treatment of discipline that has blinkered most recent accounts that are indebted to his work. Briefly stated, Foucault loses track of some important claims of the utilitarianism he is tracing because he cannot let go of the notion of punishment. In the early chapters of *Discipline and Punish,* he regularly employs the words "use," "usefulness," and "utilize," as if to indicate that he knows that he is describing the utilitarian thought of the late eighteenth and early nineteenth centuries—and, of course, Bentham in particular. Yet he is drawn to talk about what happens to punishment with the waning of the old spectacular model that displays the punishment of one person as a warning to others. Citing "humanization" and a host of other possible motives for the advent of disciplinary systems, he claims that "punishment, then, will tend to become the most hidden part of the penal process" and says that "the scandal and the light are to be distributed differently; . . . the publicity has shifted to the trial, and to the sentence; the execution itself is like an additional shame that justice is ashamed to impose on the condemned man. . . ."[15]

My objection to Foucault's account here is not that it isn't true of trials and the situations in which someone—a judge or members of a jury—is asked to determine the facts of a case and whether those facts lead them to a sense of a defendant's guilt or innocence. It is, instead, that his account does not acknowledge how far such trials are distinct from the disciplinary systems that a thoroughgoing utilitarian like Bentham was devising. Foucault's description therefore tends to treat any situation in which preferences are demonstrable as if it participated equally in a process of coercion. If you found anything preferable to anything else, Foucault suggests, you were "complicit" in societal "coercion." Yet the remarkable feature of Benthamite Panoptic structures was that they sought to do away with punishment altogether. While the subtitle of Foucault's *Discipline and Punish* is *The Birth of the Prison*, Bentham would have been more likely to describe his Panoptic structures as betokening the death of the prison, as the prison came to look more like the orphanage and the school. In Bentham's view (and that of many others in the early nineteenth century), Panoptic social structures functioned as an innovation in the moral universe because they aimed to address motivation directly. Unlike moral catechisms that even Protestants like the early Kant borrowed from the Catholic tradition, Panoptic social structures did not rest on an attempt to produce a list of statements about the specific acts that a given society valued positively or negatively. Instead, Panoptic structures made social recognition itself—praise and blame, precedence or neglect—both reward and punishment. Bentham could thus be surprisingly sanguine about the idea that schoolchildren and prisoners would need no punishment, because he thought that Panoptic schools, workhouses, and prisons would enable them to see the advantage of relative advantage. Social recognition was, like the water in "the cup we all race for" at school recess, a goal for everyone. Panoptic social structures, then, acknowledged social recognition as coercive, but this coercion did not involve enforcing a legal injunction (such as "Do not commit murder") with a punishment. Benthamite coercion rested on the way Panoptic structures gave individuals in their limited artificial societies immediate motives for acting. Persuasion did not, for them, rest on debates about beliefs. Indeed, the Benthamite approach saw itself as an acknowledgment of and response to the insight that the operations of belief are limited in many aspects of life. I would even go so far as to claim that Bentham's utilitarianism represents an extension of Rousseau's and Kant's transcendentalism in this sense: Bentham attempted to provide a concrete instantiation of the abstract transcendental account of society that Rousseau and Kant had advanced by inventing Panoptic schoolrooms, workhouses, and prisons that employed a game model of examination designed to confer a number on everyone. If

Panoptic classrooms began with a random order, they aimed to provide a rational order that converted the arbitrariness of numbering into a series of statements of the relative value of each individual in the group. Indeed, Panoptic systems favored counting because they relied on the indubitability of the sequence of the series of numbers used to count. There, saying "seventeen" after hearing the numbers "one, two, three" was more like a mistake, less like a statement of an individual's right to think and say what one believed. The "coercion" lay not in the threat of punishment or social opprobrium. "Coercion" or "obedience," in Bentham's view, was not capitulation to the views of someone more powerful than oneself. It was, instead, something closer to conviction about things that it would seem strange to question.

Whereas Foucault presented Bentham's Panopticon writings on schoolrooms, workhouses, and prisons under the aspect of the prison and punishment, I emphasize Panopticism under the aspect of the schoolroom and workhouse and the temporary transparency that they sought to lend to evaluations. What Bentham and others tried to instantiate in their artificial social structures was a situation in which persons might plausibly continue the action of other persons, might respond to a request to spell "cat" or "eleemosynary" by trying to spell "cat" or "eleemosynary," might count themselves off in their turn as members of a team. Thus, though disciplinary structures were regimented, it is hard to see them as compromising individual freedom—unless we take our freedom to be compromised any time we acknowledge generally perceptible experiences. Indeed, Bentham was known as a "philosophical radical," because he thought of this regimentation as generating greater freedom rather than less. No longer would merit be judged on the basis of what family one came from or even whom one knew. Instead, Panoptic examinations made it possible for the merit of even the poor and unwashed to become apparent. It was this feature of Panoptic social structures that their great historian Elie Halévy was pointing to when he identified them as democratic but not liberal.[16] They were democratic in that they admitted all comers; not liberal in that they restricted the range of choices. For anyone acting within their framework, they were coercive, in that they provided immediate occasions for continuing a larger group action and for acknowledging the preferences that became apparent within it. For anyone carrying the stamp of the credentials they provided, they opened opportunities and access that would have been unimaginable in a strictly class-based or wealth-based society.

The basic claim of this study is that as such utilitarian social structures began their extensive development in the late eighteenth and early nineteenth centuries in western Europe, they came to embrace sex as well. They introduced something more than the familiar manuals for managing erotic life by imagining that even sexual privacy could be presented with all the publicness and explicitation that utilitarianism lent to social structures. The product of that extension is pornography as we know it. Pornography is not only a product that can be evaluated in terms of the abundant sales that mark it as a recognizable commodity to be bought and sold. It also proceeds by generating as many narrowly defined niches and subcategories as those recognizably utilitarian institutions—the competitions of county fairs and the lists of "the best."

Pornography, as I argue in the chapters that follow, does what a number of less controversial utilitarian structures do. With utilitarians like Bentham, pornographers came to make an implicit argument that neither sexuality nor learning is noteworthy for being visible, in the sense of being available to be seen. Rather, pornographers try to capture the difference between visibility and explicitness—the explicitness of value that is a statement of the values of a group. Like utilitarian social structures that attempt to search out value and convert latent value into perceptible value, pornography provides mechanisms for underscorings: it offers up not sex but the sexiness of sex. Like those other social structures, pornography responds to the sense that visibility needs emphasis to become perspicuous. Its various procedures revolve around creating an ictus, or emphasis, that converts visibility into perspicuousness. In that sense, it does not really have to do with content per se. Instead, pornography represents the attempt to capture the "sexiness" of anything that can be said to be interesting by giving it the relative weight that it has within a particular social grouping.

I will have things to say about how that ictus—that emphasis, or relative weight—is achieved in various settings and texts in the chapters that follow. But before proceeding further, I want to draw attention to an important question about the proper place of utilitarian groups. One view of the utilitarian social structures that I am describing is to say that they produce actions and evaluations but cannot themselves be evaluated. They seem, in this account, to have their force by virtue of their operating unilaterally—having an impact on persons whether those persons choose to operate within them or not. Utilitarian social structures are public for their participants, in that everyone within their reach can observe their operation. They are, however, private to those outside them, in that they are self-enclosed institutions whose assessments are not particularly meaningful outside of their parameters. They do not resort to secrecy, because their claim is that they can provide the assessments that they do only because they know how to restrict their own parameters enough to provide analyses of the relative value of the actions that they make perceptible. Yet this very self-restriction puts them outside the reach of general pronouncements: utilitarian social structures do not lend themselves to independent external scrutiny and formulations of rules.

The self-enclosure of utilitarian social structures led Foucault and many who have seen the force of his account of disciplinarity to suggest that schools and workplaces have come to resemble actual prisons, and that modern society generally has come to resemble a universal prison. And those who are anxious about the dangers of regimented social structures are not entirely mistaken. The dangers are obvious in the historical accounts of "ordinary Germans" who were prepared to commit murderous acts merely in going along and the psychological accounts of ordinary individuals who are prepared to torture other people merely on someone else's say-so. It is clearly part of the power of utilitarian regimented structures that they make values apparent by virtue of treating themselves as powerful indexes for values. While our characteristic way of talking about aesthetic judgments is to say that their value can only be indexed to single individuals, utilitarian structures encompass a number of individuals within their embrace. What people mean by saying that utilitarianism has no concern for individuals is that they evaluate individuals, whether the individuals would choose to be evaluated or not.

The question that arises, then, is whether the values that utilitarian social structures generate and make operative ought to be recognized as themselves simply beyond evaluation. Roland Barthes, in his *Sade, Fourier, Loyola*, essentially describes the self-analyzing utilitarian social structures of these three apparently improbably conjoined figures as both a problem and the solution to that problem. Recognizing these three as "Logothetes, founders of languages," Barthes calls attention to the ways in which each of these writers uses the operations of self-isolation, articulation, ordering, and theatricalization to create self-analyzing worlds like those of the utilitarian social structures I have been describing. Yet Barthes sees these writers as essentially opposed to the utilitarian tradition in that the writers create "texts" that are "objects of pleasure."[17] Thus, while he quite rightly maintains that Sade's, Fourier's, and Loyola's texts cannot be "*summarized*," he wrongly insists on a parting of the ways between these texts and utilitarianism in imagining that pleasure has nothing to do with "justice, equality, liberty" (as he says of Fourier).[18] For it is a completely utilitarian and, specifically, Benthamite view that pleasure has everything to do with "justice, equality, and liberty." In other words, Barthes characterizes the social structures of Sade,

Fourier, and Loyola as simultaneously creating their own productive rankings and energies and as standing outside that system in the moment in which they produce pleasure. Bentham, by contrast, collapses pleasure into the utilitarian scheme by proposing that our slightest actions are pleasure-oriented. If the Benthamite project is to replace metaphysical accounts of morals with utilitarian structures, the motive is not to eliminate morality *tout court* but to give morality a new language—not that of remote moral maxims but that of representations of perceptible choice. Bentham can treat "success," "happiness," and "pleasure" as synonyms because he thinks that utilitarian social systems don't so much force people into a renunciation of pleasure as make it possible for them to see their pleasures more clearly than they otherwise might do.

Yet the obvious question that arises with the explicitation of the value, or pleasure, of actions in a utilitarian social scheme is, What can be done for those who are last in the lists and least in the rankings? The Sadean universe revolves around enclosed societies from which there is no appeal; its evaluations identify pleasure only with strength and make pornography the story of the demonstration of that hierarchy. Moreover, Sade has been a particularly compelling figure for many modern thinkers who have been interested in bracketing morality because he takes that hierarchy very seriously. The modern Sadean account, that is, recuperates fixed identities for persons by arguing that society's evaluations of them were always, from the outset, evaluations of what kind of person they were and are and will always be. The evaluations of enclosed social structures are treated simply as mirrors and by-products of more general and more enduring social evaluations. In this view, morality can only appear as moralism, and there is no recourse for the losers in any given social structure; they are losers in that structure because they are losers in life.

Democratic utilitarianism, however, has a significantly less global view of its own evaluative social structures. Bentham, for example, imagined that persons would participate in any number of different classes in schools, workhouses, and prisons, and imagined that social structures would provide positive social recognition for everyone eventually. Indeed, he puzzled out Panoptic schemes in all these different arenas precisely because he took society to be under an obligation to provide new occasions for recognizing the value of all the individuals who were part of it. Moreover, he attacked what we would think of as identity groups by arguing that social structures did not need to seek to know more about the character of the individuals that people them, and by arguing against the notion that there were any particular kinds of actions that could be seen as organizing character. (Thus, he offered something on the order of a proof that sodomy was not the deep truth of a socially harmful, or even socially delinquent, character.) Bentham did not recommend that individuals should aim to be types who perfect themselves by becoming ever more specialized and self-consistent (as Sade did when he presented his burlesque of allegorical personifications in the various representatives of what would come to be called the different perversions and when he substituted the coprophiliac for Fortuna, the masochist for Virtue). Rather, Bentham projected a utilitarianism that insisted that society owed individuals the opportunity not merely to extend their past histories but to develop, sometimes in relatively unexpected ways, in the future. For that process, relatively robust social institutions were necessary—not just schools, but also prisons and workhouses that were rehabilitative because they offered their denizens new arenas for action and new evaluations of the actions they clearly could perform (because they had performed them). Neither penitence nor penance was especially interesting for Benthamite utilitarianism.

Disciplinary social structures obviously created the conditions in which various actions could be "caught" by the structured social field and awarded their portion of social recognition. Yet utilitarianism of the sort that Bentham practiced did not go on to imagine that social structures were unimpeachable in their estimations of individuals and their actions. He knew that the social structures that he described were artificial—he had, after all, gone to a great deal of trouble to devise them. And because the rules of their operations had been self-consciously devised within living memory, the only hope of their continuance was that they not constrain individual action so much as to come to seem unjust. If they were to be true to the claim that they were local and temporary rather than metaphysical, they needed to find a way to avoid creating evaluations that would only be *newly* permanent. Bentham seemed to think, in part, that the simple possibility of multiplying institutions would suffice to eliminate the disadvantages for those who had received less advantage from the structures that had already been devised. It was as if he were proposing that new utilitarian structures would be added continually—in much the same way that the Olympics adds new events every four years. Bentham's answer to the problem of the monopolization of societal recognition was, then, to imagine that new disciplinary social structures would regularly be devised to capture previously imperceptible kinds of action and to discern their value. Value was everywhere—but latently. Panoptic structures made value explicit and in that sense gave it perceptible weight. The argument for the proliferation of utilitarian structures was that the latent value of all individuals could be explicitated if there were social procedures sufficient to the task. If individual disciplinary structures were democratic in admitting all comers, they were, as I have observed earlier, illiberal in that their very articulation of advantages made choices look more determined and determinable than free. Yet if utilitarian social structures were illiberal in their individual instances, Bentham proposed to introduce disciplinary structures liberally. His assumption was that multiplying disciplinary social structures would enable virtually everyone to find an arena in which they could assess and demonstrate whatever strengths they had.

In the chapters that follow, I hope to justify these intuitions about the importance of the diffusion of utilitarian social structures by examining some texts—Sade's *Philosophy in the Bedroom* and Catharine MacKinnon's work, for example—that directly address questions of social and political power, and others—*Madame Bovary* and *American Psycho*, for instance—that obliquely do so. In an argument I advance in the discussion of Catharine MacKinnon's work, I connect these recognition-awarding public structures (as she does) with modern affirmative action law. That law is, to my mind, best defended in terms of an essentially Benthamite utilitarian lineage that argues that diversity among the members of a group is not important simply for the sake of diversity. Rather, the question of access—the ability to enter and leave modern disciplinary social structures—has become ever more pressing as they have been incorporated into government—in the form of compulsory schooling and the like. When Catharine MacKinnon talks about how pornography involves domination and subordination, I think that her richest target is not a condemnation of the personal psychologies of pornographers or men or of pornographic actors and actresses or women. Rather, her more important insight is one that pornography itself reflects in its fascination with the scenes of education, incarceration, and the convent. For these institutions have fewer aspirations to dominate the world through their doctrines than to identify the value of an internal hierarchy. Domination and subordination—or, for that matter, any way of representing hierarchical evaluations—were essential to them rather than incidental. Even as the convent began to decline, the very effectiveness of the school, the workhouse/workplace, and the prison at allocating and reallocating social recognition made it crucial to submit the procedures for awarding social recognition to basic claims about justice.

Sade, as I argue in my discussions of his *Justine* and *Philosophy in the Bedroom*, is the first modern writer to understand the importance of sex as a social competition within a group—and to argue that sex revolved around fundamental inequalities and inequities that meant that justice should be rejected as an illusory goal. Sadean pornography recommends carceral human communities not so much because one must escape the conventional world since one can be explicit about sex only in private. Rather, he focuses on the evaluations that sexual games produce for all of the members of the community so as to insist on the hierarchy of hierarchy—so that one can know who's boss. Sex without a group is sex at least half wasted: Sadean pornography anticipates Henry Kissinger's observation that power is an aphrodisiac by arguing that there would be no sexual pleasure without the demonstration of power. In a Sadean vision of the group, the distribution of power is never open to appeal. Justice is irrelevant.

Sade's work, as I suggest in the chapter called "Justine, or The Law of the Road," already feels obliged to set itself up against the notion that individuals have value only within fixed communities. It does so specifically in its effort to demonstrate the futility of tort law, which revived the Roman law that treated accidental or unintentional injury as a matter for law. The law of torts is known as private law, largely because it relies on a basic principle—what the Romans called *alterum non laedere,* the intolerance of harm to another—rather than on a written code or the artificially constituted groups that someone like Bentham saw institutions as providing. It rests on cases, many of which revolve around the improbable but actual effects of a farmer's cow straying onto the road and causing a highway accident. If the claim of law is that written laws can be devised for people who recognize themselves as a people, the basic claim of tort law is that harms to persons—torts—may be perceptible even when one is outside a predefined social group. Indeed, this point is obvious in the fact that many of the key cases in early western European and American tort law are cases that assume that our capacity to travel will put us out of the reach of both the laws and the customs with which we are familiar. It retains its standing as a law of the road in being the kind of law at stake in traffic accidents that occasion injury to property and persons. Tort law is necessarily common law—law that must proceed by way of decisions on cases and commentary on those cases rather than statutes since it aims to speak even to the accidental. It already contains within it an implicit assertion that law is not merely geographical, so that one can, with Sade, simply withdraw from a community and create an arena that observes only the laws one would choose for oneself. A harm does not cease to be a harm simply because one had not known the person whom one harmed or hadn't committed an action with the intention of harming them. In that sense, tort law establishes a new social group that includes harmer and harmed—no matter how much they may be strangers to one another. It attempts to assign a value to sociality without sociability—albeit in less finely articulated ways than the Benthamite social structures do.

While Bentham thought that the solution to the problem of inadequate social recognition was to multiply the social structures available for mining latent value and making it explicit, for taking apparently insignificant action and giving it relative importance, tort law proceeds in the opposite way. It begins with a negative consequence, seeks a line of action that produced it, and projects a social world that links harmer and harmed. While utilitarian social structures attempt to coordinate a public world of highly articulated perceptible facts and perceptible values, tort law basically claims that the perception of a demonstrable injustice is the basis for a social world that goes past the boundaries of sociability and personal exchange. Moreover, while tort law may involve only two persons who have been joined by an action (the one as initiator, the other as recipient), its procedures involve rationalizing the value of that action. The monetary awards that tort law distributes as a way of making amends for demonstrable harms are, in keeping with that rationalization, not simply retributive and punitive. They address not just the possibility of harm but its value in terms of life chances, the projectable future possibilities that an injury destroys or compromises.

It is in the context of the genealogy of utilitarian social structures and tort law that this study situates pornography and treats it as one among an array of exercises in social valuation. Both pornography and utilitarian social structures of a perfectly respectable cast are concrete transcendentals: they provide an overarching microworld within which everyone may be evaluated hierarchically and in which there is no appeal. They produce continual evaluations with certainty, and both Sade's world and that of the Panoptic classroom offer equally legible demonstrations of the relative value of the persons who act within their confines. Yet to observe this resemblance is only to get at a portion of the importance of the reemergence of pornography in modernity.

For a key fact about pornography is that novelists in particular—as opposed to writers in general—are the ones who revive the term. Discussing the importance of the question of pornography in relation to specific novels (rather than police reports or sociological studies) makes it possible to see that there is an important link between pornography and obscenity, because debates about whether texts are pornographic or not involve something other than simple moral judgments about what those novels depict. They involve an understanding, however hazy, of the fact that representations have a central role in our conception of how actions and individuals should be recognized and evaluated. The novels that I discuss have, in the moments of their appearance, been regularly described as pornographic, and they have, as regularly, been exonerated of that charge. They have been judged obscene rather than pornographic, insofar as they offend society's image of itself and of a generalized idea of culture and cannot regularly be correlated with harms to individuals. Legal decisions have regularly been made that suggest a modern consensus in the view that Charles Rembar has called "the end of obscenity"—that societies should not be in the position of trying to police the descriptions and evaluations that are made of them.[19]

Yet simply to acquit these various novels of the charge that they are, in and of themselves, pornographic is to ignore their importance as episodes in the development of the objectification of sex—and of modern life. In a classic study such as *The Rise of the Novel,* Ian Watt argues that the novel arose in connection with the transformation of socioeconomic conditions, and he stresses the historical coincidence of the rise of the middle class and the rise of the novel. On the one hand, his account emphasizes the validation of individual experience.[20] A novelist like Richardson, in his view, endorsed the claim of a character such as Pamela Andrews to take her own experience seriously and to see her "true" worth as rivaling that of her social superiors. The novel was committed, in other words, to discovering the interest of new kinds of persons—the unheroic—and new kinds of actions: the routine or the commonplace event of a wedding rather than the epic founding of a nation. It thus specialized in characters with names approaching the distinctiveness of "John Doe" and discarded traditional plots of the kind that Shakespeare had regularly mined.

Although Michael McKeon has qualified Watt's account in his brilliant reexamination of the early novel, *The Origins of the English Novel: 1600–1740,* by pointing to the importance of the "anti-individualizing and idealizing tradition of romance,"[21] he has in the process also called attention to an enormously interesting feature of the novel that does not entirely emerge in Watt's survey. While Watt emphasizes the coincidence of the rise of the middle class and the rise of the novel in such a way as to suggest that the novel expressed middle-class interests, McKeon points to a more self-contradictory figure, "the familiar middle-class upstart whose middle-class identity is defined by nothing so much as a self-negating impulse, a will to be assimilated into the aristocracy." Watt's description of the formal features of the novel, McKeon argues, does not adequately describe many texts (such as Fielding's *Tom Jones*) that are generally acknowledged to be novels, and any description of the middle class must concede the instability of the classification.

McKeon concludes by saying that the flaw in Watt's "highly suggestive theory of the rise of the novel" is that it tries "to correlate two categories [the novel as a form whose features can be detailed and the middle class as a class], neither of which can be made to have any definitional stability."[22]

McKeon's aim is to provide an adequate social and literary history of the early English novel. My own involves a narrower band of the literary tradition. Where he sets forth the variousness of the different kinds of novels in an effort to provide a fuller sense of the dialectical unfolding of the genre, I look at novels that have been viewed as pornographic and ask two related questions: What is the significance of the fact that the novel was for two centuries the literary form most likely to be treated as pornographic? And, what can supposedly pornographic novels tell us about the novel form more generally?

In *Desire and Domestic Fiction,* Nancy Armstrong suggests, but does not develop, a link between pornography and the novel form when she emphasizes the importance of surveillance in the novel. In her account, the observation of other people develops as a domestic activity, so that it might seem an easy step from the voyeurism that *Pamela* traffics in to pornographic viewing. Yet while many critics have argued that the domestic fiction Armstrong discusses creates separate spheres and awards domestic spaces to women and public spaces to men, Armstrong's argument has a different emphasis. While she does stress the importance of the novel in the rise of a discourse of sexual difference, she also suggests that women's domestic surveillance came to provide the model for public surveillance, that ideas of government followed on the domestic model instead of competing with it. She therefore sums up her discussion by referring to "the power of all the domestic clichés" as a "power that was given to women and exercised through them" to establish "the preconditions for a modern institutional culture."[23] In her view, the novel, then, helps to demonstrate the contribution of supposedly private experience to public life. The importance of this insight can scarcely be exaggerated, because Armstrong discerns a key feature of the novel—that even in the moment in which the novel seems most concerned with private life and the enclosed domestic sphere, it introduces a narrator and a reader to observe that privacy and make it public. In this regard, Armstrong's account and mine concur in significant respects. Yet for all Armstrong's insightfulness in discovering improbable distributions of power, I differ from her ultimately in stressing the increasing importance of actions, as opposed to agents, because I take one of utilitarianism's great insights to have been that the capacity for modification and transformation of identities—what usually goes under the name of class mobility—is best served by social structures that do not focus on categories of persons but on constant comparisons of actions.

If the term "pornography" was revived by novelists, and novels were the literary forms most likely to be prosecuted, part of the reason for that convergence has to do with the very instability of the form of the novel and the instability of the class identity of many of its protagonists. While Watt sought to identify various formal aspects of the novel, it was inevitable that his list would be incomplete, because Bakhtin's definition of the novel as a form without form has always, ultimately, been the most persuasive. The novel, by contrast with a sonnet or other traditional poetic form, has no predictable way of distributing its beginning, middle, and end. Yet this formlessness of the novel, far from merely representing a default position that designates all the writing that cannot manage to achieve highly wrought form, is a very significant aspect of its functioning. Novels, as we know them, typically achieve their completion in the moment in which the characters have been hierarchically ranked. The very formlessness of the novel creates the demand for the evaluation and ranking of the characters, so that the novel form revolves around how it comes out. In other words, what Frank Kermode has called "the sense of an ending" is definitive of the novel form.[24] Like games, novels can be played at one length or another, deploying one convention or another, but they end in the announcement of evaluation.

The novels that I will discuss at length in this study all carry the process of ranking to an extreme. Yet the extremism of the cases that have been viewed as pornographic should not distract us from seeing the importance of this feature of novels more generally. Richardson and Austen, after all, accustomed us to the novelistic convention in which characters are introduced as if wearing their financial statements on their sleeves (so that the entire drama of *Pamela* revolves around the question of the possible relationship between a well-to-do gentleman and a poor-but-honest young woman, so that we know exactly how much money Bingley and Darcy have to make their status as eligible bachelors conspicuous for the marriageable daughters of a middle-class family in a place like Highbury). Courtship in such examples of the novelistic tradition involves posing a question and creating an occasion for making a decision, and the marriages provide all of the satisfactions of a successful resolution to a problem.

Novels, by virtue of not having any facts of the matter to attend to, are able to register their concerns and evaluations without being gainsaid by new information. Moreover, the novel as it develops from the eighteenth century on has become preeminently the genre of social evaluation, the genre that does not merely deliver the deep texture of a society but that also (as Ian Watt has argued) renders that society in the mode of philosophical realism—by presenting the organization and hierarchization that a rationalized account of that society involves. This is to say that it judges its characters and treats them as if they could be evaluated. And it accomplishes this process both through showing social reaction and through devising plots to produce the sense of outcomes. The ending of a novel displays its characters as winners and losers—with a host of intermediate and mixed examples. And it is this strong drive toward displaying not just the sense of its social reality but the reality of its evaluations that makes it preeminently the literature of the modern social field.

Yet to point to the novel's hierarchizing tendencies is not to claim that the novel displays evaluations in such a way as to endorse them. Indeed, Sade, at the beginning of the pornographic tradition in modern Western writing, frequently presents characters who continually object to the ways in which social fields convert their thoughts into actions. In *Justine,* for example, the title character continually maintains that her "virtue" is intact because she never meant to engage in the various acts of debauchery in which she participates and never meant to produce the catastrophic consequences that regularly attend her acts of Good Samaritanism. All of her actions are equivalent to checks marked "paid under protest." Even as they are cashed, she insists that she did not mean to write them. Yet the protest itself underscores the newly important place of action as collective action. Sade will himself engage in his own rearguard gesture in *Philosophy in the Bedroom* as he attempts to come to terms with the way in which the thinking of Rousseau and Kant captures individual intentions and gestures in a framework that causes them to extend past the moment in which they were authored. There, incest—among several generations—becomes a means of arguing for an insistence that bodies and the things that they do cannot be extended through time, in the way that modern societies founded on Rousseauvian and Kantian accounts of the general will necessarily made unborn generations important participants in any action. For Sade, the very notion of a national debt conspicuously involved intergenerational debt. National debt was, he thought, a way of diluting not just the authority of the seigneur but of actual persons, a way of yielding too much to persons who might only be conjectured, and who were certainly not available to make any compacts with anyone.

After discussing Sade, I move to a consideration of Flaubert's *Madame Bovary,* in which I track the significance of Flaubert's depiction of the externalization of desire, so that, in René Girard's words, "Triangular desire has now become the most common form of desire." One's desires, he claims, become artifacts (rather than authentic emotions) in the modern era because individuals desire things and persons because someone else desires them. Girard speaks of this externalization as a sign of "the progress of ontological sickness" that an author inevitably documents in a novel and claims that "curtailing the role of spontaneous desire in the universe of the novel" betokens this sickness—rather than "an author's whim or his particularly peevish humor."[25] In my account, by contrast, the emphasis falls less on sickness—ontological or otherwise—than on the ways in which individuals come to rely on utilitarian social structures to produce motives and affections in themselves. Indeed, I argue that Flaubert's literary role as the archivist of boredom dramatizes the importance of utilitarian social structures for conceiving action in deontological rather than ontological terms. In his treatment, we can see how the nineteenth century had developed many of the utilitarian structures that Bentham (and Sade and Fourier and a host of other less notable figures) had devised and can also see his repudiation of the notion that utilitarian social structures would make moral action and happiness easier to achieve.

Lawrence's *Lady Chatterley's Lover* presses the question of the relationship between sexuality and happiness. Foucault famously observes in his *History of Sexuality* that Lawrence presented himself as the priest of sexuality, a development that Foucault greeted with a certain amusement.[26] In my discussion of *Lady Chatterley's Lover*, I track the ways in which Lawrence makes sexuality look like the chief motor of individual character and like the most important instigator of change. With Lawrence, I argue, sexuality comes to override both money and class, to make it possible for individuals to act not out of "class spite, but in spite of class."[27] As sexuality replaces money and status and even love as the leading motive for individuals, character becomes open to conversion, as individuals reclassify themselves on the basis of their responsiveness to new sexual objects. In that sense, Lawrence is every bit as much the prophet of sex as Foucault suggests, because sexual experience is not simply sexual experience but soul making.

In the epilogue I address *American Psycho*, Bret Easton Ellis's satirical commentary on sexuality as the seat of individual spirit and individual distinctiveness. The culture of sex, drugs, and rock and roll that Ellis depicts is one that dissipates Lawrence's commitment to sexuality as the most revelatory aspect of one's character in favor of the jaundiced view that personal names are interchangeable with brand names. Anyone—and, as it seems in the novel, everyone—can wear Ralph Lauren and Giorgio Armani. Yet if the circulation of brand names makes it impossible for individuals to be distinctive individuals, that indistinguishability has infected the proper names of individuals as well: Bateman is continually greeted by people, supposedly friends, who call him by the names of other people. Patrick Bateman could be anyone at all. Bateman's violence, moreover, could be directed against almost anyone. He kills the homeless and women, but he also kills rich white men like himself. The violence is, however, neither exactly random nor exactly motivated. The difficulty that characters in the novel have in identifying friends and foes and in distinguishing between themselves (who they are) and what they wear (who they take themselves to be) makes it clear how far Ellis's novel is from Sade's and Bentham's view.

The claim that I advance about Sade and Bentham is that they specified environments and collected individuals in them so as to provide assessments of the relative strength and value of those individuals and their actions. They continually treated action as a modification of individual identity. In *American Psycho,* the constant search for excessive distinctiveness—the best of the best and the sexiest of sex—issues in its opposite, the inability of any individual to perform an action that can be connected with his name by other people.

1 Pornography, the Theory

In this chapter I undertake an exposition and assessment of Catharine MacKinnon's anti-pornography argument, which asserts that "pornography is central in creating and maintaining the civil inequality of the sexes" and that "pornography is a systematic practice of exploitation and subordination based on sex which differentially harms women."[1] She argues that pornography should not be handled under obscenity law but should instead be treated under the rubric of the civil law that guarantees equality of social access and should be seen as a form of unlawful discrimination. I try to address the various aspects of MacKinnon's argument without being dismissive, but ultimately conclude that only two of MacKinnon's claims are tenable—that pornography ought to be actionable when pornographic performers are injured in the performance of their work and that pornography ought to be actionable when it is used for the purposes of sexual harassment. Sexual harassment, I argue, enables one to identify a situation in which pornography could be used to do harm to an individual by excluding him or her from the groups that are artificially constituted by workplaces and schools. While I accept the portion of MacKinnon's arguments about pornography used for sexual harassment, I disagree with the terms of her explanation. Where MacKinnon affirms that "equality is guaranteed" in the environments of the workplace and the school,[2] I argue that the crucial reason why the workplace and the school are important is that they are public social structures that have assumed a privileged role in capturing the differential value of individual actions through a process of ranking that ultimately distinguishes the value of each individual action from every other. These utilitarian social structures are significant, then, not because they enact equality, but because they aim to create a social objectification for actions by rigorously delimiting them and establishing a basis for comparing one person's actions with another's. Access to that process of ranking and hierarchization is, I argue, a crucial feature of modern society, and even rather contentless representations ought to be seen as "pornographic" when they become the instruments for debarring individuals from those structures that enable persons to see their value increased through the public objectification of their actions. One chief virtue of utilitarian social structures such as the workplace and the school is that they objectify actions and make them discernible—without trying to derive accounts of the value of actions from claims about property rights or previous personal history.

What does Catharine MacKinnon mean by "pornography"?[3] What account of pornography is she putting forward when, in "Francis Biddle's Sister: Pornography, Civil Rights, and Speech," she writes that pornography is "a practice of sex discrimination" that "combines a mode of portrayal that has a legal history—the sexually explicit—with an active term that is central to the inequality of the sexes—subordination"?[4] What do she and Andrea Dworkin mean to accomplish, and what do they accomplish, by talking of what pornography does rather than of what pornography is?[5] In the essays MacKinnon wrote on pornography in the 1980s, she spoke of "pornography as a practice of sex discrimination" and of "what it does behaviorally."[6] More recently, in *Only Words*, she speaks continually of pornography in terms that treat it as an action—or a variety of actions—rather than as an object, or a collection of objects. This is a formulation or verbal habit sufficiently interesting to require some examination. We could portray it as simply a matter of rhetorical escalation, a histrionics designed largely for demagogic effect.[7] Or we could render it fatuous by paraphrasing it as a statement that all speech is behavior, thus making pornography look like a subset of language in general and like merely one example among the myriad examples of the operations of prose. The aim of this chapter is to set aside those two dismissive accounts of MacKinnon's position, to examine some of her opponents' arguments, and to locate what I take to be the most interesting aspect of the MacKinnon-Dworkin position, namely, its attempt to suggest a connection between pornography and action that continually demands a revision of the ways in which the law acknowledges and, indeed, formulates action.

There are, however, considerable difficulties that one must engage in advance. First among these is that MacKinnon's opponents continually represent her position as necessarily involving censorship, with censorship being traced through its full pedigree for suppression of dissent. (Indeed, the "feminist anti-censorship" position has made its act of self-naming an implicit characterization of the MacKinnon-Dworkin position; and the free-speech position—whether linked with or uncoupled from feminism—has repeatedly argued that the potential "chilling effect" that would be produced by the enforcement of any civil rights ordinances against pornography would be the functional equivalent of censorship.)[8] Second, there is the problem of MacKinnon's recurrent use of statistical studies as if they indicated clear causal patterns between pornography and imitative crimes including rape and murder. It has been a simple enough exercise to find statistical studies that appear to maintain the reverse.[9] Moreover, leaving aside the studies that seem to acquit pornography in the aggregate, commentators have found it all too easy to make the point that pornography must be a relatively indirect or remote cause of serious crimes against women if pornography is as nearly omnipresent as MacKinnon says it is and if substantial numbers of women nonetheless take themselves not to have been harmed by it.[10] This is as much as to say that although many have claimed that MacKinnon cites only studies overstating the number of rapes and acts of sexual abuse, even her comparatively large numbers are not large enough to make the case for anything like a regular causal connection between pornography and crimes against women.[11]

In the following discussion, I attempt to locate what I take to be a fundamental insight of the argument that MacKinnon and Dworkin, individually and together, have articulated against pornography. I take that project centrally to involve the claim that pornography is only significant insofar as it involves acts—as it puts representations to use. (Moreover, I see that claim as entirely consistent with the assertion that positive uses of pornographic representations are indeed positive and that they would call for no legal action.) In the process of analyzing and defending what I see as the most powerful aspects of this position, I shall also be arguing that neither censorship nor a simplistic claim about pornography directly causing readily predictable instances of extreme violence is central to that position. With regard to the question of censorship, I am not so much arguing a new point as simply recognizing and following the logic that MacKinnon herself has repeatedly laid out. With regard to the question of pornography and behavior, I am proposing a modification of what her position sometimes—perhaps even frequently—appears to be.

Briefly, I see MacKinnon as addressing a central question for modern self-governing societies—namely, how can such societies modify their own tendencies to replicate the power structures that already exist? How can they avoid simply responding to the precedential appeal of the stereotypes that are stereotypes because they come with all the recommendation of existence? However far political thinking may qualify its truth claims to insist upon the impossibility or unavailability of knowledge apart from the conditions of our knowledge, that is, some version of those claims reemerges in the perception of value. Stereotypes are stereotypes because they reflect judgments of value, judgments that have particular force as implicit maxims because they claim the authority of what has been credited over what has not.[12] They represent what has been called—usually with a certain edge—the dividend of membership in certain groups, in recognition of the relative value of advantaged groups; and they carry an analogous penalty as well, in recognition of the relative value of disadvantaged groups.[13]

When feminism has occupied itself with pornography, it has done so because pornography, in its appeal to viewers, clearly emphasizes the issue of evaluation—the value that is placed on a person or a thing in the literal or metaphorical marketplace.[14] The visibility of pornography is thus important not because it involves a tacit claim that visual imagery has an unusual immediacy by comparison with other representational media, but rather because of its obvious orientation toward viewers and their evaluations. It emphasizes individual value as it is assigned, that is, rather than a notion of intrinsic worth (as it might be postulated by an abstract account of individualism) or a notion of self-worth (as it might be postulated by someone's constituting him- or herself as an ideal market or audience for him- or herself).

Adherents of a variety of political perspectives are willing to grant a value to what has been credited, but they draw widely different conclusions about the proper way of recognizing it. On the one hand, an essentially libertarian view affirms that experience continually ratifies existing distributions of power and that efforts to counteract the ratifications of daily experience are at best pointless.[15] On the other hand, classical liberalism has frequently been seen as enunciating a strong argument for individuals as political equals that tries to offset the value of what has already been credited by suggesting its contingency, the possibility of things having been different from what they in fact were. As critics of classical liberalism have repeatedly suggested, however, seeing the essential or potential equality of conspicuously different people does not in itself alter their practical inequality, the inequality of their capacities for action and of the values that other people attach to them. In other words, the classical liberal analysis of politics as something other than a continuation of the status quo may argue in favor of a basic notion of the equality of individuals, but that analysis tends to stop short of providing accounts of the possible redistributions of the conditions of equality. (Indeed, insofar as classical liberalism argued for the equality of individuals by claiming that individuals could form ideas and judgments and actions that went beyond the norms of previous actions and perceptions, it could plausibly seem to make specific models and examples look like a distraction.)[16]

Both the economic analysis of Marxism and many of the policies of the modern welfare state have attempted to address this problem of liberal abstraction—a problem that is, arguably, not really so much one of abstraction as of a reluctance to see existing examples as bounding the field of possibilities. Yet, whatever the successes of these approaches, they have had considerable difficulty addressing the inequality that attaches even to the effort to advance equality in the most basic economic terms. For, even in the process of rejecting the liberal focus on the value of the individual, they have tended to imagine that inequality can be dealt with almost exclusively in the present, whereas, as Pierre Bourdieu suggests in his sociological investigations of the operations of class, "precocity is an effect of seniority."[17] Precocity in Bourdieu's analysis is what we might recognize more generally as the recommendation of membership in a group, the increased likelihood that others will value an individual in ways that track the way they have valued other individuals who resemble him or her by virtue of membership in the same family, association, race, religion, or gender. It is the condition of being able to be credited with quickness for not having had much distance to cover.

The interest of MacKinnon's work, as I see it, lies in its implications for the question I have briefly been identifying—the question of the valuing of persons—and in its analysis of the resources available for altering the values of individuals as they have been assigned in the present on the basis of registrations of past value. Of the efforts to claim that one can identify the value of individuals as anything other than a recognition of present norms and values, the two most prominent are the law of torts and the liberal assertion of the fundamental equality of persons. Each of these approaches makes a more or less compelling argument for insisting upon the superiority of an assigned value that differs from that of present circumstances, and a brief canvas of their central features can serve to indicate the uses and limitations of each.

Tort law makes claims about the proper value of an individual largely by identifying an incident that interrupts the value that a person would have had in the most plausible projection of his future as a direct extension of his past. That is, it assigns persons property not only in all the things that are most obviously property but also in a variety of extrapolations of actual physical property (potential earnings over a lifetime, psychological distress, reputation, and so forth). It makes claims for the value of what would probably have occurred as opposed to the value of what actually has come to be and tries to compensate an individual for the value that an unblemished reputation, undamaged property, or uninjured limbs would have had for him or her.

The applicability of a modified version of the tort approach to women's equality suggested itself in MacKinnon's early work *Sexual Harassment of Working Women,* in which she describes sexual harassment as "tort-like." In its tort-like aspect, sexual harassment constitutes an interruption of an individual's projectable property in their job (with whatever compounding might seem appropriate).[18] Yet if tort law continually pleads the case for a plausible value against an actual one, its limitations in attesting to the values of persons who have not yet been valued are significant if not always obvious. Tort law requires that imagined losses become visible in conjunction with an actual past, and it primarily criticizes the current valuation of a person by way of a contrast with the value that one would have predicted for a person who had a particular recognizable value in the past. Insofar as it argues against the justice of a present assessment of value, it does so by reference to a past in which a higher value was clearly perceptible. Tort law does not attempt to redress past imperceptibility or deficient perceptions of value in the past.[19]

The equality model of liberalism, by contrast, does attempt to set aside such deficient perceptions of value in the past. Yet it does so largely by seeming to argue that the recommendations of experience ought simply to be rejected. In that sense, it seems abstract, committed less to countering the weight of specific examples than to dismissing them. Understood as an abstract affirmation of an abstract equality, liberalism may seem, as it does to MacKinnon, to claim that increasing the freedom of one always increases the freedom of all; it may seem to see its work as complete at the outset when it affirms the priority of virtually universal human faculties over particular circumstances.[20]

In the one case, that of tort, the notion of value is converted into a version of property, so that past possession seems the crucial means of asserting a claim to value. Tort law, for all its attentiveness to the significance of omission as well as to positive action, fails to provide a sense of potential value apart from a perceived past. In the other case, that of liberalism, the notion of value is treated in terms of potentiality in and of itself, so that it provides no counterweight at all to the images of past experience. The one gives all too much weight to experience in imagining the future as a direct extension of the past; the other, too little in seeming to imagine that the only way of repudiating the recommendations of present evaluations of individuals is to affirm that individuals are in principle equal.

In the following discussion I am essentially arguing, first, that MacKinnon's characterization of contemporary society as "a world made by pornography" is right insofar as it tries not simply to see pornography as an occasion for a judgment of value (a decision upon whether *it* is appealing or disgusting), but also to acknowledge the recommendation implicit in any representation as both an object for evaluation and also a representation of an evaluation. Second, and more importantly, I am arguing that, despite the difficulties MacKinnon's analysis has in describing women as a group, her account of pornography as sex discrimination helps us to appreciate the problems that attach to the often-invoked injunction to treat everyone like an individual. Finally, I am suggesting that her account enables us to see the importance of artificial environments—the workplace, the school, and public spaces conceived on their model—for creating artificial groups that importantly alter the value of individuals. The right of access to value-altering groups is, I am arguing, a crucial one, and the case against pornography can be pressed most strongly against pornography as it is used to try to restrict access to such groups.

The Minneapolis Ordinance that Dworkin and MacKinnon coauthored in 1983 identified pornography in terms of "civil inequality" and stated in part that

the [Minneapolis City] Council finds that pornography is central in creating and maintaining the civil inequality of the sexes. Pornography is a systematic practice of exploitation and subordination based on sex which differentially harms women. The bigotry and contempt it promotes, with the acts of aggression it fosters, harm women's opportunities for equality of rights in employment, education, property rights, public accommodations and public services; create public harassment and private denigration; promote injury and degradation such as rape, battery and prostitution and inhibit just enforcement of laws against these acts; contribute significantly to restricting women from full exercise of citizenship and participation in public life, including in neighborhoods; damage relations between the sexes; and undermine women's equal exercise of rights to speech and action guaranteed to all citizens under the constitutions and laws of the United States and the State of Minnesota.[21]

This statement, like the Minneapolis Ordinance in general, has most frequently been seen as making the claim that pornographic images produce misogynistic behavior imitatively and that eradicating pornographic images would eliminate at least some misogynistic behavior.

That characterization is, of course, partially right. The Minneapolis Ordinance seems to suggest—if only in the somewhat guarded language of "promoting," "fostering," and "contributing"—that pornographic images function as a pattern language. Pornography, in this sense, looks as though it "gives people ideas," and the question is whether one can hold pornography responsible for the actions that result from those ideas. Someone like Robin Morgan, whose memorable phrase "Pornography the theory, rape the practice" I am adapting in the title for this analysis, seems to, when she speaks of pornography as simply the first stage of a continuous process culminating in rape.[22] Someone like Andrea Dworkin seems to, when she speaks of pornography as inseparable from rape.[23] In these extended accounts of action, being able to imagine a particular action is continuous with and functionally equivalent to producing an action; implementing such an intention appears as a necessary and unproblematic extension of it. Representations, in this sense, appear simply to distribute the intention and the execution of an action among persons (so that a pornographer might not depict an actual rape but might produce a simulation that led to its being effected).

Against such a strong view of the inevitable connection between representations and actions, or of the view that a representation produces a mere repetition of the represented action, anti-censorship feminists and various proponents of a free-speech argument about pornography have focused on the weakness and unreliability of the connection between seeing pornographic images and acting them out. Thus, Sara Diamond attacks the MacKinnon-Dworkin position on the grounds of its supposed literalism, its not being able to distinguish between a representation of an action and an action, and Ann Snitow calls attention to its "misplaced concreteness" in thinking that images always depict actualities.[24] Lisa Duggan, Nan Hunter, and Carole Vance amplify this line of attack on MacKinnon's anti-pornography position when they describe it as equating images with actions as if there were no escape from the lockstep of the trajectory projected by an image one has seen. In their view, MacKinnon and Dworkin adopt an especially narrow version of behaviorist psychology in equating images with actions and imagining a straightforward causal connection between the sight of images and one's subsequent behavior. There are, they argue, so many images that cause behavior that it is mistaken to single out pornographic images alone for attack. Having made that point, however, they proceed to advance two additional suggestions that they see as nullifying the negative force of pornography.

They claim, in the first place, that religion has historically been more misogynistic than pornography and proceed to suggest that any cause other than the most important is not merely subordinate but insignificant as well. As they put it, "It need hardly be said that pornography did not lead to the burning of witches or the English common law treatment of women as chattel property. If anything functioned then as the prime communication medium for women-hating, it was probably religion." (If not always a principal cause, then never a principal cause.) In the second place, they claim that insofar as pornography is sex, it is good, enlightened, and progressive: "... the existence of pornography has served to flout conventional sexual mores, to ridicule sexual hypocrisy and to underscore the importance of sexual needs."[25] In their view, pornography serves a variety of purposes, with the balance falling on the side of those that are desirable rather than harmful. (If unconventional, then good.) Basically, that is, some anti-censorship feminists have adopted what appears to be a strange form of relativism on the way to absolutism. If one possible cause of harm can be arguably trumped by another, more important cause of harm, it is assumed not merely to be a lesser cause but basically a nonexistent one.

This style of arguing for pornography or arguing against censorship is sufficiently remarkable, in the first place, for seeing the two issues as the same. It is, however, equally remarkable for the all-or-nothing logic by which it advances, in suggesting that any but the most important and most thoroughly negative cause of misogyny is no cause at all—or else that it is good. The assertion that an anti-pornography position must resolve itself into a version of censorship, in other words, converts itself into the assertion that being opposed to censorship also involves endorsing pornography. Under this approach, anti-censorship feminists move almost effortlessly from arguing that pornography is not invariably bad to arguing that there is a readily recognizable category of things called pornography that is relatively stable and, on account of its irreverence for authority and authoritarianism, preponderantly beneficial.

Having, that is, begun by questioning the inevitability of a link between an image and behavior that would in some sense re-create or reenact that behavior, anti-censorship feminists have reinstalled a strong claim for just such a link. Thus, the trajectory that the feminist anti-pornography argument traces is one that advances from skepticism about the regularity of the effects of pornography when those effects are seen to be negative to a strong claim about the positive benefits of pornography. For example, Gayle Rubin, in a series of essays, and Linda Williams, in her current project, argue that pornography not only doesn't cause harms to women but that it serves a positive educational purpose.[26] Pornography, in their treatment, has developed to the point of dividing into a variety of genres with a variety of target audiences; it performs a major service by educating a self-selecting audience into the possibility of sexual self-realization. The meaning of the pornographic object, in other words, is its audience's self-image. From this perspective, pornography teaches by giving one anticipations of certain actions that are merely an incidental expression of the sexual identity one has already (if only proleptically) achieved. Here one sees an important argument of feminist historians—that consumption is a considered and significant activity—developing into the extraordinary claim that consumption is inviolable, in that the process of consumption is an act of evaluation treated as if it could never fail, because the consumer's evaluation is treated as if it were determinative of the value of every object. This particular version of the anti-censorship view, in other words, supplements the maxim that the customer is never wrong with the corollary insistence that the customer is also never wronged.

Now what is puzzling about the anti-censorship position is that it moves in two contradictory ways. On the one hand, it accurately captures a crucial problem of censorship—that it has a hard time registering the different uses to which pornographic representations may be put and, therefore, condemns the pornography of positive effects along with that of negative effects.[27] On the other hand, its central assertion—that even the images that produce negative impressions for some may have positive and instructive value for others—tends to be undercut by a renewed effort to generalize about the effects of pornography that now reclaims it for self-affirmation and group affirmation. That is, a position recognizing that a pornographic object's meaning changes with its various uses by various audiences converts itself into a question of the rights of various audiences to have and use pornography.[28] Pornography thus comes to look like something you might have—as you might possess an object or hold a belief—rather than like something whose meaning is constituted by its use. The very right to be a group comes to be bound up in the right to have expressive forms, of which pornography would simply be one conspicuous example.[29]

The difference between anti-censorship feminists and MacKinnon here is instructive. Where they argue that the meaning and the effects of pornography essentially express a positive relationship to a group, MacKinnon does not see group membership as resolving the issue.[30] Although MacKinnon and sex-affirmative feminists would be in fundamental agreement with one another in resisting censorship, MacKinnon's argument against censorship is in fact significantly stronger than theirs. Sex-affirmative feminists continually point out that censorship creates problems of recognition, that it scapegoats minorities in the name of protection for persons and rounds up the wrong suspect. Yet MacKinnon's position, however much it may have been seen to be functionally equivalent to censorship, provides a critique of censorship that reaches much further than mistrust of the motivated perception of the censors. For pornography, in her account, essentially does not depend on depicting actions that one would endorse or repudiate if they were to be acted out in one's presence or on the notion that one can establish meaning as a function of its meaning for identity groups. This is to say that MacKinnon ultimately stakes very little on the notion of content, if content can be understood either as offering an image of an action that might be repeated or as emphasizing the likeness or identification between an actor depicted in a representation and the viewer of that action. Rather, MacKinnon is concerned with what action a representation is used to perform.

Thus, far from being naive about representation or unable to tell the difference between an act and the representation of that act, the strength of MacKinnon's position is precisely its focus on the representation as act. A representation may have considerable overlap with an action—as in the cases that MacKinnon stresses most strongly in her earlier work in which her interest in coerced performance is an interest in showing that the production of a representation of a rape could sometimes itself be rape.[31] On the other hand, it may have little resemblance to actual persons, as in the case of cartoons or graffiti, in which the representation may work less as a lesson for imitation than as the assertion of the power to insult. What MacKinnon most importantly emphasizes about representations is not their capacity to frame actions for imitation or avoidance but their transitiveness. This is the point at stake when she and Dworkin describe pornography not as a description of sex but as sex, or speak of it not as a depiction of an idea of sex as a product that can be made, sold, bought, and used to produce at least the action of masturbation.

In the Minneapolis Ordinance and the essays in which she explained its rationale, MacKinnon approached the question of pornography's intermittent identity with sex in a variety of ways. She emphasized, first, that it was a product expressly made to produce masturbation, that it was not merely the random occasion for a series of erratic associations. Second, she asserted that pornography was a causal factor in some rapes. Third, she stressed that a camera-based pornography involving live actresses collapsed the distinction between having sex and representing sex for those actresses. (Moreover, she argued that, insofar as the legal system finds the two situations functionally indistinguishable, the law is itself functioning as an incentive system. In its strong version, this claim is that rape may be open to criminal punishment but that pornography, by virtue of being treated as yet another instance of representation, makes the notion of a documented rape look completely unavailable.) Finally, she outlined the view that pornographic representations might serve the purposes of harassment, in being used to intimidate on the basis of sex.

The first of these claims—that pornography is a product of an industry that can continue in existence because the product delivers not just another reading experience but the activity of masturbating—puts in place MacKinnon's emphasis on action in discussing value. Her amplification of it—that pornography works by eroticizing abuse, at worst, or by eroticizing inequality, at least—attempts a comparison of intention and effect that would expose a view as ideological by pointing to the contradictions of its practice. If sexuality is taken to be an expression of affection, she asked, why does it take the form of apparent violence?

This view expresses a certain brilliant literalism in seventies feminism that had tried to argue that sexuality simply enacted hierarchy and inequality every time it got down to acts.[32] Yet that line of thinking had a hard time explaining just what the component parts of sexuality were and how one might locate the properly literal action and the properly framed intention that it was seen to express and contradict. Working within the framework of ideological critique, such accounts, like the instances in which MacKinnon tries to describe sexual violence as such, suggest that it is easy enough to identify the elements that will provide appropriate reciprocal commentary on one another—that you can know something crucial about social domination and subordination, for instance, by looking at a pornographic image that seems to literalize domination and subordination in individual sex acts and their representations. Failing such confidence in identifying the parts and wholes of sexual action and in establishing the correctness or incorrectness of their relationship to one another, however, it has been hard to say exactly when pornography fits or misfits its purposes.

The second aspect of MacKinnon's position—that rapists frequently use pornography as a kind of preparation for rape—also has its flaws. As we observed earlier in commenting on the importance of lesbian-, bisexual-, and gay-affirmative pornography, there may be widespread agreement that pornography may have causal effects, but it is hard to describe those effects except in the rather vague terms of something like self-recognition in terms of a group identity. If a central claim of sexually affirmative accounts of sexually explicit and sexually inexplicit representation is that representations help one to begin imagining oneself as part of a community, that they give you home thoughts from abroad about who you are, then that basic position rightly separates self-recognition from imitative action. Indeed, it would seem to suggest just the reverse; if the corrupting effect of pornography is imagined to be that you may recognize yourself in images of people doing things you have not done, then self-recognition is already detached from the notion of action. Individual identity—and identification with a group— need not resolve itself into a generalization about one's actions; and, once again, the notion that one's character or one's intentions might be contradicted by one's actions comes to seem peculiar, if only because the experience of having a character, seeing oneself in terms of a group identity, is hard to correlate simply with the production of actions.

MacKinnon's interest in camera-based pornography, however, addresses a more powerful challenge to pornography. As her recurrent use of the Linda Lovelace/Linda Marchiano example is designed to demonstrate, two different views of pornographic representation collide in the case of photographic pornography.[33] On the one hand, one may take pornography to operate according to a conventional separation between actor/actress and action that is an underwriting condition of theater. As with other cases of acting for a camera of any kind, pornographic acting does not, in this view, involve the actors or actresses in feeling what they represent their characters as feeling. The represented emotions and sensations need not coincide with the actual emotions and sensations of the actor or actress.

On the other hand, one may see pornographic representations in live performance and for the camera as importantly imaging some form of representational collapse, in which the representation of action involves the action. Sometimes the perception of such a collapse extends past the recognition of the possible identity between action and representation to a renewed affirmation of their separation. Thus, the Williams Committee on Obscenity and Film Censorship justified the prohibition of live sex acts by drawing a distinction between representations and actions and by arguing that "what artistic or dramatic requirements do not involve is the performance of real sexual activity" while "the presentation of actual sex on the stage immediately introduces a presumption that the motives no longer have any artistic pretension." As they put it, "the situation is changed completely when the spectator is confronted with, where that involves *being in the same space as,* people actually engaged in sexual activity," because that shared space provides "the ground of a relation between performer and audience which is not present with, for example, a film of the same activity."[34]

The burden of the Williams Committee's account of representational collapse thus falls on the representational distance between an action and the spectator observing it. Because, that is, their account essentially maintains that an action does not become a representation simply by virtue of being watched, they are concerned with the difference it would make to spectators to watch, on the one hand, simulated sexual activity in a camera image or, on the other, actual sexual activity occurring in their presence. MacKinnon and Dworkin have, however, sorted out the collapse between action and represented action quite differently. They have insisted, in the first place, that the camera is dependent on real action for its representations. Dworkin's lurid assertion that pornographers "write their sentences with our bodies" attempts, in other words, to short-circuit arguments about the conditions of representation by trumping them, in claiming that representations may do without many things but that they cannot do without the things they are made of—in this case, the bodies of pornographic actors and actresses. Pornography, whatever else it may do, alters behavior at least for the persons who appear in it.

In MacKinnon and Dworkin's treatment, the emphasis therefore shifts from a question of the motives for the representation to a question about its very materials—now identified as the actors and actresses whose bodies become its medium. In their view, pornography exists as a direct product of the actions of its willing or unwilling actors and actresses. Moreover, they see the legal treatment of pornography as effectively eliminating the possibility of distinguishing between consensual and nonconsensual pornographic performance. From this vantage, they point to pornography as the culmination of a formalist account of representation and the incentive system that it could be said to produce. For their analysis proceeds by emphasizing, with considerable shrewdness, that all of the legal attempts to deal with pornography have essentially revolved around judgments of the pornographic object alone, so that its subsequent effects have seemed a more considerable issue than the effects of its production. While only live sex acts may raise the question of "a relation between people"—between actors/actresses and spectators—MacKinnon would stress that such relations are constantly at issue for pornographic performance before the camera. Thus, in her account, the camera continually captures actions but, paradoxically, nullifies the possibility of their being witnessed by the very act of displaying them as representations. Acts are treated as fictitious representations merely because of their being watched by a camera and, subsequently, by an audience.

In its fullest extension, MacKinnon's position on camera-based pornography reconciles itself into the claims that Susanne Kappeler, in *The Pornography of Representation,* and Andrea Dworkin, in *Intercourse,* have made about non-camera-based representations of women—that the formalist account of art that takes representations to exist in a separate space from actuality functions not simply to deny the links between art and actuality but also to make artistic representation into an alibi.[35] In this account, imitative actions—or, instances of actions that are substantially the same—can occur in actuality in both situations, but in the representation the action is continually treated as if it were fictitious (because the basic motive of producing a representation is taken to override all other motives and to make them incidental). Representation, that is, provides quotation marks that may allow a perfect reproduction of an action and, at the same time, may suspend any interest in the effects of those actions.

In this third aspect of her critique of pornography, then, MacKinnon attempts to portray the inability of our present laws to distinguish the voluntary from the nonconsensual pornographic performance and to point to a fundamental inequity that potentially obtains in the treatment of pornographic representations. Such inequity might result from a complex set of assumptions about fictitious representations—that, for instance, aesthetic objects necessarily involved something more than or different from the process of their production, that their being aesthetic objects meant they could never retain documentary status.[36] Such inequity might result, as Richard Posner suggests, from the simple fact of the illegality of pornography, which consigns all of its participants to legal incredibility.[37] But whatever its causes might be, MacKinnon's claim is that pornography is the concrete and visible manifestation of what we cannot see.

When MacKinnon argues that pornographic camera images lose all their rightful value in documenting actual injury because they are continually treated as mere simulations and actuality is subjected to the conventions of fictitious representation, her analysis treats the pornographic representation as a disseminator of action. In consuming pornographic images, one need not commit further acts of injury in imitation of those images because the act of consumption and the techniques that govern its conversion from the documentary into the artifactual already function as actions. Insofar as the consumption of pornography is the production of an incentive for making more pornography, MacKinnon sees not tolerance for different sexual tastes but a "protection racket," in which treating pornographic images under the sign of fictitious representations simply abrogates the recognition of the effects of one's act of consumption.[38] Since the claim is that the continuing refusal to acknowledge the possibility of coercion is itself a recurrent and ongoing action, MacKinnon portrays the possibility of coerced performance as contaminating pornography in its various subsequent uses.

The drawback to that line of argument is its illimitability. In emphasizing conditions of production and consumption, it makes each individual act of consumption look as if it were answerable for all possible effects of that act. On the most practical level, the repeated assertion of the reality of injuries to women becomes a decision—simply on the basis of the images themselves—about which performances were consensual and which nonconsensual. As such, it converts what is at bottom a claim about a probability—that there might be producers of pornography who would recognize how to align pornography with the conventions of fictitious representation and thus create a cover for their coercion of porn performers—into a uniform law of pornographic production. MacKinnon's conclusion, that is, may be different from the claim that pornographic images need no regulation, but she pursues similarly general procedures of argument. Where the opponents of regulation emphasize that artistic and dramatic representations do not necessarily entail the performance of real sexual activity (with the suggestion that we must assume, as a working hypothesis, that none does), MacKinnon emphasizes that some pornographic performances do involve the performance of real sexual activity (with the suggestion that we must assume, as a working hypothesis, that all do). In either case, the effort to describe what happens in pornography moves immediately into an account of the conventions governing pornographic representations as instances of fictitious representations in general.

The attractiveness of this third aspect of MacKinnon's argument is that it does not simply accept a broad set of conventions for dealing with visual images but raises the question of pornography as a technological change in the production of images. Further, this aspect of her argument gestures toward the possibility of historical change not just in technology but in the acknowledgment of individuals. Just as we take earlier practices for instantiating equality to have failed in ways that are now conspicuous, so, MacKinnon suggests, will our own come to look deficient. Indeed, MacKinnon's comparisons between the legal situations of women and blacks continually recall the ways in which earlier versions of equality look conspicuously inequitable from the vantage of the present.[39] Inasmuch as one can see the difference between the equality that the eighteenth-century framers of the Constitution produced in practice and the equality of the United States at the end of the twentieth century, one can imagine that many of our own practices will to later generations appear neither equitable nor even neutral, that they will seem like conspicuous contradictions of many of the principles that we take them to illustrate.

Yet the very attractiveness of this line of reasoning is also its greatest weakness. As a critique of ideology, it can provide a check on the sense of the inevitability of one's own ideology, but it can do only that. MacKinnon's gestures toward the future and the strangeness it will impose on the present, like Dworkin's adaptations of literary classics to expose their misogyny by retelling them in tendentious paraphrase, may work to suspend our confidence in our views. Yet, as with ideological critique generally, the crucial difficulty is one of application, of translating a general notion of possibility into an available attitude about one's own circumstances and actions.

This is to say that MacKinnon's description of how "all the *unspeakable* abuse: the rape, the battery, the sexual harassment, the prostitution, and the sexual abuse of children" is in pornography "called something else: sex, sex, sex, sex, and sex, respectively" sweeps too broadly in imagining that one needs to root out both the unconscious and the conscious "lies" of ideology.[40] It ends up creating categories that appear to exist independent of their use—so that coercion into pornographic performance must be treated as the clear-eyed account of even apparently consensual performances; and the difficulties of redressing abuse within family units must be converted into evidence of the abusiveness of the family unit itself.[41]

MacKinnon's strong claim—that we cannot see the harms of pornography "in a world made by pornography"—is in fact so strong as to be ineffectual.[42] It would seem, at this juncture, that MacKinnon's attack on pornography has included a variety of ways of describing pornographic action, but that none of them has amounted to a case against pornography. If pornography produces an action in producing masturbation, we have nonetheless had a hard time extending that causal sequence to establish that violence, abuse, or domination is a necessary component of its erotic charge. If pornography can be said to depict abusive actions and in the process to teach abuse, the regularity of that connection has been difficult to sustain. And if MacKinnon describes pornography as appropriating conventions of representation in such a way as simultaneously to display actual abuse and to treat it as a simulation, that description of pornography continually suggests a standard of reality that is unattainable. We are thus left with MacKinnon's argument against pornography as a vehicle for sexual harassment. The sexual harassment argument does not, however, stake anything on a claim that one can assess, on the basis of an image alone, the mixture of actuality and fictionality that it represents. Therefore, the question of what pornography means need never ask what it meant for its performers or its producers, need never explain what the general conditions of theatrical performance are. For the argument about pornography in sexual harassment simply concerns its use in a specific situation, not its history or genealogy.

In this, the argument that focuses on sexual harassment does not preserve the insistence upon eliding individual consent or nonconsent with the imagined or enjoined consent of a group. Under the coercion-into-performance argument, MacKinnon had identified the consumption of pornography with participation in a network of incentives and exchanges that would, eventually, turn out to have actually violated someone's consent; she had, that is, suggested a strong connection between the consent of the performers and the consent of the viewer, as if the choice of theater—the individual viewer's ability to remain in the theater or depart from it—could not exculpate pornography so long as such freedom was not open to everyone involved in every stage of its production and circulation. She had thereby made the idea of the performers' consent look as though it was relevant because it somehow implied the consent of others. If pornographic performers were always volunteers, she had suggested, there might be a genuine erotica; but if "Linda Lovelace had to be coerced into making *Deep Throat*, doesn't that suggest that *Deep Throat* is dangerous to all women anywhere near a man who wants to do what he saw in it?"[43]

Under the sexual harassment argument, however, the extension of consent or nonconsent from one person to another becomes unnecessary. If MacKinnon has suggested that a viewer's consent to see a pornographic image should not retroactively be used to establish the presumption of the performer's consent to act in it, the sexual harassment argument about pornography does not rely upon preserving similarity between pornographic performers and viewers in this regard. For the sexual harassment argument emphasizes that pornographic images may be put to use without regard to their previous histories of use. Moreover, it insists that not even the consent of pornographic performers can ensure that its subsequent uses will reenact such consent; even if Linda Marchiano had consented to perform in pornography, her consent would be irrelevant to the question of the viewers' consent to watch that performance.

Essentially, I have been criticizing the aspects of MacKinnon's argument against pornography that revolve around resemblance or likeness, or rather, to the aspects of that argument suggesting that resemblances—between one woman and another, between an action and a representation—provide a useful index to the value of the images. Whether these versions of her argument extrapolate from a represented action to the possibility of a similar action, or whether they suggest a similarity between one woman's freedom or coercion in pornography and other women's freedom or coercion, they emphasize similarity of actions (between pornographic representations and imitated actions) or similarity of effects (on one woman and on other women). And even when MacKinnon insists upon the similarity between action and representation in pornographic images in which actions are simply recorded, to argue that an action does not become a representation by being watched, the logic of resemblance is used to cast suspicion on all that it touches.

With the sexual harassment argument, however, MacKinnon is able to make a rather different point: an action may not become a representation by being watched, but a representation may become an action by being watched. As the proponents of sex positivity maintain, it can create a kind of compact; as the analysts of its use in harassment argue, it can make the communication of an image from one person to another an assertion of difference. Like a variation on irony, with its rehearsal of the same words with a different meaning from that which they have previously carried, the harassing image is harassing not so much because of its content, what it says, but rather because it uses an image as a conspicuous expression of the difference between the parties who view it. A pornographic image need not be offensive in itself, need not even be sexually explicit, to be used in harassment. It need only be used as an ostensive definition of an individual's difference from the other members of a group.

The sexual harassment argument brings out a perhaps surprising aspect of the previous versions of MacKinnon's arguments against pornography—namely, that resemblance (between real and simulated sex for pornographic performers, between one woman and other women) is less central than the effort to identify women as nonassimilable to the artificial groups that do not so much confirm the value we already have as persons as add to our value. She has, in other aspects of her argument against pornography, insisted upon resemblance (in the similarity between simulated and actual instances of voluntary and coerced pornographic performance, in the similarity between one woman who had to be coerced into pornographic performance and all women) to suggest that a collective image (of women in general) affects women as individuals and to suggest that restrictions on pornography will importantly serve to revalue that image. Women, who are now women by virtue of social assignment, would be revalued in the process of altering the elements of the images through which that assignment worked.

That account plausibly stresses the importance of the image of the group one is assigned to, but it has a hard time stating what a properly valuable group image might be and when one would know it had been achieved. Richard Rorty makes a version of this point in his essay "Feminism and Pragmatism," in which he urges that MacKinnon withdraw her claims about the nature of pornographic objects and the reality of women's testimony and instead emphasize the importance of women as a group. Paraphrasing Marilyn Frye, he affirms that "individuals—even individuals of great courage and imagination—cannot achieve semantic authority, *even semantic authority over themselves,* on their own," that getting authority over oneself means hearing "your own statements as part of a shared practice," and that "people in search of such authority need to band together and form clubs, exclusive clubs." One might, in his view, discard the claim that all women ought to be feminists and simply recognize the importance of feminism as an affinity group, in which the group as a community with mutually reinforcing views enhances the value of each of its members. As he says,

> I am suggesting that we see the contemporary feminist movement as playing the same role in intellectual and moral progress as was played by, for example, Plato's Academy, the early Christians meeting in the catacombs, the invisible Copernican college of the seventeenth century, groups of workingmen gathering to discuss Tom Paine's pamphlets, and lots of other clubs which were formed to try out new ways of speaking, and to gather the moral strength to go out and change the world.[44]

In Rorty's view, feminism would profit from identifying itself more clearly in terms of affinity groups, collections of individuals who band together out of a sense of shared values and whose mutual agreement increases the authority of each.

Rorty's approach, politics by voluntary association, converts group membership into an expression of individual belief (much as the sex-affirmative arguments we have encountered earlier). In that, it sidesteps the difficulty we have encountered with MacKinnon's arguments that emphasize resemblance. Those arguments—that a real action might imitate a simulated action, that real actions involving injury sometimes occur in the making of representations of those actions, and that membership in the class of women is "an assignment made visually"—continually de-emphasize the importance of individual beliefs.[45] Insofar as you are who you are because of someone else's perception of you, group membership occurs, in MacKinnon's account, as a possibility that may be both positive (when one finds oneself surrounded by persons who imagine you to be like them) and privative (when one finds oneself, by virtue of one's membership in a stigmatized group, incapable of being seen to act outside of the pejorative stereotypes of that group and vulnerable to the images that constrain one by applying those pejorative stereotypes).

The sexual harassment argument presents still another account of the significance of groups. Whereas Rorty emphasizes the voluntariness of association in a common cause and whereas MacKinnon sometimes speaks of the global visual assignment of women to the category "woman," MacKinnon's focus on sexual harassment stresses that representations like pornography may be useful in the positive constitution of affinity groups only insofar as representations like pornography may also be useful (albeit negatively, for various disadvantaged groups) in the constitution of groups to which people do not intend to belong. And the fact that pornography may promote sexual freedom in promoting identification with a group is part and parcel of the fact that it may also promote sexual inequality whenever it is used to expel a person from a group.

By describing groups as products of common beliefs and interests, as expressions of affinity, Rorty makes an individual's membership in a group look continually like a positive assertion—a voting that one does with one's feet by staying in one place rather than going to another, by joining this group rather than that. Moreover, the description of pornography in terms of theater, which spectators ratify or condemn with their presence or departure, maintains a similar approach—that what you do, including what you are willing to see—expresses your beliefs and choices, and that a group can promote that process by hearing, ratifying, and echoing them.

Rorty's recommendation, that an individual define herself in terms of the maximal consistency of her beliefs and values with those of a group, would, that is, confirm MacKinnon's feminism. But it would do so by disregarding the claim that MacKinnon's account of sexual harassment rests on—that spaces like the workplace and the school are not mere locations but fundamental vehicles for framing action, and that sexual harassment is pornography not by virtue of its representation of bodies but by virtue of its action on the body of its victim, its effort to deny access to the group economies created by such environments.[46]

This is to say that when Richard Posner observes that "pornography is not about relationships," one can take his meaning—that pornography does not concern itself with lasting emotional ties, with mutuality and affection—but can also see the plausibility of the obverse, that pornography is about nothing but "relationship"—the ways in which pornography revolves around the reliance of individual action on other persons.[47] On the one hand, a group seems most completely a group when the individuals in it share a maximal number of beliefs, as did the early Christians; freedom and authority alike stem from the capacity to function as a group. On the other hand, there is a less psychologically immediate account of groups that specifically minimizes the place of common belief. That account, articulated most clearly in Bentham's descriptions of the schoolroom and the workhouse, dispenses with a host of beliefs and common attributes as the basis for a working relationship, because these are social organizations that do not so much reflect common views as substitute for them. In this account, the factory system magnifies individual action in the process of specializing it (so that the turn of a screw might become a recognizable act in the building of a car); the schoolroom continually revalues an individual's answers and omissions by routing them through the answers and omissions of others (so that individual merit—the rank in one's class—continually displays itself as both agreement with and difference from other individuals).[48]

However much the school and the factory have been viewed as instruments for inducing conformity, that is, the Benthamite description of them suggests their unique importance in revaluing individuals and their actions. The artificial group that can restrict its claims on common beliefs to something very close to the mere belief in the group and its very restricted action—that this is going to school, that this is doing work—revalues the importance of individual action by giving it significance in relation to the economy of the group. As opposed to the various analyses that attempt to look at action simply in terms of its expression of what one believes, the artificial group can be assimilative precisely because it has so comparatively few requirements for entry and participation.[49]

If MacKinnon once presented her anti-pornography position in terms of its connection with "a mode of portrayal that has a legal history—the sexually explicit," I am suggesting, she was relying on the wrong legal history.[50] Inasmuch as that legal history has been seen in terms of the rights of groups to be groups and the rights of the individuals who represent those groups to express their views freely, it has been hard to explain how the assault on sexual explicitness would not advance some groups at the expense of others.[51] MacKinnon's argument from sexual harassment, however, suggests the importance of these environments for creating groups that have, and need, relatively little agreement and resemblance among the individuals that form them. For sexual harassment in her account requires no more or less than the effort to treat these artificial environments and the groups they produce as if they could be reconverted into statements of affinity and the groups that they determine. The harm of pornography, in other words, does not lie in the fact that it takes images that one might consent to see in private and makes them public, nor in the fact that pornography may in this sense be assaultive and act-like. Rather, the harm of pornography used in sexual harassment is that it would effectively eliminate the publicness of the public sphere, in continually trying to reread the minimal agreements of modern public spaces as if they ought always to resolve themselves into private compacts and to reconstrue the minimal actions of secular groups as if they always involved unanimity about not one action but many. I take this to be the essential meaning of her statement that "the workplace and the academy are the sites of this confrontation [between free speech and discriminatory expression] not only because inequality is crucially enacted there, but because equality is crucially guaranteed there."[52] The question that argument poses is not why there is not full equality in every instance and in every context. It is, rather, why we extend the artificial environments of the school and the workplace only intermittently and restrict their claim that school and work, public accommodation and housing should not be a matter of similarity of belief or its physical equivalent.

The pornography debate, in other words, raises the question of toleration as fully as virtually every commentator has suggested. What I have been arguing is that we can crucially misconceive the nature and value of that toleration when we continually appeal to a genealogy of cases that treat that public sphere as a demilitarized zone in which the conflicting views of a variety of groups may, and indeed, ought to be expressed. For if we frequently do what we do out of a commitment to the beliefs that we hold and acknowledge by our membership in groups, then the artificial environments that constitute an important aspect of the public sphere also (and perhaps more significantly) promote toleration by lightening the grip of individual beliefs and the group memberships that they entail and express. By contrast with the view that, with enough performative ingenuity, anyone can become anything he or she can identify with, the logic of these artificial environments opens individuals to act in concert with a group to which they do not already belong. Its aim is to render irrelevant the aspects of individual identity (the gender and race continually resurrected by visual assignment) that are minimally susceptible to change on the basis of one's beliefs.

2   Justine, or The Law of the Road

I treat Sade's novel *Justine* as emblematic of a distinctively modern and utilitarian account of action and its significance for representations of individual intention. In the episodic structure of the novel, Sade recurrently presents his hapless heroine as a dupe of her own conviction that clarity about her intentions is significant. Thus, while Justine continually speaks of preserving her virtue in spite of the acts of debauchery in which she participates, Sade depicts this virtue as merely a "sentimental chastity," a notion conspicuously at odds with what he takes to be a proper acknowledgment of the physical conditions of action. Sade presents his argument that action is always physical and material, rather than metaphysical and immaterial, through two devices. First, he regularly assembles, at various locations along Justine's path, groups in which persons are physically present to one another but have no real communication, so that their actions are continually evaluated in a competitive utilitarian scheme, one that is concerned not just with posing abstract questions about the value of actions, but with giving explicit statements of their relative value in a concrete social group. Sade's depiction of the importance of sadistic domination and masochistic subordination thus emerges from a representational scheme that is not designed to capture the deep psychological motives that make those positions appealing; he simply advances the view that the crucial and ineradicable feature of society and social organization is competition among its members that transfers the power of some to the account of others. Second, Sade arranges Justine's actions so that, for all the vaunted innocence of her intentions, she regularly inflicts grievous injury on other people and brings about the deaths of persons whom she had meant to save. Her actions can therefore be seen in the terms of tort law, a law that began redeveloping (along lines recognizable in classical antiquity) in the eighteenth century. Tort law provides the model for seeing actions as created by the presence of an injured party, whether or not that injury was intended. In tort law, an action is treated as producing a relationship even between persons who are unknown to one another, and tort law offers up the most basic pattern of objectification for action, in which the perception of injury constitutes the action without needing to have recourse to an account of the agent's intentions.

In the wake of New Criticism and its emphasis on taking the poem, the story, the novel as the unit of analysis, literary criticism has recurrently found itself asking a set of questions that center on literature in its relation to what is, if not real, then at least nonliterary. It has seemed important, in other words, to identify the kind of work literature can be seen to do and to engage the question of how it relates to its messages. And nowhere have those questions seemed more urgent than in two apparently quite different types of studies—the accounts of the emergence of aesthetics and of the emergence of pornography.[1]

On the one hand, critics have seen aesthetics and pornography as completely distinct, as in Adorno's account of the eighteenth century's (and specifically Kant's) relegation of art and pornography to separate spheres.[2] If pornography was pornography by virtue of its insistent materialism and its appeal to affect, art was art by virtue of what came to be seen as the sublimation effected by formalism—the claim that art necessarily detached itself from the world and its representations. On the other hand, it has seemed to many critics that affectivism linked pornography and aesthetics: while the two might have different objects of representation, a similar emphasis on reception and affect suggested their affinities. In fact, some arguments have stressed affective recognition as so important to the constitution of art objects and pornography alike that their relative explicitness or inexplicitness did not matter.[3]

The following account of Sade's *Justine* offers a reading of that novel in the service of a hypothesis about pornography and aesthetics—namely, aesthetics and pornography can emerge as distinct spheres of philosophical speculation and legal regulation only in relation to the question of civil society as it emerges in the eighteenth century. Many histories of aesthetics trace the story of the abandonment of reference and reality in the emergence of the formalist argument for art, and many histories of pornography document what might look like the relatively steady advance of laws repressing sexuality and its expression in pornography and the various "victimless" crimes. Both sets of tendencies, however, obscure at least as much as they reveal (and do so for what is fundamentally the same reason—that they conceive art and pornography as involving epistemological transactions in which someone produces a discrete object with implicit or explicit messages that is more or less effectively received). Between the view that formalist aesthetics increasingly identifies art as the anti-didactic because it speaks in terms so formal as not really to have a message and the view that pornography's value lies in its speaking to a sexuality that needs never to be learned, there lurks a view to which we have insufficiently attended. It is that the evolution of civil society in the eighteenth century did not—or did not merely—extend democracy and replace monarchs with republics; it also registered how deeply civil society made itself a whole that was simultaneously more and less than the sum of its parts. Civil society, in other words, is not mass society by virtue of disseminating its products and its privileges more widely. Rather, civil society—in its extension of education to the many rather than the few, in its suggestion that art might serve as an anti-type to property, in its rediscovery of pornography—enables us to see the obsolescence of privacy even in the rise of protections for it, or the evacuation of individualism even in its triumph.

There are three basic points that I should like to make in relation to Sade's pertinence to these basic issues. First, I will claim that *Justine* is an example of pornography that does not so much challenge the law *tout court* as contribute a very specific position to the extensive eighteenth-century discussions of it. Second, I will argue that Sade's relentless punishment of Justine in the novel is not enacted just for the sake of being true to his character or nature (being Sade and therefore sadistic), but rather because he is implicitly making an argument that the very practices of domination and subordination that we take to be crucial to Sade and Sadeanism have already been replaced by the dissemination of punishment through society. And third, I will indicate the ways in which my reading of Sade involves a critique of the Foucauldian account of modern social organization.

Justine, published in 1791, epitomizes Sadean monotony, if we regard monotony as involving the relentless consistency of the novel's elements. In saying this, however, I do not mean to talk about the fact that the same thing arguably happens over and over again—though it does, as Justine goes from one miniature world to another, falling victim to one tyrant after another and to their either explicit or implied force. Rather, the repetitiveness of the various scenes in Sade's novel prevents there from being anything like plot, if plot is understood to involve anything like additive action. To state the obvious, *Justine* is a picaresque novel.[4] Yet *Justine* is not, I would argue, just another eighteenth-century picaresque, an example of the early novel's commitment to looking as if it were not yet art and were still preoccupied with the notion of imitating real and realistic narrative. Over forty years after *Tom Jones,* it repudiates the kind of novelistic advance that had enabled Fielding to produce the apparently random, episodic plot as the infinitely determined one (when Tom wandered long enough to be brought to the point of thinking that he was verging on marrying his mother), so that all roads might look as though they ended in the archetypal signature of plot that marked literature as literature. Moreover, it repudiates the artistic advance of well-formed plot in part by having Justine continually resume her original attitude, with her disposition to future action always looking uninfluenced by her own past. If Fielding had made the picaresque accommodate the modest recognitions of a virtually ineducable character (Tom), Sade insisted upon the episodic nature of his plot in part by preventing Justine from making any connections that seem to rise much above the level of the merely grammatical.

The novel *Justine,* that is, manages to be resolutely picaresque not merely by virtue of its employing the device of the journey, but also, and primarily, by virtue of the character Justine's inability to recognize any resemblances between one episode and another, her inability to adapt what she might have learned from one situation to another. I think particularly here of the ending of the novel, which features Justine providing a capsule summary of the novel's incidents as if she sees the elements of her cumulative history in explicitly causal terms but still cannot apply them to the future.

During my childhood I meet a usurer; he seeks to induce me to commit a theft, I refuse, he becomes rich. I fall amongst a band of thieves, I escape from them with a man whose life I save; by way of thanks, he rapes me. I reach the property of an aristocratic debauchee who has me set upon and devoured by his dogs for not having wanted to poison his aunt. From there I go to the home of a murderous and incestuous surgeon whom I strive to spare from doing a horrible deed: the butcher brands me for a criminal; he doubtless consummates his atrocities, makes his fortune, whilst I am obliged to beg for my bread. I wish to have the sacraments made available to me, I wish fervently to implore the Supreme Being whence howbeit I receive so many ills, and the august tribunal, at which I hope to find purification in our most holy mysteries, becomes the bloody theater of my ignominy: the monster who abuses and plunders me is elevated to his order's highest honors and I fall back into the appalling abyss of misery. I attempt to preserve a woman from her husband's fury, the cruel one wishes to put me to death by draining away my blood drop by drop. I wish to relieve a poor woman, she robs me. I give aid to a man whom adversaries have struck down and left unconscious, the thankless creature makes me turn a wheel like an animal; he hands me for his pleasure's sake; all fortune's blessings accrue to him, and I come within an ace of dying on the gallows for having been compelled to work for him. An unworthy woman seeks to seduce me for a new crime, a second time I lose the little I own in order to rescue her victim's treasure. A gentleman, a kind spirit[,] wishes to compensate me for all my sufferings by the offer of his hand, he dies in my arms before being able to do anything for me. I risk my life in a fire in order to snatch a child, who does not belong to me, from the flames; the infant's mother accuses and launches legal proceedings against me. I fall into my most mortal enemy's hands; she wishes to carry me off by force and take me to a man whose passion is to cut off heads: if I avoid that villain's sword it is so that I can trip and fall under Themis'. I implore the protection of a man whose life and fortune I once saved; I dare expect gratitude from him, he lures me to his house, he submits me to horrors, and there I find the iniquitous judge upon whom my case depends; both abuse me, both outrage me, both accelerate my doom; fortune overwhelms them with favors, I hasten on to death.[5]

If its heroine's name begins to identify the novel with the justice that Justine continually says she doesn't get, the novel's commitment to its picaresque mode locates its view of justice. For the picaresque here announces itself as the principle of geographical relativism, the view that the one transcendental rule is that laws are always local. This version of the law of the road represents might as making right within the domain that it can oversee. And if the initial joke of the novel is that Justine keeps failing to "learn," to carry over from one experience to another, the joke on the joke is that she is the purest geographical relativist of the novel: only she imagines that the sun might not rise tomorrow, only she believes that there might be a genuinely sympathetic individual over the horizon.

The argument in favor of geographical relativism had, of course, been put forth most famously by Montesquieu, in *De l'esprit des lois* (1748), and its care in outlining its account of government as a functional equivalent of collective intention established it as a particularly important moment in the eighteenth century's emerging debate between intentionalism and consequentialism in law. Although it deserves a lengthier critique than I can give it here, its undisputed importance seems to me a function of its incarnation of a "mentality" position, the view that individuals may not have intentions but that the groups in which individuals exist have intentions for them. As in Weber's later understanding of the Protestant spirit, the group, the geographically and culturally constituted state, functions as a disembodied individual, a repository of individual traits expanded and overblown by virtue of the fact that mere individuals don't have to be their bearers. As a compromise formation between transcendentalism and absolute individualism, it suggested that laws and customs inevitably extend past the individual; as a hybrid between intentionalism and consequentialism, it insisted that individual intentions were always the consequence of a social organization. Like a form of the weak social constructionist argument that is frequently attributed to Foucault, Montesquieu's description of governmental organizations keeps funding itself through the constant recirculation of its own terms: the individual is collective, et cetera.[6]

I take *Justine*'s concern with law and with government to involve a purification of geographical relativism: thus, Justine's imagining that the laws might really be local and therefore different over the next hill; thus, the prominence of the sovereign individual in Sade's work. If picaresque law is the nontranscendental law of geographical relativism, it is also the law of the nongeneral will. Sovereignty, according to its principles, must be individualizable, even if that sovereignty can only realize itself through an intensification of the policing powers of an individual subordinating all others to his will.

Another way of putting this point would be to say that Justine's plight, her repeated victimization, challenges the eighteenth-century project of democratizing action, the century's obsession with the question of how a government can be capacious enough to accommodate more than one set of intentions. It makes a simultaneous claim that intentions may constitute one's—specifically Justine's—sense of conscience *and* that intentions are irrelevant to anyone except oneself. Moreover, a distinctly utilitarian line of reasoning enables Sade to demonstrate that Justine's being an orphan, being deprived of a certain obfuscatory protection afforded by family life, immediately increases the likelihood that other people will see her less for her intentions than for her body. Strangers may not, in other words, understand what she means by virtue, but they continually find something to do with her body. As Dubourg, the rich man from whom she initially seeks aid, says:

> The thing which least flatters men, that which makes the least favorable impression upon them, for which they have the most supreme contempt, is good behavior in your sex; ... what does the virtue of women profit us! It is their wantonness which serves and amuses us; but their chastity could not interest us less. (470)

Justine as a picaresque novel forces the orphaned Justine to travel, and travel looks as though it ought to teach her a particularly intense version of Montesquieu's account of laws: that right and wrong are less ethical terms than geographical ones, dependent less upon what you do than upon where you are. Yet while Montesquieu had imagined that one could produce an empirical catalog of types of governments and the kinds of actions that each might favor without imagining an ideal type that all individuals ought to attain, Sade implicitly attacks even the notion of government that is local rather than transcendental as itself too strongly committed to intention. Sade produces a narrative that, as I suggested earlier, enlists Justine in a cartoonlike commitment to the primacy of her intentions. It does not matter, in her view, that her body has been through the proverbial wars. She can, she thinks, preserve a mental chastity. Thus, even after her body has been ravaged, she implores Saint-Florent to rescue her from the band of robbers, imagining her honor as the "unique treasure" that she has salvaged from her wreck of her body. She can recount being obliged to satisfy the wishes of a gang of robbers and gloss it with the remark that "at least my honor was respected even though my modesty assuredly was not" (486). As Rodin and Rombeau use her own argument against her and say that her conscience will remain unsullied through their rape because they promise that she "will have been vanquished by force" (556), as they brand her with the mark of the whore, she affirms cheerfully, "Whatever had been my trials until that time, at least I was in possession of my innocence" (557). Severino the monk can introduce her into the monastery as "one of the veritable wonders of the world, a Lucretia who simultaneously carries upon her shoulder the mark stigmatizing girls who are of evil repute, and, in her conscience, all the candor, all the naivete of a virgin . . ." (564). She reapplies the taunts of others as if they were comforting: she cherishes what Dubois the procuress calls her "sentimental chastity" (705). Like a strange variation on high Calvinist antinomianism and its claim that election constitutes a spiritual state that may go so far as to nullify the significance of individual acts, Justine's chastity is "sentimental" in its refusal to acknowledge acts that she has not meant to commit. Her position is, in the first place, completely plausible. If the mere physical act of sexual intercourse, regardless of the intention to have intercourse, counted as an action, we would not have the notion of rape and the corollary notion of a rape victim. Justine is not, then, entirely absurd to imagine that her virtue is not compromised by acts she was coerced into committing. Western criminal law constantly relies upon just such a distinction; it is intention that sorts the criminal from the innocent, the criminal from the victim.

Yet even though Nietzsche characterized Western law as having increasingly abandoned the Greek moral understanding of "the value or disvalue of an action . . . from its consequences," the outcomes of one's actions,[7] the history of law in the eighteenth century defines a different trajectory altogether. Kant, certainly, was perfecting the intentionalist argument for ethical action by suggesting that one entered into the equivalent of an illusory contract with oneself in the absence of any sense of inevitable reward and in the absence of any sense of inevitable contractual exchange with anyone else.[8] Yet the burden of legal consequentialism in the work of figures like Beccaria and Bentham was an assertion of the irrelevance—or, at least, the reduced relevance—of intention.[9] If the intentionalist approach to law and morals involved hating the sinner who could mean to commit a particular act, the consequentialist approach eliminated the criminalization of apparently ignoble states of mind by asking if the practices they involved really resulted in harm to anyone. (Thus, Bentham's famous defense of usury freed it from its socioreligious history and identified it instead in terms of an analysis of its productive effects.) *Justine*'s particular spin on these issues is to foreground the question of bodily liability. For if Justine is continually being falsely accused and framed for the very crimes she refuses to collaborate in, her vulnerability to being framed comes from the fact that she keeps being physically located at the scenes of crimes, and that her physical presence has infinitely more weight than her statements of her intentions and her innocence. Her refusal to participate in crimes becomes the immediate cause of her being accused of crimes.

Moreover, false accusation is only the simplest version of Justine's problem with her body, as she becomes what she calls "criminal through virtue." And "virtuous criminality," Sade's most brilliant stroke in the novel, involves Justine in committing a crime in order to cover the tracks of an innocence that looks like guilt. As Monsieur du Harpin the avaricious thief brings charges against her to "be rid of a creature who, through possession of his secret [thievery], had become his master" (479), the novel lays down its key pattern. Justine sees herself "upon the brink of having to pay with my life for having refused to participate in a crime"(479); and then she knowingly witnesses an arson at the Conciergerie in which "many people" are burned (480). Now Dubois the arsonist who arranges the actual torching of the Conciergerie glosses the matter by simply suggesting that virtue suffers while crime pays: "A misplaced delicacy led you to the foot of the scaffold, an appalling crime rescued you from it . . ." (480). Yet that simple reversal, the neat chiasmus in which good intentions produce bad consequences and vice versa, may epitomize Dubois's views, but it by no means captures the extent and complexity of the matter. For the trick of the plot is continually to take an innocent and turn her out as a criminal, and to do so without ever corrupting her mind—and, indeed, *without so much as needing to corrupt her mind.*

This is to say that *Justine* depicts recruitment to pornography by virtue of making her examination of her own motives continually free her to commit new crimes. Justine, in other words, may take comfort in the fact that her performing as a slave or a servant exonerates her of having acted willingly (640), but the very process of self-examination enables her to function as an increasingly effective tool of destruction. In describing her encounter with Coeur-de-fer and his band of robbers, this seems like merely a matter of choosing the lesser of two evils: faced with the possibility of being forcibly sodomized or vaginally raped, she remembers, "I was going to abandon myself and become criminal through virtue" (490); and only the coincidental arrival of travelers for Coeur-de-fer to rob saves her from choosing against one crime not by actually choosing but merely by appearing to choose the other.

Justine is put in an increasingly problematic position. Her being a slave by virtue of being an unprotected woman establishes her as repeatedly dependent and as necessarily being repeatedly a "sneak in bondage" (647). But she does not merely accept the appearance of complicity in crime in order to avoid committing a crime, as when she agrees to aid the Comte de Bressac in his plot to kill his aunt precisely so that she will be able to save the woman. Refusing to collaborate with the comte would not save his aunt; appearing to collaborate enables Justine to perform a virtuous action by means of the appearance of perfidy. But Sade has Justine commit to consciousness that her virtuous motives must, perforce, commit her to the vicious action of lying.

Le parjure est vertu quand on promit le crime, one of our tragic poets has said; but perjury is always odious to a delicate and sensitive spirit which finds itself compelled to resort to it. My role embarrassed me. (526)

The embarrassment of conscious duplicity, however, will become the least of Justine's difficulties. For her efforts to enlist herself on behalf of other unfortunates and to create leagues of women—from Madame de Bressac to Rosalie in the convent, to Madame de Gernande, the wife of the blood-sucking count, to Suzanne, sister and mistress of Roland the counterfeiter—will be punished and will multiply the sufferings of the very victims she intended to aid. The lie that she sees herself enlisted to produce continually enlists her as part of the project of torture. And never having intended any wrong itself becomes part of the extension of the wrong.

Toward the end of the novel, one reaches the apogee of this pattern, and Justine's double agency ceases to involve the contradiction between what one says and what one really means to do and involves instead conspicuously deficient intention. Justine, having taken refuge from the pursuing Dubois in a Villefranche inn, wakes to find the place in flames and everyone around her in panicky flight. She hastens from the inn with a woman with whom she has recently joined forces on the road and

> ... at this point I remember that my conductress, more concerned for her own than for her child's safety, has not thought of preserving it from death; without a word to the woman, I fly to our chamber, having to pass through the conflagration and to sustain burns in several places: I snatch up the poor little creature, spring forward to restore her to her mother: I advance along a half-consumed beam, miss my footing, instinctively thrust out my hands, this natural reflex forces me to release the precious burden in my arms.... [I]t slips from my grasp and the unlucky child falls into the inferno before its own mother's eyes; at this instant I am myself seized.... (712)

If Justine has regularly reassured herself that, as a servant or a slave, she never acted willingly in anything whatsoever, the meddlesome commitment to virtue that makes her more solicitous of the child than its own mother here emerges with considerable clarity. No one has made her pick up the child; and even if a "natural reflex" forced her "to release the precious burden in [her] arms," no one has made her drop the infant.

This "crime" is the one Justine stands accused of as she relates her story to her long-lost and recently refound sister Juliette and her lover Monsieur de Corville. But it is an especially peculiar crime in a novel obsessed with an analysis of the rewards and punishments of crime. On the one hand, the novel has repeatedly challenged the wisdom of a criminal law that can, in the process of trying to discourage the crime of robbery with capital punishment, actually provide an incentive for a robber, who already potentially stands under a capital sentence, to commit murder as well.[10] On the other hand, it is difficult to see what kind of disincentive, what kind of exemplary punishment, one might offer to discourage the crime of tripping and falling, the misdeed of dropping and breaking.

For in a novel in which there are many intentional crimes that Justine herself may not have intended, Justine's abortive rescue—the good deed–cum-murder—is the first purely unintended harm. And its occurrence marks an important shift in the understanding of the law and its relationship to Sadean pornography. For the ultimate rebuke to Justine's virtuous intentions is not that other people interfere with her ability to effect them but that a thoroughgoing consequentialism would begin to erode the value of that virtue. That is, the eighteenth century's major contribution to Western law would occur less in the form of any codification of the law than in the evolution of a law of torts to supplement the criminal law. Here, in making this claim, I am of course employing a concept that would not necessarily have had a clear definition for Sade, since the law of torts emerged irregularly throughout the eighteenth and nineteenth centuries and would receive its first histories only in the 1920s in England and America. Suffice it to say, however, that tort law came into being largely as what one can think of as a law of the road. It did not rely upon the justice or honor of thieves (the assumption that might makes right); but, on the other hand, it almost completely bypassed a transcendental argument that implicitly established some version of contract—or an appeal to the durability of intentions—as the basis of law. Rather, as an essential complement to mercantilism, it emphasized a law of physical persistence over time and space. Against the credit economy's emphasis on relating individuals and their rights and obligations to the property that gave them incentives for character, for stability of disposition, the very circulation of goods in the mercantile economy produced an argument that ultimately had very little to do with the notion of the value of the goods. For tort law assigned a liability for possession that matched and perhaps overmatched the privileges of that possession, as tort law came to hold persons responsible for their effects and for the effects of their objects. The paradigmatic early cases established a law of the road by claiming that a person's carriage did not cease to be his/her carriage even when it was out of his/her control. In the eighteenth century's early versions of the laws that presently require us to carry insurance against the damages we might unwillingly and unwittingly commit against others, it might be a defense against the criminality of our intentions that we could have no motive for doing harm to someone we didn't know (and thus would have no feelings about) if we saw no possibility of gain to ourselves. The logic of causation, however, operated to emphasize the material persistence of persons, of objects at the expense of intentions. Not only was ignorance of the law, in the materialist account of tort law, no excuse; one could never really be anything but ignorant of the law so long as the future remained invisible. And therefore the notion of rewards and punishments for actions—indeed, the very notion of actions—was considerably refashioned.

One way of describing the effect of tort law would be to say that it mistakenly tries to assert social control over the accidents of fate. But it seems to me that one major element—both cause and effect—of tort law is to demonstrate the limits of quietism, or the activity even of inaction. If the existence of tort law exposes what Bernard Williams has called the "moral luck" of those of us who are able to have relatively clear consciences because our cars have not gone out of control and accidentally caused us to kill or maim anyone lately, it is especially important for funding the errors of omission as well as the errors of commission.[11] Tort law, that is, makes incapacity count as an action.

That Justine should have begun to do harm as the unwilling servant or instrument of others, that she should have ended by being unable to have avoided doing harm begins to clarify certain otherwise mysterious elements of Sade's novel. They are, moreover, issues worth addressing because they speak to the question of Sadeanism—its sadism, its masochism—quite directly. These are, first, Sade's strong argument against contract because contract presupposes an unattainable equality; and, second, his handling of the question of punishment.

In the episode involving the Count de Gernande, serial vampire to a succession of wives, Gernande delivers himself of an eloquent denunciation of the illogic of contract in marriage (and far more so in the civil state).

"How are you justified," he asks Thérèse/Justine, "in asserting that a husband lies under the obligation to make his wife happy? . . . The necessity mutually to render one another happy cannot legitimately exist save between two persons equally furnished with the capacity to do one another hurt and, consequently, between two persons of commensurate strength. . . . I can agree not to employ force against him whose own strength makes him to be feared; but what could motivate me to moderate the effects of my strength upon the being Nature subordinates to me?" (645)

A passage that lends support to the claim that sadomasochistic contract is not a particularly Sadean notion, it seems to enlist itself on the side of an insistent assertion of the physically enforceable will. Yet it follows on a description of Gernande that correlates his merciless practices with his incompetence or incapacity.

It was then I noticed, [Thérèse relates], not without astonishment that this giant, this species of monster whose aspect alone was enough to strike terror, was howbeit barely a man; the most meager, the most minuscule excrescence of flesh or, to make a juster comparison, what one might find in a child of three was all one discovered upon this so very enormous and otherwise so corpulent individual. (641)

What seems to me to be suggested by the various elements of the Gernande episode is what one might think of as a theory of progressive action, analogous to a theory of progressive taxation. In the legal economy, one should only be expected and required to act according to one's ability to act. As Clément has repeatedly declared to Thérèse/Justine during her incarceration in the monastery, "It is the most barbarous and stupid intolerance to wish to fly at" the throat of the individual, who singular and extravagant, is "no more guilty toward society . . . than is . . . the person who came blind and lame into the world" (602).

Taken alone, Clément's arguments might simply be taken as advocacy of pluralism (with sexuality made the paradigm of what it might mean for the senses to be abled or disabled, functional or dysfunctional); taken alone, Gernande's repudiation of contract might seem to continue its claim that the freedom to act is fundamentally asymmetrical and unequalizable. Together, and with the account of the "fatal apathy" of Gernande as an epitome of "the true libertine soul" (644), these views indicate the massive changes that the logic of the law of torts effects upon the body of criminal law. While it may be difficult, even impossible, for an individual to perform a virtuous action, to satisfy a contract implicit or explicit, Sadean sadism is the process of recognizing harm to another as a kind of prosthetics of agency. The unlovable and the incompetent may have no positive capacity to please, that is, but harm is something one can accomplish without charm or resources—"apathetically."

Indeed, all the mechanisms of the Benedictine monastery suggest how far apathy may be from asceticism. For the trick of the monastery involves not merely converting the young women who have been abducted at the monks' behest into the servants of their pleasures. It includes a transfer of agency so extreme that the young women's actions are completely detached from their intentions. This is, in the first place, a matter of their facing up to the inevitability of their fates, to the "impunity guaranteed [the monks] by this impregnable retreat" (580). As young women who are bereft of observers, of people who will sound any alarm at their disappearance, they are transported into an enclosure whose rules contradict their wills so thoroughly that their wills become obviously irrelevant, and, indeed, "all resistance" comes to seem "pure affectation, pretense, and useless" (567).

In the moment that resistance comes to be defined as "feigned" whether one means it or not, the importance of the notion of the restricted group or class in Sadean pornography becomes clear. The regimentation of the Monastery of Saint Mary-in-the-Wood, that is, may involve an interest in imposing discipline, in producing an arbitrary system that is inflexibly maintained, but even more importantly the regimentation assembles groups of people—four classes of four women each, twelve procuresses who provide twelve young women a year for the monks, circles of debauchees—so as to transfer agency. Thus, the penal code of the monastery must be detailed to each new inmate, but the code is one that is arbitrary not by contrast with some standard of naturalness but because one has no way of conforming to it. Some offenses are punishable even though they have occurred "either through misunderstanding or for whatsoever may be the reason" (581); and if others, such as pregnancy, are punishable, their remedies (abortion) are as well.[12] As Omphale, the "superintendent" who explains the system to Thérèse/Justine, makes clear, the monks are interested only in sexuality as infinitely repeated rape, sexuality always separated from consent.

They do not absolutely confine themselves to virgins: a girl who has been seduced already or a married woman may prove equally pleasing, but a forcible abduction has got to take place, rape must be involved, and it must be definitely verified . . . ; they wish to be certain their crimes cost tears; they would send away any girl who was to come here voluntarily; had you not made a prodigious defense, had they not recognized a veritable fund of virtue in you, and, consequently, the possibility of crime, they would not have kept you twenty-four hours. (587)

And, in the ultimate conceit for the monastery's dislocation of the will, the young women who have been abductable by virtue of not being watched are required to maintain a constant vigil, to become "Girls of the Watch," each of whom "must remain awake all night throughout the whole of the term she spends with her master" and each of whom is made responsible and punishable for his every action and inaction—"who is always wrong, always at fault, always beaten" (585). The perfection of the monks' power, in other words, is that they can inflict suffering even in their sleep (611). And whatever deterrence effect might be achieved by a system of punishment with an ongoing effort to establish the law as an incentive system to individual action must contend with the transfer of both actions and their consequences.

Sadean pornography, in the account I'm giving of *Justine,* is thus important for establishing the notion of class action. But unlike the notion of class as an economic group defined by a relationship to the means of production, and unlike the notion of class as a group assembled through a classification of similar individuals or similar aims, class here functions as a conspicuously self-divided term. The Sadean enclosure, that is, operates not just to seal an individual from any world outside it, but (like the parentheses that identify a mathematical grouping or class) also to create the possibility of distributing action among the members of the group.

For what Sade describes in *Justine* is neither sadomasochism as a plausible version of sexual contract (establishing a class of sexual deviants) nor sadomasochism as what Lacan identifies as the opposite of the categorical imperative—an individual's right to demand unremittingly that others supply one's needs and desires (in which class domination and class subordination provide the model).[13] Instead, an enclosure creates a class less as a conceptual term, an epistemological statement, than as a tool for the redistribution of the consequences of action. As tort law supplements criminal law, there is no mere extension of the old law of the servant, which held a master accountable for the acts that a servant had committed at his behest. Instead, tort law identifies everyone except the sovereign individual (who becomes increasingly rare, increasingly elusive) as a servant to the very idea of the civil state, the law of society that is always verging on putting one in the wrong, by holding one accountable less for intentions than for consequences—or by holding one accountable for both simultaneously. And it is the simultaneity of these dual regimes of law that makes it particularly difficult to track their operations precisely, since the triumph of utilitarian legal arguments did not so much replace intentionalism with consequentialism as insist upon applying both at once. Acts that had long been criminal, such as murder and theft, remained criminal and thus found punishments that were designed to be disincentives; therefore, Sade is able to present the counterfeiter Roland as the perfected criminal less because he commits more crimes or more serious crimes than other characters than because he has unleashed the power of the legal system of disincentives. Loving being punished, having himself hanged for pleasure, his every action is charmed, and he can exist within a happy orbit of intentions in which even what he hasn't chosen seems like a reward. In tort law's distribution of rewards and punishments, he becomes a sovereign individual less through strength of will than through an accident of adaptation that enables him to experience punishment as a reward.

Though Sadean criminality has recurrently been seen as a conscious violation of conventional morality, I think that the existentially thrilling account of the Sadean hero who chooses his necessity and demands the punishment that others might impose on him is fundamentally flawed. For whatever else Sade may have been doing (and whether or not he liked what he was describing), he was providing one of the most effective ways of identifying the way in which tort law funded a host of new forms of action.

To some extent, my view of tort law coincides with Foucault's account of the disciplinary society, with its particular reliance on Bentham's Panopticon as an emblem of the importance of visibility.[14] Within the various Panoptic structures of society, Foucault's argument says or implies, certain kinds of technological efficiencies occur. A Panopticon, by giving one superintendent a central position from which he can view a host of people, replaces the relative cumbersomeness of a social contract model of society (with one-to-one agreement providing a paradigm for the agreement of many) with the control of many by one. By an effort of architecture, the Panopticon resolves a basic dilemma of the law: Why it is that when those who have been taken to be criminals assume the majority, they don't simply overtake the minority and make criminality the new law? The superintendent's impersonality, his having no personal views of those he supervises, further diminishes the contractual nature of the interaction, and being visible seems thus to acquire a particular resonance from its opposition to the notion of a potentially verifiable contractual agreement.

A great deal is almost instantaneously plausible about this version of Foucault. Yet its particular way of treating the relationship between penality and social action tends to make surveillance seem a sufficient consequence in itself, as if the expansion of visibility were itself a regulative process.[15] In this form, the Foucauldian account suggests how changing the odds of detecting a crime might act as a disincentive to further crime; and self-surveillance appears as an individual's tendency continually to represent probability as inevitability, likelihood as event. Yet what seems mistaken about this account is that it fails to register how fundamentally the consequentialism of the law of torts precipitated a reconfiguration of both action and its evidence. As much as Bentham wanted to have the Panopticon built, as much as he favored the reduction of the law to statute (what could be known in advance of action) rather than common law (what was always in danger of being invented on the spot by judges), his work on morals and legislation is important for having supplemented the anticipatory causation of intentional action with the retrospective causation of consequential effect. And in that maneuver, he underwrote tort law as a law of class that does not know itself because of being observed but recognizes itself as action because of what it has done. Thus, certain kinds of involuntary action—the damage caused by your property run amok that I mentioned earlier—come to count as moral action; indeed, certain kinds of omission become actions, as when eighteenth-century law identifies professional misconduct as one of the earliest examples of a tortious harm. In this process, the Panopticon is merely one instance of what it means for there to be such a thing as class formation. Like Wesleyan Methodism, with its introduction of the twelve-person class, and like the Lancasterian schoolroom, with its creation of large numbers of small grade levels for classes, the Benthamite account of causation produces class actions. While all of these social structures have been seen as implementing social conformity and establishing oppressive disciplinary regimes in every conceivable direction, they are, instead, crucial in making action look as though it were only possible through other people. (The examinations in a Lancasterian classroom, for instance, continually correlate your achievement with that of other people; indeed, they speak the message of class even as they ostensibly inaugurate the expansion of education beyond the ranks of the aristocracy and the gentry by making your class standing depend not merely on your knowledge but also on someone else's failure or lapse of knowledge.)

This is as much as to say that Sadean pornography joins Benthamite consequentialism and a host of class-forming practices in eighteenth-century civil society to make actions more visible in relation to other people than in relation to individual intention. The importance of the visibility of pornography is, thus, not that it assaults the eyes (with sight taken to be the most involuntarily transmissible sense), not that it offends the public good, the public interest, the public morals. Rather, it is that *Justine* presents pornography as the model of action in which morality is extremely imperfectly assimilable to rules of conduct, codes of behavior that may be taught. For pornography, in this view, commits itself less to affect (the production of further responses and consequences) than with effect (the manifestation of the visible consequences of what one has already done). As *Justine* keeps telling its heroine, "There's no justice," or, "Now look what you've done."

This particular account of Sadean pornography, as instanced by *Justine*, may serve to suggest how important it is to revise what has come to be a conventional antithesis between Kant and Sade, aesthetics and pornography. As I have argued elsewhere,[16] the Kantian sublime founds Kant's version of idealist aesthetics on the insistence that aesthetic experience essentially involves a reconfiguration of our notion of objects. From the moment that Kant distinguishes the sublime from the beautiful principally on account of its being natural—its not having been produced by human beings for human beings—the aesthetic appreciation of nature becomes something quite distinct from a *recognition* or *understanding* of objects. The aesthetic appreciation of what was never made to be appreciated, that is, eliminates the need—and, indeed, the possibility—for certain kinds of justification and explanation; it cares less about evaluating a beech tree, for instance, as a specimen of beech trees than about producing what one can only call a new object from what may be accidental or transitory or incidental features of the old.

The account of the sublime, in other words, enables Kant to make the aesthetic the vehicle for the notion of ontological relativity. What I have been arguing about Sadean pornography in the case of *Justine* is that it provides a similarly relativized account of what an action might be, to correspond with

Kant's relativized account of what an object might be. As civil law in the eighteenth century increasingly supplements criminal law's emphasis on intention with an emphasis on consequence, it reconfigures even the notion of personal intentions and individual character by making the material persistence of the body of the messenger (Justine and her equivalents) override any message that she might want to deliver.

Thus, pornography and aesthetics, however strongly they have been distinguished from one another as the most material and most immaterial poles of our experience of representations, are not nearly so much opposed as similar. They are similar in their shared commitment to the interimplications of medium and message, and to the ways in which those interimplications enable the reconfiguration of both objects and actions by expanding the role of effects in defining them. They are similar, that is, in making effects so much more important than intentions that the aesthetic can lay claim to a pleasure that was never meant (since the sublime is, in Kant's view, concerned only with a pleasure in what was never designed for our perception or our pleasure), and the pornographic can attach blame to a harm that was never intended (since the pornographic is, in Sade's view, concerned only with the physical and "unsentimental" effects of one's actions). This is as much as to say that the relativity that both Kantian aesthetics and Sadean pornography attach to objects and actions conspicuously erodes the abilities of either aesthetic objects or pornography to "express" personal or ideological commitments, because the effective meaning of such objects and actions is no longer in the eye of the maker or the beholder.

3

Eugénie, or Sade and the Pornographic Legacy

In this chapter I describe how Sade's *Philosophy in the Bedroom* works out his view that understanding the centrality of human usefulness has profound implications for political thinking. "Use," he argues, can no longer be used as a synonym for custom. By the same token, however, the notion of use should not be extended into the future, as a projection of what might be useful at some unidentified time in the imaginable future. Sade's discussion of politics thus attacks the notion of abstract rights, as enunciated in the Declaration of the Rights of Man (which Bentham had referred to as "nonsense upon stilts")[1] in favor of a defense of the importance of the ready to hand. Although Sade ultimately develops an account of the rights of the sovereign that suggests there might be a relatively stable elite with the right to enforce its use of others, the main engine of the novel's perverse recommendation of intergenerational incest is Sade's attack on the Enlightenment privileging of the child. The pedagogy that initiates Eugénie into sexuality refuses to acknowledge children as a separate category of being, as Sade suggests in saying that the problem with modern societies based on abstract rights is that they barter the only experience one can actually have—the experience of persons and objects in the present—for the abstraction in which both children and potential children become the justification for political decisions. If Sade continues the critique of metaphysical accounts that he had begun in *Justine*, he also deepens that discussion by arguing that modern rights-based governments put themselves in debt to the future by crediting unuseful persons with rights, making it a condition of present action that living individuals act in the name of the barely born and the unborn. The abstract rights of the Revolutionaries thus come to look as pernicious and as unavailable for experience as the religious views that they had opposed.

My subject in this chapter is Sadean pornography and the function of outrage in establishing its place. As many have observed, hostile responses to Sade—his acts and his work—forwarded his literary career: public outrage over his private sexual acts sent him to prison, where he became even more an author than he had been before.[2] From that perspective, the story of Sadean pornography seems to be a story about the centrality of reception to any determination of the meaning and value of literary works. What Sade did and meant, in this light, looks less important than the fact that his writing comes to look symbolic, like a public relation. In the argument that follows, I shall be suggesting why I see Sadean pornography, with its ambiguous relation to the rise of Republicanism in France, as mounting an attack on the very relationship between the public and the private on which the conception of outrage is based. No matter how much Sade may have come to sympathize with Revolutionary ideals, that sympathy was continually constrained by Sade's attack on the notion of publicness, which he treated not so much as an alternative to an idea of privacy as the inauguration of a mistaken conception of persons.

The twentieth century has embraced Sade's writings with an enthusiasm so intense that it once appeared that writing about Sade was almost a predictable stage in establishing an intellectual career; what the writing of pastorals and epics had classically done to demonstrate poetic seriousness, writing about Sade did for writers like Blanchot, Bataille, Beauvoir, Barthes, Lacan, and Foucault. One might want to speculate that Sade's writings exerted their peculiar appeal in part because they emerged as suddenly as do fossil remains; although they were from the end of the eighteenth century, they had almost no historical baggage. The brute fact of their having initially inspired outrage had eliminated the possibility for much of that history, as the complexities of publishing the works had continually jeopardized the manuscripts' survival. It was not merely that Sade's works existed in the world of clandestine bookshops. It was that Sade's denials of authorship (for works like *Justine*) and his ruses of posthumous publication (for works like *La Philosophie dans le boudoir*) themselves were indices to the texts' extreme vulnerability. If Sade's incarceration made him both committed and prolific,[3] the hazards of imprisonment continually jeopardized the mere physical existence of his manifestos—most conspicuously when he lost control of some fifteen manuscripts during his transfer out of the Bastille ten days before it was stormed.

This is as much as to say that even though Sade's writings obviously came from the period surrounding the French Revolution, they were attractive in part because the regulations and the accidents governing their public appearance had insulated them from tradition. Custom could not stale what had been lost. What had been lost in turn preserved the freshness of what had been saved. With the lost texts haunting the available texts, with the history of earlier suppression and obstruction, Sade's writings have not merely provided examples for arguments about the necessity of free speech and unrepressed sexuality. Indeed, they have become icons of a cultural heritage made even more valuable because it is one that we were very nearly denied. With the preciousness of narrowly averted scarcity and possible extinction, they have functioned as central illustrations of the argument that censorship and repression violate a text's right to cultural transmission, a public's right to receive a canonical legacy as broad and diverse as possible.[4]

What concerns me here, in part, is the tension between the arguments defending access to Sade's work and the arguments put forth by that work itself. Some defenses of the right to read Sade seem to be grounded not merely on the claim that there should be as capacious an intellectual marketplace as possible but also on the assumption that the utility of that capaciousness emerges only as one realizes that Sade was "right." In this spirit, Angela Carter urges her view that nothing is inevitably not public, that time-bound social constructions continually alter the line between the private and the public. Sade must finally escape the censor by having, according to her lights, become true, and the very possibility of recognizing Sade as the contemporary of twentieth-century feminists like Carter herself can occur only if any given generation anticipates its obligations to its own posterity.[5] Censorship, outrage, and even inattention fail to register opportunities, as is implicit in her "Polemical Preface: Pornography in the Service of Women" in *The Sadeian Woman,* where the emphasis falls on an ongoing process of adaptive reception in which one learns to recognize one's own interests and image in the taboos of the past.

Pornographers are the enemies of women only because our contemporary ideology of pornography does not encompass the possibility of change, as if we were the slaves of history and not its makers, as if sexual relations were not necessarily an expression of social relations, as if sex itself were an external fact, one as immutable as the weather [*sic*], creating human practice but never a part of it.[6]

From this standpoint, changes in the reception of texts do not at all bespeak the irrelevance of reception. Instead, the assumption is that reception will eventually validate almost anything that has been preserved. One must inherit things like pornographic texts not to replicate them but to accumulate a range of choices for one's own "making" of "history." One preserves and publishes Sade because writing like his may come in handy, may come to look like an expression of the value of unrepressed sexuality.

In other words, the notion of a cultural debt, in the form of an obligation to preserve even what one may hate for the love that some future generation may have for it, has been instrumental in liberating Sade's texts from both intentional and accidental censorship. Yet for this particular line of argument to have preserved and indeed promoted Sade's work represents a considerable irony. If Sade's pornography epitomizes the notion of writing for affect, of depicting the differences that bodies can make to bodies, it constitutes an absolute alternative to such cultural tolerance. For the cultural pluralism that tolerates Sade justifies itself not in the name of affect but in the name of a projection of what affect might be for unborn beings in worlds not yet realized. As I shall argue, it is precisely the commitment to the linked notions of intergenerational obligation and intergenerational inheritance—a commitment that has in part served to protect Sade's writings—that Sade's writing most vehemently attacks.

The writing on Sade's work quite rightly centers on communicability, emphasizing the shifting social norms that condition communicability and the intersubjective implications of pornography respectively. The first of these positions—the one most frequently cited in publishers' prefaces that tell us that we can repress our sexuality only by risking our political freedom—credits Sade with having discovered a symbolic weapon in the sexuality that virtually all people would seem to have available to them. Pornography, in this account, shifts the burden of sexuality from sensation to representation, and its chief accomplishment is to register the extension of sexuality from individual bodies to the political world. Pornography, thus, registers the symbolic capital even of apparently private experience and sees that the symbolism rests upon a reversal of the valence of that private experience. Private pleasure evokes public outrage, as the depiction of sexuality pits its affective origins in sexual pleasure and its affective reception in outrage against one another. In this account, indeed, this opposition between the two sets of affect is the pornographic message. Pornography exists less as sexual explicitness than as the contest between competing accounts of health and abnormality, private and public, social obligation and individual self-assertion.

Yet the reaction of enlightened tolerance that both develops this line of argument and embraces Sadean pornography can be seen as well to involve a somewhat desperate combination of motives—wanting, that is, both to learn from pornography's message and also to avoid learning from it. If the political force of pornography lies in its capacity to offend against proprieties, then a society acculturated to pornography will be simultaneously informed by its account of proprieties and immune to its attack. The society that imagines itself uncommitted to proprieties, uninterested in outrage, is likewise the society that has already cut its losses. Treating pornography primarily as a matter of its affect and effect, being invested in the outrage that it can inspire, the progressive view accepts pornography. Yet having identified pornography as outrage, the very acceptance of pornography counts as a veritable kiss of death. To define pornography as outrage involves only the pleasure in imagining that one identifies with an outrage to someone else. From this standpoint, Sade, in setting up Eugénie's mother as a pornographic victim by virtue of her being an agent for social propriety, demonstrates something less like outrage than like a new cultural cliché. It adopts a progressivist view that an increasingly unrepressed society can make public the sexuality that had once been expressed in private or as an affront to the public sphere. Sade and Freud thus become intellectual partners in the smug and familiar story of the cultural annexation of previously private and taboo areas. In contemporary culture's rivalry with its own past, today's proprieties disappear in a convenient scapegoating of what we take previous mistaken norms to have been.

This is to say that, in a curious self-reversal, the apparently progressive, apparently tolerant view obliges itself to manufacture monsters, to create antagonists in the form of one's contemporaries or one's ancestors so that one can demonstrate outrage at their outrage, or complacency in the face of their offense. Pornography becomes, in this view, a contest of affect. The metaphysical illusions that the heuristic physicality of pornography would seem committed to dispelling reemerge as audience reaction.

Against this emphasis on response and reaction, another position has been, I think, more powerfully if less broadly influential. This account—one that I associate with the work of Blanchot, Bataille, and, most recently, Bersani—treats pornography as politically significant in setting a limit to politics—if by politics one means anything that has to do with interchange or exchange between persons. This second position treats Sadean pornography as pointing to an outrage so ineradicable as to be beyond mere affect—namely, that sexuality remains so private as to constitute a barrier to intersubjective communication in general (between persons and, indeed, within persons).

The first of these positions sees Sade as using the physical to make an attack on metaphysics, seen as the excessive incorporeality of justifications of political power. Insofar as it emphasizes the symbolic as a contest of affect, however, it reintroduces metaphysics as a political by-product. The second of them (to which I shall return later) likewise sees him as attacking metaphysics by means of an insistence on the body's capacity for sexual physicality, but it emphasizes that that physical capacity does not establish a new political position. Sadean pornography, by virtue of having scandalized fathers and mothers, may make sexual explicitness look like a symbolic weapon. It has not with this gesture, however, so much established a new political insight as registered the impossibility of political solutions. For sexuality, in the work of Blanchot, Bataille, Beauvoir, and Bersani, ultimately and continually refers to the physical; and sexuality establishes inequality as a necessary, rather than incidental, element of pleasure. The sexual exchange that seems to narrow the social contract to its most basic units does not, for these writers, produce loving mutuality in a private encounter seen as a refuge from and counter to a public and unjust world. Rather, inequality begins in sexuality.

In the discussion that follows, I shall be, essentially, taking up various aspects of the view that Sade attempts in the *Philosophy in the Bedroom*: to write a political dialogue that would be as material—as physical and as unmetaphysical—as possible. In that sense, understanding pornography as a genre with specific claims embedded in its medium seems important. For pornography's medium—or its heuristic medium—would avoid representational metaphysics; it would write in bodies (as in the passage at the beginning of the *Philosophy* in which Madame de Saint-Ange offers herself up as an instructional aid, the living embodiment of an anatomy chart).[7]

In addition to arguing that Sade's interest in the pornographic is generally anti-metaphysical, however, I shall also be claiming that Sade's *Philosophy in the Bedroom* is specifically anti-cultural. Culture, which in the *Philosophy* comes to represent the transmissibility of civil society from one generation to another, also amounts to a notion of intergenerational inheritance that emerges specifically in the context of the French politics of the national debt. The legacy of the French Revolution, in the terms of Sade's *Philosophie,* is at least as much a dissemination of indebtedness as of entitlement, as individuals come to secure equal rights by means of a national process of buying out individual inheritances (church lands as well as the public offices that, by virtue of being bought and sold and by virtue of being treated as heritable, had been converted into property) with public funds. The attempt to maximize intragenerational equality, that is, becomes the vehicle for promoting intergenerational inequality, for inaugurating the national debt as the emblem of the modern state as illimitable shared responsibilities.

Recently Sadean pornography has been of interest to historians of the French Revolutionary period (Lynn Hunt and others) because it participates in the eighteenth century's discovery that politics could be waged by sexual means.[8] Sexuality, in this view, is less physical than symbolic. Pornographic pamphlets and cartoons, particularly those directed against the royal family, made private sexual acts look like public crimes. If their sexuality made Louis XVI and Marie Antoinette look human rather than divine, Louis's rumored sexual impotence and Marie Antoinette's supposed incest with the Dauphin made them look less than human, as if sexual abnormality clearly vitiated any claims to legitimate inheritance of sovereign power. Pornography, in this account, collapses the king's two bodies into one, exposing the noncorporeal body as a sham and indicting the royal family of libertinage; their sexual excesses assimilated themselves to the same pattern of pretension that had enabled the king to claim two bodies, instead of the one that is standard issue for the rest of mankind.

Within the context of the growing political exploitation of pornography during the last years of the ancien régime, in other words, it makes sense for Sade to have been incarcerated for libertinage. Thus, for historians uncovering the politics of pornography, Sade's protest in his famous letter of 20 February 1781 appears more than a little disingenuous:

Yes, I admit I am a libertine and in that area I have imagined everything that can be imagined. But I have absolutely not acted out everything that I imagined nor do I intend to. I am a libertine, but I am not a criminal or a murderer.[9]

If the logic of political pornography of Sade's era was to annihilate the royalist claim to a nonphysical body, the politics of pornography made libertinage itself a crime. Yet the analogy between political liberty and sexual liberty does not completely explain Sade's versatility as an equal-opportunity offender and his remarkable ability to return to prison under the old regime and the new, under the Monarchy, the Republic, the Consulate, and the Empire. If the crime of the pornographer against the monarchy was to decry the royal presumption to a metaphysical body, his crime against the Republic in turn was to charge that it had consistently attacked the wrong target. Where the Republic had attacked bodies that seem associated with the illusions of religion, monarchy, and feudal property rights, Sade suggests an implicit conservatism even in this approach. The gothic illusions that had accompanied various physical entities, that is, may attach to the progressive as well as the royalist position.

Sade's dogged materialism, his dispatching of spirit and presentation of nature as merely matter in motion without recourse to any metaphysical external cause, suggests the difficulty of assimilating him to a particular progressive or regressive politics. In the twentieth century, the rediscovery of Sade has involved a second position—an enthusiasm for the sexuality of his texts that examines the aesthetics of a writing that eschews what I am calling metaphysics by appeal to individual privacy. Blanchot's account of the inevitable egoism of sexual experience can thus be read as an insistence upon Sade's pornography as establishing an ineradicable domain of solitude.[10] However much the modern democratic state may nationalize and publicize, Sadean pornography announces the limits of the public arena. However much sexual pleasure in Sade relies upon the presence of others, it nonetheless remains, for Blanchot, supremely private. Sexual pleasure comes to be the epitome of the bodily sensation as absolutely ungeneralizable (nontranscendental) experience.

Indeed, as Bataille builds upon Blanchot's reading of Sade, the notion of sexual pleasure as a version of contact without communication becomes increasingly clear.[11] Those characters whom Bataille titles "sovereign beings" demonstrate not merely that one person's sexual pleasure does not operate to disseminate sexual pleasure to his/her partner(s); they also indicate for Bataille the ways in which sexuality continually reinaugurates societal inequality. The sovereign being, that is, happily produces the pain of his/her partner for the sake of his own pleasure. As the most private of all private experience, sexual pleasure makes tyrants of us all, because it constitutes an assertion that one's pleasure does not rest on a transmission of pleasure (a solicitous regard for one's partner[s] as expressed in the question "Was it good for you?"). From an entirely non-Bataillean perspective, pornography might register a kind of equality by undressing people and making bodies rather than clothing or any external ornament the focus of attention. From a Bataillean perspective, pornography does not stress equality by dwelling on the fact that all persons, whatever else they may have, have bodies. Instead, it insists that inequality begins with the body, as the pain or discomfort of the "superior individual's" sexual partner comes to look like an essential rather than an accidental part of that pleasure. As Bataille puts it in *L'Erotisme*:

The kind of sexuality he [Sade] has in mind runs counter to the desires of other people . . . ; they are to be victims, not partners. De Sade makes his heroes uniquely self-centred; the partners are denied any rights at all: this is the key to his system. . . . Communion between the participants is a limiting factor and it must be ruptured before the true violent nature of eroticism can be seen, whose translation into practice corresponds with the notion of the sovereign man. The man subject to no restraints of any kind falls on his victims with the devouring fury of a vicious hound.[12]

As Bataille elaborates the argument, Sadean pornography not only reveals the fundamental equivalence of sexuality and violence; it also comes to represent an inequality absolutely fundamental to even the apparently egalitarian Republican state. Thus, even though Bataille sees Sade as, in part, having "sided with the Revolution and criticised the monarchy," he also sees Sadean pornography as providing a consolation for the loss of that monarchy. Sadean pornography becomes the aesthetic replacement for monarchical glory. Indeed, Bataille continues this line of argument by affirming that Sade "exploited the infinite possibilities of literature and propounded to his readers the concept of a sovereign type of humanity whose privileges would not have to be agreed upon by the masses"[13]—and that, for Bataille, is important precisely because they could not be agreed upon by even two persons, much less the masses.

The place of pornography for these commentators becomes abundantly if ambivalently clear. Pornography, as the absolute opposite to even vestigial notions of contract that control many nineteenth-century accounts of aesthetic experience, registers the possibility of material affect. It alters the terms of exchange for the contract of pleasure, insisting that it was never designed to create equality or equilibrium but rather to identify inequality, violence, and sexuality. Sexuality for Sade is merely the inherent motion of matter, with that motion being so much a property or attribute as to render any external motive or spirit conspicuously redundant.[14] And as such motion, sexuality is as inimical to equality as it is indifferent to a divinity.

All acts of heterosexual intercourse thus look as inequitable as Catharine MacKinnon and Andrea Dworkin have claimed that they are.[15] Bataille had made the egoism of sexuality appear an invalidation of the social contract as such—until, of course, the symbolic significance of the sovereign individual came to function as a collective social myth that did not so much challenge society as sustain it. The "infinite possibilities of literature," that is, resurrect the religious, royalist, and feudal standards that the egoistic sexual self would seem to have renounced. Pornography writes the story of sexuality as inequality, an inequality that is intrinsic to every sexual act involving more than one person.

Although MacKinnon and Dworkin have identified all heterosexual acts as intrinsically inequitable, revolving as they do around some positional version of domination and subordination, the inequality of sexuality has continued to surface even in accounts of gay and lesbian sexual acts. Thus,

Leo Bersani—in his brilliant extension of Bataille's position in "Is the Rectum a Grave?"—has argued that not even sexual acts between gay men escape the taint of inequality that sexuality brings to human relations.[16] Were all men created equal, the argument runs, they would cease to be so with the advent of sexual relations. Natural inequalities between bodies exist, but even if they did not, sexual acts would invent them, establishing domination and subordination within even the most egoistic and asocial experience open to humans. Yet where Bataille establishes the sovereign individual as a surrogate for the monarch, Bersani makes sexual egoism its own state, in which the will-to-domination of the sexual self also entails the shattering of that self; the very pleasure that it arrogates to itself as its own egoistic portion constitutes the selfishness of the self as the instrument of its own annihilation.

If Dworkin and MacKinnon define the inequality of sexuality in terms of gender identities, Bersani's account emphasizes the way in which sexual acts themselves destroy identities. Yet what is particularly striking from my perspective is that the language of domination and subordination for these accounts falls largely on power disequilibria between contemporaries, between sexual partners. Bodies mobilize themselves in sexual acts and do not so much incidentally express inequality between partners as they enact it. Thus, Bersani writes, in part of his extended argument, that "human bodies are constructed in such a way that it is, or at least has been, almost impossible not to associate mastery and subordination with the experience of our most intense pleasures. This is first of all a question of positioning."[17] And he goes on to suggest that the reproduction necessary to the continuation of the species can only (until recently) proceed by an act of biological injustice. The end—the preservation of the species—requires that sexual acts be politically incorrect.

But if the means of reproduction themselves carry the taint of inequality, that end—the continued generation of persons—constitutes for Sade an even more massive inequality, one in which we recruit the unconsenting for society and continually announce the simultaneous hold of the social contract on persons who succeed one another in time. Writing an educational treatise that would conform to our own current accounts of sexual harassment,[18] Sade presents *The Philosophy in the Bedroom* as if the inequality of sexual acts were an inequality so mild as to constitute a veritable antidote to the inequality of human succession.

What is pornographic about Sadean pornography is not, or not merely, that it establishes the limits to communication in language or the limits to equality in sexuality. It is, rather, that pornography would, with the privacy and self-shattering self-interest of sexuality, undo a metaphysics that is always extending matter in time and space to create causes and histories as if matter could not, did not, take care of itself.

This anti-metaphysical position emerges, most conspicuously, in the pamphlet "Yet Another Effort Frenchmen, if You Would Become Republicans," that Sade encapsulates in the *Philosophie*. In the latter half of *La Philosophie dans le boudoir*, Dolmancé, the arch libertine, introduces the pamphlet that he has supposedly bought just that morning outside the Palace of Equality and offers it to the group. It ought, "if one can believe the title," to provide an answer to the question Eugénie, the initiate, has been invited to ask—"whether manners are truly necessary in a governed society, whether their influence has any weight with the national genius."[19] What is, in other words, the place of custom in civil society?

This pamphlet makes its appearance *ex machina*. As if it were an antitype to the objects that exist in *Robinson Crusoe* almost as pretexts for anticipation and regret, for budgeting and recalculation, the pamphlet appears on the scene as if to make the very existence of objects identical to their immediate use. If Defoe sets Robinson Crusoe to an endless process of taking inventory, the pamphlet's sudden appearance, by contrast, indicates a peculiar fact about the Sadean scene: even as one knows it to be a world of privilege with recognizable class configurations that make Madame de Saint-Ange and her gardener Augustin equals only for the space of the sexual contract that they continually negotiate in their contact, there is no excess. The *Philosophie*, that is, presents a remarkably uncluttered and indeed Spartan decor. While the interior spaces may emblematize as relentless an enclosure as Barthes has said they do,[20] they involve no housekeeping. Indeed, part of the point of the enclosed spaces is to keep people from imagining the transportation of objects across the boundaries of the particular rooms they occupy. Remarkably undecorated and oblivious to fashion, the characters do not acquire or accumulate, do not dress for success or pack for tomorrow.

To frame the matter differently, as the pamphlet suddenly materializes almost out of thin air, we see yet another manifestation of Sade's commitment to tracking metaphysics to its physical bases. For a pamphlet, a whip, or a dildo to emerge as always ready to hand but never in the way, as there when you want it and never needing to be fumbled with or searched for, is for objects to have lost that annoying character of temporal duration that continually harnesses material objects to the most metaphysical lines of argument.

Sadean pornography, in other words, does not consist (or does not merely consist) in treating persons as though they were things, mere objects to be subordinated by the Sadean "sovereign individuals," in Bataille's phrase. Or rather, it involves treating persons as though they were things—and as though things were especially volatile entities, the materialism of a relentlessly idealist world in which things ceased to exist when people left the room. Rousseau had written in *Emile* of the importance of objects in educating a child, because objects do not respond to the child's will, do not accommodate or yield to the child's demands. Sade depicts the reverse—objects that come only when they are called, like the pamphlet that appears only when a question has been asked. An object of infinite politeness, it speaks only when spoken to.

Thus, even though the pamphlet and its audience never become equal in the sense of being similar kinds of things, things that might be mistaken for one another, it epitomizes Sade's thinking about equality in two ways—as statement and as example. As statement, it rehearses the arguments of Sadean equality (one owes nothing to one's parents because they invested no labor in one's production; a woman's husband has no property right in her not because a woman has, like any other individual, inalienable property rights in herself, but because every man has a property right in her; and so on). The equalities that it states, rather, are both temporary and limited. As an example, it is similarly temporary and limited. It appears, is read, is approved, and disappears. While it represents positions so compatible with Dolmancé's that it could have been written by him, it is a pamphlet of anonymous authorship. The parallels with Sade's refusal to attach his name to various works (including the *Philosophie,* which appeared in 1795 as "a posthumous work" by the also anonymous author of *Justine*) may make this look merely circumstantial, or like a clever joke on the political and judicial climate in which Sade wrote. Anonymous authorship was, after all, a gesture toward avoiding the blame for writing that kept accruing to Sade's account and kept him in one prison or another for twenty-seven years. It was, also and more importantly, a strategy for avoiding the patronymic, the passing on of the name as if identity, either for human or literary progeny, could be transmitted.

This is to say that the *Philosophie* continually elaborates the difficulties of living in the material world as a problem of inheritance. Burke had written in his *Reflections on the Revolution in France* of 1790 that we wish to derive everything as an inheritance from our ancestors, and the French Revolutionaries had conceived the state as salvageable if one could, among other things, reconfigure property relations. For Sade, heritability was a rather more basic issue, involving as it did for him a challenge to both the duty-

Eugénie, or Sade and the Pornographic Legacy 87

based and the rights-based accounts of the social contract. For if the Burkean account clearly converted custom into an emanation of nature on the basis of the inevitable connectedness of generations, the Revolutionary account was unsatisfactory because it failed to realize how little difference the Revolution made to the understanding of the relation between law and custom. Eugénie's question, that is, was an infinitely more serious one than either the anti-Revolutionaries or the Revolutionaries were prepared to admit: "Je voudrais savoir si les moeurs sont vraiment nécessaires dans un gouvernment, si leur influence est de quelque poids sur le génie d'une nation." (In the lame translation of the Grove Press edition: "I should like to know whether manners are truly necessary in a governed society.") She does not ask if laws are necessary to a society based on custom. She asks, rather, if customs are necessary to a law-governed society.

As the *Philosophie* proceeds to address the question, it comes to appear in a still more radical form: Are customs themselves supportable in a law-governed society? Or, isn't it the whole function of law to replace custom? Sade's pamphlet's call for a "few laws" that should be "good ones" may, in its insistent vagueness, be directed against the Revolutionaries' efforts to coordinate the variety of laws governing marriage, divorce, children, and inheritance into a single unified system for the nation. But instead of making the Burkean argument for custom as the expression of nature, Sade makes custom itself the antagonist of nature, on the basis of an attack on the family as itself unnatural, the point at which nature ceases being nature and becomes instead customary.

Just as objects become metaphysical in the process of becoming property, so laws become metaphysical in the process of becoming custom. Custom, in short, is another name for an overextended law. In its Burkean form, custom treats nature as if it were civil society, as if the existence of land could come to count as an argument for the existence of persons whose merely nominal connection to landed property gave them authority less on account of their being persons than on account of their being emanations of the land. Custom represents the ghostly version of nature, the point at which the entire interest of nature for Sade—its physicality—gets lost.

The Revolution, seen only as the abolition of feudal rights and duties, looked like the end to feudalism that Lefebvre's modernization hypothesis has maintained that it was: the Revolution was effected in part as an acknowledgment of the rising middle class in its attack on inherited claims to offices and property rights.[21] It curtailed obligations to the feudal lord as a landed, human version of religious illusion.

Yet the aspect of the Revolution that many recent historians have explored—its attempt to formulate and promulgate a new symbolic culture—must have looked to Sade like a peculiarly self-vitiating gesture. From Sade's standpoint, the problem with feudalism was not the systematic inequity of its operation or its favoritism for the nobility. It was, in the end, that it read one physical entity, land existing in nature, as if its connection to persons could be sustained in their absence, and another physical entity, a person, as if its connection to other persons could have similar metaphysical persistence. This is as much as to say that for Sade the project of the *Philosophie* is essentially rather than accidentally pornographic.

If Andrea Dworkin emphasizes that pornography is "the graphic depiction of whores,"[22] Sade's bedroom more or less explicitly repudiates nonpornographic, symbolic writing that can operate by incorporeal means. The message of anti-feudalism, then, is not (or not merely) that the ancient aristocracy and the old system of land tenure were unjust. It is, in Sade's account, that any nonpornographic society is illusory and unjust. A nonpornographic society, in short, continually emphasizes custom as a storage system that eviscerates the very bodies that seem to be its basis. Even as the Republican constitution extended the vote to "over half the adult male population; or to more than two-thirds of those over the required age of twenty-five,"[23] it enabled those voters to vote only for electors whose eligibility for office depended upon their being a version of self-storage. They had accrued credit for their own and their families' pasts. For the electors were not merely to have the means to supply their needs; they were defined as those whose property specifically constituted an accumulation of labor. In cities of more than six thousand inhabitants, one could qualify as an elector by owning "real property assessed on the tax rolls at an annual income value equivalent to 200 days' unskilled labor" or by leasing "a dwelling worth an annual income value (or rental of 150 days' labor)."[24] In smaller cities and towns, the amount of stored labor that was required was less, but the same principle obtained. If the feudal lord was no longer able to treat a laboring peasant as his accumulated savings, the Revolution produced governmental equality by making property holding the freedom that was based directly on one's own industry. This reallocation of governmental access limited the heritability of property in office. It did so, however, by substituting a metaphysical and unavailable self for a physical self; in basing political privilege less on use than the ability to forestall need, it also established the individual as his own potential heir. Property bespoke freedom precisely by denying the freedom to use.[25]

Although the reform of the criminal code had taken precedence over that of the civil code, the outline of the civil code was perceptible from a very early stage of the Convention's discussion. "Three things are necessary and sufficient to man in society: to be master of his person; to have the means to satisfy his needs; to be able to dispose, in his own best interest, of his person and his goods. All civil rights resolve themselves thus to those of liberty, property and contract."[26] As the Assembly's legislation circumscribed paternal prerogatives and provided for the equal division of estates among heirs, it substantiated those principles in the name of equality. The fraternity of the Revolution was the equality of brothers, specifically conceived as an equality that neither paternal authority nor birth order should constrain. By the custom of united succession, equal shares in the real property of a deceased had been consolidated in one heir, the eldest son in France succeeding to the burgesses' tenements (just as the youngest son in England succeeded to tenancy). Thus, primogeniture reproduced within generations the very inequality that paternal authority had produced between them.

In the Revolutionary period, and (as William Doyle has recently demonstrated) even more importantly in the pre-Revolutionary period,[27] the attack on property involved in part an attack on the gross imbalances in the distribution of property and prosperity. It was an imbalance most strikingly apparent when the peasantry found itself with an increased tax burden in the 1780s (as the government tried to fund its payments on the debt it had assumed to support, among other things, its participation in the American Revolution) and when that increased tax burden coincided with "poor to catastrophic" harvests "almost everywhere" in 1788.[28] For even though the nobility had felt tax increases very keenly (as the capitation, the "head tax," fell upon everyone with a body), it had also been able to pass along even the burden of that tax by raising agricultural rents. The most basic right that the Convention registered—a citizen's right to have the means to satisfy his needs, was a strictly material right, the claim for a person as a body to maintain itself. From that physical right would seem to be derived the right to self-sovereignty, the right to be master of one's body. Had the body gained a self through use, through supplying its own needs, the physical economy would have been sustained. With the use of property to designate that self-sovereignty, however, the individual could only configure itself as anticipated need.

The reformulations of the person-property distinction in the pre-Revolutionary and Revolutionary period were, as has been frequently observed, a break with feudalism. And feudalism looked Gothic not merely because it represented an inheritance from the medieval period, but because its systematic workings had converted property from a concrete to a conspicuously immaterial notion. In Doyle's words, "Long before the eighteenth century lordship and ownership had ceased to be synonymous." Feudalism had come to mean that a seigneur had rights that were only erratically related to his property rights. "It was rare to find a lord who did not own any of the land over which he exercised rights; but it was equally rare to find a lord who exercised rights only over his own land."[29] Among the rights of lordship that would be challenged by the Revolutionary reforms, none were more significant than the rights of access or use that enabled a lord to hunt; shoot; establish monopolies in milling, baking, and wine pressing; and, most importantly, to levy dues (exact duties).

In its ability to call on the rights of use or access, lordship represented the social and economic form of the relationship to objects that I described earlier. For though it related to property, it had the peculiar advantage of enabling one to treat property as most perfectly one's own when one didn't own it—or didn't have to own it, but could instead invoke the duties of those who did. As the tax rates increased in the 1780s, they exposed the competition between rights of sovereignty and rights of ownership in a particularly graphic way. It was not merely that the nobility enjoyed exemptions from more taxes than the peasantry, or that they were taxed at a disproportionately low rate in relation to their ability to pay. It was, more importantly, that the feudal duties made the aristocrats' taxes the peasant landowners' taxes. If the Lockean account of property distinguished property from nature on the basis of the investment of one's labor in it, seigneurial rights constituted a heritable right to reward without labor. Sovereignty was, in short, the demand for the satisfaction of one's needs without any obligation to anticipate those needs. Rights of sovereignty converted other people into the functional equivalent of one's own forethought. While Crusoe must continually ration his property to himself, doling out portions that create immediate scarcity for the sake of his anticipated future needs, the feudal sovereign has a right in other people's property that is the material equivalent of anticipation. Other people and their labor become his savings account.

It is, then, as an attack on the metaphysics that underwrites both the landed and the laboring versions of inheritance that Sade stakes his argument for use. Rather than extending the rights to property and public office that had attached to the nobility, he would extend the only seigneurial right of any value—the right to access, to use. In the *Philosophie,* moreover, the right to sexual use contends directly with the family. The family and sexuality are sharply distinguished in Sade's bedroom, not merely because parental authority (and specifically paternal authority) operates as the same kind of metaphysical projection as religion and royalism. Instead, the family builds metaphysics into nature. Making generation look like a consequence—an inheritance—of sex, the French family around the time of the Revolution makes sexuality look assimilable to heritability.

Generation, in short, continually operates less as an inconvenience or necessary risk that always attends properly pornographic sexuality than as an essential statement of injustice. This injustice does not, however, involve Sade's extreme sensitivity to what for Burke and even for Freud is a lamentable fact of human existence: that persons, being born of other persons, inevitably discern the limits of their own independence. Rather, generation, for Sade, becomes unjust at the moment at which one person's existence comes to seem the consequence of another person's intention.

As Dolmancé reads the rights of birth, they involve neither an inheritance of property nor an inheritance of property rights in children: ". . . we owe nothing to our parents."[30] Eugénie has suggested that the satisfaction of individual needs may yield to ties of affection (in a version of Lawrence Stone's description of the companionate marriage), and Dolmancé counters by supplanting the social contract with coition. "So long as the act of coition lasts, I may, to be sure, continue in need of that object, in order to participate in the act; but once it is over and I am satisfied, what, I wonder, will attach the results of this commerce to me?"[31] Sexual partners "who, exclusively thoughtful of their own pleasure," begin to call themselves spouses or parents may be praised for having given one life or blamed for "having given us nothing but an unhappy and unhealthy existence."[32] Parental authority converts mere temporal priority into a claim to property rights in an individual. Fear (in this case, fear on the part of parents) causes them to create themselves as (former) gods: "These latter relationships [of marriage and consanguinity] were the results of the terror of parents who dreaded lest they be abandoned in old age"; "the politic attentions they show us when we are in our infancy have no object but to make them deserving of the same consideration when they are become [sic] old."[33] Parenthood, in sum, involves a contractual structure in which an accident (conception) is misrepresented as an intention, and inequality is insisted upon by the contract itself; the trade is always of one party's incapacity for the other's capacity, the weakness of the child or the aged for the strength of an able-bodied adult.

It is in the context of such a critique of implicit contract, the contract of custom, that one can understand the catalog that Dolmancé and Madame de Saint-Ange compile of family relationships—a list of pretenders to other people's bodies. Women cannot be mothers, because "that which we women furnish has a merely elaborative function," and "the child born of the father's blood owes filial tenderness to him alone"[34] on account of the father's having been alone in desiring "our birth." Men, similarly, cannot be fathers, because conception operates by chance. Indeed, a man's inability to cause procreation at will becomes the basis for the impossibility of his denying his paternity to any child of a sexual partner. As Madame de Saint-Ange puts it to Eugénie, "Provided I sleep with my husband, provided his semen flows to the depths of my womb, should I see ten men at the same time I consort with him, nothing will ever be able to prove to him that the child I bear does not belong to him."[35] If any claim to paternity is to be allowed, all possible attributions of paternity cease to be deniable. "Immediately it can be his, it is his...."[36] Although parental relationships continually invoke the language of intentional causes and obligated effects, the cause-and-effect relationship can only be achieved in the sexual exchange itself. Nature produces children by accident; sexual partners produce one another by use.

The sequence of disqualified relationships continually seems to award rights in a child more to fathers than to mothers, more to mothers than to fathers, more to children themselves—only to proceed to disqualify all intergenerational and nonsimultaneous relationships as a basis for heritability. The family, as a unit spanning generations, ceases to exist—which means that the incest that Sade proposes to counterbalance the family comes as an illusory remedy to an illusory wrong. On the one hand, biological connection looks impossible to establish, so that sexual acts that offend against biological connection look equally impossible to establish. On the other hand, Sade insists that both history and nature sanction incest. First, biblical history adduces the case of Adam as the most tightly wound case of incest imaginable, a version of partial onanism or sex with one's own body part. Second, nature not only tolerates the continued existence of an anonymous incestuous friend of Dolmancé's but enables him to produce sexual partners almost at will.

One of my friends has the habit of living with the girl he had by his own mother; not a week ago he deflowered a thirteen-year-old boy, fruit of his commerce with this girl; in a few years' time, this same lad will wed his mother: such are my friend's wishes; he is readying for them all a destiny analogous to the projects he delights in and his intentions, I know very well, are yet to enjoy what this marriage will bring to bear....[37]

Incest makes this genealogical tree (could one quite diagram it) not so much foreshortened as increasingly flattened. The man sleeps with his mother to produce a daughter, the man sleeps with this daughter to produce a son, the man sleeps with this son—as if the point of sexuality were to erase cross-generational inequality. The man who sleeps with his son is, for the space of their intercourse, equal to his son, even though he is simultaneously father of his son and also grandfather of this same son on the maternal side. Dolmancé has rehearsed the most basic genetic argument for incest: the appeal of incest (like the appeal of homosexuality, in the current arguments that Bersani would counter) lies in its approximation of equality: "If, in a word, love is born of resemblance, where may it be more perfect than between brother and sister, between father and daughter?"[38] Resemblance as likeness approaches sameness or equivalence. Yet the movement from the intragenerational pair—brother and sister—to the intergenerational pair—father and daughter—progressively strains the notion of resemblance. The pleasures of "carnal connection with the family," in sum, do not so much rely upon the inherent appeal of resemblance as they create resemblance. Only, that is, in terms of the systemic equivalence of each of the individual elements in the sexual arrangements that Sade disposes does a woman resemble a man and a child resemble her parent.

Incest enables the lateralization of the vertical hierarchy produced by generation. If the Republic's abolition of the law of primogeniture made it possible for all heirs to succeed equally to an estate, incest makes it possible to end the tyranny of succession by identifying the benefactor with the beneficiary, the settler with the heir. The significance of incest in the *Philosophie,* then, is that it demonstrates exactly why the French need "yet another effort" to "become Republicans." The Republic had attacked the notion of heritable office, but it had at the same time left the basic structure of heritability intact. Public office had been opened to ability rather than heritability as the Republicans attempted to equalize the relationships between members of the same generation. Yet just as heritable property in office had been abolished with the one hand, heritability had been incalculably strengthened on the other. The state, in ending the venality of public offices (through which members of the bourgeoisie had entered the nobility at a profit to the royal treasury), had foreclosed a crucial source of income. The seizure of church lands and the issuing of *assignats* backed by that church land attempted to replace some of those funds. This was the financial situation that Burke was responding to when he saw the confiscation of church land and the paper-money economy as creating an abstract and inflationary system that attempted an impossible break with the fact of human successive generation. For Sade, the problem must have seemed both different and more severe. Even though France had supported an extremely high level of government borrowing for two decades, the venality—the vendibility—of public office had served first to make public office-holding the privilege of birth and to make wealth the privilege of manufacturing the privilege of birth. Public offices that were purchasable and, thus, heritable by virtue of not having been themselves inherited had, in addition to providing an (admittedly narrow) avenue for upward social mobility, tended to disguise the publicness, the omnipresence and nonexclusiveness, of the national debt. The debt, as something that the king could pay in part by minting new men in exchange for their money, looked like monarchical and ministerial debt. As the Republic abolished the sale of heritable office, however, it explicitly established the debt as national and secured the abolition of such heritable office by funding it through an announced nationalization of the debt. Heritable office was thus replaced by heritable debt, in the foundation of "a consolidated national debt, the *Grand Livre de la Dette Publique*" in August 1793.[39]

More than one commentator has referred to national debts as inaugurating civil society generally, and many have traced to classical times the use of a national debt for funding such extraordinary expenses as wars.[40] Yet however time-honored the basic structure of national indebtedness may be, for the France of the 1790s in which Sade wrote *La Philosophie dans le boudoir,* the explicit nationalization of the debt made the state itself insist upon replacing heritable property with heritable debt. The national debt, that is, makes the state's power ineluctable. As intergenerational debt, it operates with a violence that is no less illimitable for being abstract. Against the Sadean account of sexual violence that enforces inequities and insists upon the right of men to compel women's submission "not exclusively, . . . but temporarily,"[41] the nationalized debt becomes the sign of the inevitable inequality of the modern state, whose contract is most binding precisely because it applies only to those who could not, by definition, have had any part in its formulation.

In 1783 Sade wrote angrily from prison objecting to the fact that his eldest son, Louis-Marie de Sade, had been named sublieutenant in the Rohan-Soubise Regiment. Instead of complaining that his son had not received a properly exalted position, Sade protested that his son had not been appointed as a legacy. He, the marquis, had wanted Louis-Marie to serve in his old regiment and wear the same cavalry uniform he had worn. This rather extreme insistence on heritability—on intergenerational hand-me-downs—waned, however, in the 1790s. In 1792 another son, Donatien-Claude-Armand de Sade, aide-de-camp of the Marquis de Toulongeon, deserted and Sade legally disavowed his son's emigration. This gesture was, on some level, purely expedient. The Republic had decreed that parents were responsible for the actions of their children, and Sade had, as it were, to divorce himself from his son in order to escape legal liability for his son's actions.[42] On the argument of the *Philosophie,* Sade's disavowal could not, however, have been purely expedient. For the *Philosophie* insists that intergenerational inheritance, whether forward, from fathers to sons, or backward, from sons to fathers, inaugurates political culture as the essentially metaphysical, and as the diametrical opposite to a pornography that knows how to keep its place.

4 Emma, or Happiness (or Sex Work)

In his most famous novel, Flaubert used a concrete novelistic technique, *style indirect libre,* to indicate his adoption of an objectifying mode for his work as a novelist. The presentation that resulted, as Lukács observed, left the novelist in the situation of identifying all that was most dispiriting about the organization of modern social life without allowing himself to lodge a protest or propose an alternative. In Flaubert's treatment, modern utilitarian structures seem to operate so efficiently and effortlessly, and to penetrate personal life so completely, that individuals continually have recourse to their objective measurements of their happiness—while they also lose the capacity to imagine themselves as moral agents. Flaubert frames the matter as a problem about action that arises when morals become the kind of exact science that Bentham and his followers sometimes projected. Moral objectification seemed to be able to operate without benefit of persons, and without any need to rely on their emotions and opinions for legitimation. Action and the judgment on its happiness (or success) or unhappiness (or failure) seem, in the novel, to come only by report, as if the possibility of understanding one's actions in terms of their objective effects damaged the possibility of forming and representing one's own choices and opinions. In that, it echoes, in tones of resignation, Sade's more enthusiastic pronouncements on the irrelevance of individual opinion and emotion.

In 1857 three men stood as defendants, charged by the state with having corrupted the public morals in bringing *Madame Bovary* into the world. They were Léon Laurent-Pichat, editor of the *Revue de Paris,* in which *Madame Bovary* first appeared in installments; Auguste-Alexis Pillet, printer for the *Revue*; and Gustave Flaubert, author of the novel. Although the defendants were all acquitted, it has been difficult (or, in other words, all too easy) for modern readers to see why the prosecution was brought in the first place. Historians and critics generally conclude their inquiry into the matter by quoting Flaubert's remark that the authorities wanted to strike a blow against the *Revue* and that they almost accidentally charged him in the process. When the prosecution of *Madame Bovary* is mentioned, it is nearly invariably seen under Flaubert's rubric of the random or misdirected prosecution.[1] Yet that view minimizes an important feature of Flaubert's writing that has intrigued and disquieted many, something that is difficult to localize and yet so palpable that Sartre explicitly names it the desire to demoralize and makes it the chief burden of his magisterial (if incomplete) biography; Jonathan Culler, by contrast, connects this element with Flaubert's desire to induce reverie, to lead people to withdraw from the world of purposeful activity.[2]

In what is the most sustained attempt we have yet had to explain the importance of this prosecution, Dominick LaCapra points to a pattern that has come to characterize obscenity trials more generally.[3] The prosecution identifies the shortcomings of the novel's central character and pronounces the book an insult to public morals and religion. The defense counters that it is reading the same pages, attending to the same acts and events of the novel, and, indeed, quoting all the same passages that the prosecution has.[4] Both Flaubert in his letters and Jules Sénard in his defense of the novel derided the ignorance of a prosecution that could take issue with the scene at Emma's deathbed in which most of the words are merely formulaic. Drawn from the sacrament of extreme unction and reproduced, as Flaubert said, as closely as one could reproduce them without actually plagiarizing, these are words, the defense argued, that can hardly be seen as disrespectful of religion—unless one were to imagine that the church routinely set out to mock itself. The prosecution and the defense went toe-to-toe in addressing the same portions of the text, but the defense insisted that the text's significance is absolutely determined by its outcome. The defense, that is, treated the novel as morally unimpeachable because its chief sinner suffers at the end, dying a tormented and absolutely unenviable death—a death of such agony that Lamartine, the novel's most improbable admirer, provided a letter attesting to the fact that he found it insupportable.[5] The defense argument was, in other words, that the novel provides its own judgment, its own punishment to such a degree that there was no need for the court or anyone else to do a thing. The tragedy is complete not merely because the protagonist, by virtue of having "ceased to exist," will not be able to act again—for good or ill. (This would be the pattern for the virtuous sufferers of classical or

Shakespearean tragedy.) Instead, in the defense's view, the novel is complete because it has already settled its scores; the tragedy can't grow by an inch or an ounce because Emma has not simply died but has died a death that is a punishment.

Now, it is easy enough to see the debate between prosecution and defense as simply the negative and positive judgments of the same thing and to see this particular trial as one of the many recurrent instances of such dissensus. In this scheme, one needs a strong version of individual or political motivation—an overzealous prosecutor, a repressive government—to explain the fact of the trial. Were we to cling to this scenario, we would be left with a frequent impasse in discussions of pornography—one that suggests that there are virtually no grounds for deciding that a particular work is pornographic or obscene. Written and visual signs, in this view, cannot be said to have meaning reproducible enough for texts and images to do anything more than provide an occasion for the exercise of individual fantasy. While Sartre was interested in particular persons as examples of singular universality, much of the work I'm thinking of here establishes the fantasizing self as an alternative to the kind of epochal universality that engaged him. Instead, proponents of that contrary view see selves, however discontinuous they may be, as ultimately impervious to their epochs because fantasy enables them to specialize their perceptions. Insofar as a trial is not simply a contest between opposing sides but an effort to determine which evaluations an epoch attempts to make its individuals heed, the very notion of a trial looks irrelevant or absurd on the face of it.

As suspicious as I am of that line of reasoning, I must nevertheless concede that, in the case of *Madame Bovary*, the question of what provocation the text provided for a trial is peculiarly difficult to answer if we think in the readily available terms of sexual explicitness or bad moral example. For the prosecution proceeded even though one of the defendants (Laurent-Pichat) had already cut the most suggestive passage (the carriage scene with its car sex *avant la voiture*) from the novel before it ever appeared in print. We are left with the familiar conjecture that the story of an adulterous young wife—even without sexual detail—might provide sufficient ground for legal action in the Second Empire, in which a prosecution would succeed only a few months later against Baudelaire's *Fleurs du mal*.[6] Yet the surprising aspect of the court's judgment is that *Madame Bovary*, a novel that might seem to have all the shapelessness that had historically been attributed to the novelistic form, was seen more obviously as art than Baudelaire's poetry, which the court judged more harshly. While Flaubert had repeatedly written in his letters that poets had it easy, that they had traditional forms to give them some sense of what was required of them, this assessment of the standing of the two types of writing comes to look suspect in the face of Flaubert's acquittal and Baudelaire's conviction.[7] Poetry's historic privilege over prose was publicly renegotiated in those twin prosecutions. If Flaubert seemed simply to be announcing a chauvinistic attachment to his medium when he declared in his correspondence that, although poetry is the ancient literary art, the advantage of prose is that it was invented yesterday, he was also claiming their prose had actually been *invented* as a publicly available medium for literature. And this was the case in part, I would argue, because the novel's condemnation of its heroine to death seemed to make the novel more obviously complete than even the sonnet form might do for Baudelaire's poems.[8] In the moment that the judge announced that "le tribunal les acquitte de la prévention portée contre eux et les renvoie sans dépens," he provided at least as much support for the notion of "art for art's sake" as did any of the psychologico-familial and socioeconomic conditions that Sartre and Bourdieu detail in their accounts of Flaubert.[9] Doubtless, as Sartre says, Flaubert saw himself as repudiating medicine, the bourgeois profession of his father and brother, and law, the twin to medicine that was just inferior enough to be perfectly suited to the younger son of the family, the one who was seen as never quite managing to live up to the family's standards for success.[10] Doubtless, as Bourdieu says, he was willing and able to commit himself to his art because he enjoyed the peculiarly high bourgeois privilege of not needing to think of his work as a livelihood.[11] As someone who would worry about the scale of his inheritance rather than earning his next meal, Flaubert could work with a time frame quite different from that of most workers. Some might work for their daily bread; others, like his father and brother, had professions that exerted a constant pressure on both their individual actions and their earnings; Gustave, however, worked on a scale disconnected from both the dailiness of life and a lifetime career—not because he didn't care deeply about his work, but because he insisted upon largely ignoring the effects that his work might have on his life. Since his writing would never enable him to have the truly fabulous and life-changing wealth that he toyed with in his imagination, he maintained a peculiar detachment from the popular success and the sales of his first novel. (Indeed, the most pronounced emotion that he expresses is the sense of irritation at not being left alone, an irritation that he describes in the peculiar idiom of not being allowed to be released from his novel.)[12]

Sartre's and Bourdieu's accounts of Flaubert's motives and situation explain a great deal about Flaubert the individual and the larger world of family and society in which he could be Flaubert. Yet because they seek to recapture the crucial terms of Flaubert's own point of view, they are not particularly concerned with what the judge thought in making his decision, which neither affirmed Flaubert's disrespect for the bourgeois professions nor his decision not to have gainful employment, to "have" or inherit money rather than to earn it. Given that the judge doubtless disagreed with many of the views that commentators have seen in the novel and Flaubert's handling of it, the question that we must ask is, What made it possible for the judge to send the novel and its producers off scot-free? For the judge's view—which literary historians have greeted as enlightened—was, improbably enough, that of a literary critic. Indeed, the judge's decision (down to and including the observation that there were a few blemishes, that Flaubert had failed to realize that some of his remarks might mislead the unsuspecting reader) is one that Saint-Beuve immediately adopts as his own and acknowledges in making his summary assertions that "the work now belongs to the domain of art, and art alone" and that the project of the critic is not simply to rehearse the glories of past art but to acknowledge art that is contemporary.[13] Thus, the perhaps surprising fact is that the judge's ruling established the notion of autonomy for the work of art to a degree previously unimagined. Art—whether in the form of fiction writing or painting—might not have organized curricula like medicine and law; it might not speak the specialized language of law. Yet when the judge ruled that "literature, as art, does not have only to be chaste and pure in its expression to accomplish the best that it is called upon to produce," he essentially accepted the notion that it had spoken in its own terms.[14] That is, the judge accorded Flaubert's novel the same kind of standing that the logics of the professions enjoyed. The judgment established the strong view that literature did not need, any more than medicine and law, to justify itself in its incidentals. Although art could not command assent any more than the recognizably established professions could, an author need not, any more than a physician or an attorney, pause to defend his every word. Art was, in other words, being treated as a special field in which one could make the same kinds of statements that were sensible in medicine and law but nonsensical or shocking if they were taken as the language of daily life. It was granted professional jargon, even as that jargon was seen to be coextensive with the natural language.

It was thus not simply that Flaubert's first published novel enjoyed a *succès de scandale,* that its notoriety provided it with more attention than it might otherwise have had. It was also the case that the judge, in deeming Flaubert's novel to be art, made him an artist. In making that assertion, I don't mean to suggest that Flaubert was not what we would call a meticulous craftsman or that he didn't sweat the bullets he says he did in writing the novel. I mean, rather, to insist that the judge provided Flaubert with a new confidence that he had indeed "finished" *Madame Bovary* and provided him with a way of imagining that there was a rationale for thinking that he didn't, as he had so often before, need to renew his labors on the novel. For the judge essentially affirmed that the novel had developed such internal consistency that no one would take its words as if they meant what they might outside of its pages. Although the question of the novel's realism could always be broached on a scene-by-scene or an image-by-image basis, the judge was treating it as if it had managed to establish itself as the exact equivalent of a professional language. In other words, technique had won the privilege of the technical.

It is a distinct peculiarity of the modern era that many artists have received some of their most intense acknowledgment as artists through the circuitous route of being tried and acquitted of affronting public morals. Even though most commentators lament the repressiveness of governments and praise the radical nature of art, one of the most important effects of obscenity trials is that they give government a role in authenticating art as art.[15] The inefficiency of the process may serve to remind us of how imperfectly professionalized art was (and, to a lesser degree, remains) when public prosecution served as its means of acknowledgment. Yet the obscenity trial and the review are simply different aspects of the argument that art is art not simply by virtue of its author's conviction but by virtue of its having a recognizable value to its readers. It is, thus, not really surprising that obscenity trials have regularly included testimony from critics and from other writers and that they have treated such testimony as expert. Nor is it surprising that Sainte-Beuve would see the trial as in part an exercise in literary criticism and adopt its language and conclusions or that Flaubert himself would write to one correspondent that he was increasingly interested in literary criticism.[16] For the trial and the review merely offered various avenues toward a recognition that Flaubert had already incorporated into his work when he appointed his friends as a kind of review committee and read passages aloud to them to be sure that his writing passed muster. (The work was not done until an auditor could declare that it was done; and Flaubert's commitment to making fine distinctions between the moments for *style indirect libre* and direct discourse, along with the red-penciling he did in his letters to Louise Colet and Louis Bouilhet, is part of the process of coming to define art in terms of its revision and its having already taken into account the project of not just self-presentation but also self-justification.) Thus, when the prosecution began by taking the words of the novel for descriptions of incidents that might occur in the real world, it quickly became clear that those words are not merely descriptive but also justified. As the trial concluded that the novel's words speak of incidents only in the novelistic world, the decision thus convinced both those who witnessed it and the novel's author that the novel provides a valid new measure of work, a new unit by which action may be measured.

In describing the prosecution and the verdict in this way, I disagree with a host of critical commentaries on the novel that stress the uncertainty of identifying the attitude of the author in relation to his character. That view—classically represented in Henry James's remark that Flaubert refused to stand and fight it out in his writing—takes two forms, one suggesting that the prosecution would never have been initiated if the court had recognized that Flaubert himself was not speaking (and was not therefore endorsing) Emma's thoughts as represented in the *style indirect libre* of the novel, the other suggesting that the prosecution could never clearly identify who was speaking and, therefore, did not know where to attach blame.[17] What seems mistaken about those positions is that they suggest that the novel left something open, that it appeals equivocally to its reader, when the novel's most surprising element is that it left nothing open at all in its insistent reach toward professionalism for art in prose. Such criticism has stressed exactly the sort of thing that Flaubert would have identified as getting Baudelaire into trouble—the appeal to the reader, the address to the "hypocrite lecteur" that represented Baudelaire's understanding of the imperatives that would enable the ancient art of poetry to survive in the modern world.

Flaubert made prose a profession, gave it ways of justifying itself if not of exactly following rules. While it is true that poetry in mid-nineteenth-century France became more committed to sublimity (if we temporarily restrict that notion to the idea that a work will insist upon its completion in its readers' consciousness), Flaubert aimed to make prose the art of the beautiful in making the novel an insistently complete form that has no real reliance upon or appeal to its readers. The beauty that he was continually chasing in the novel is, in that sense, impersonal, not simply because one can't exactly form an image of the novelist who speaks, but also, and more importantly, because Flaubert had recognized the significance of having the novel become scientific: "It's there that the natural sciences have their virtue: they don't care about proving anything."[18] Thus, while gossip will become important for many writers, in his novel, demonstration replaces opinion. And the project of "demoralization" is not, as Sartre would have it, a desire to inspire dejection but rather a desire to remove all the opinions, all the moralizing assumptions, that have hedged the novel previously.

The significance of Flaubert's move toward pure demonstration not only becomes apparent in the trial's outcome but also emerges in Flaubert's way of writing about "criticism" in various letters. He could write that criticism seemed of particular interest and that there was something useful for his novel about the idea of criticism (generally rather than particularly conceived) because he was not simply acknowledging that someone like Sainte-Beuve already practiced it. (He would say that Sainte-Beuve's critical work represented an adequate example of criticism's possibilities.) Rather, he was imagining that a novel of demonstration rather than morals or opinions would be an appropriate object of criticism because it would already have subjected itself to that very same process of justification; it would continually have insisted that its observations were simply the A + B of demonstration. Indeed, the most remarkable thing about Flaubert's relationship to his profession is that he aligned himself much more closely with the critic than with other novelists. However much he may have luxuriated in the reading of Rabelais and Sade, he continually identified the limitations of the novel—both in the sentimental form that Rousseau and Lamartine gave it and in the anti-sentimental form in which Balzac produced it. In the one mode, tears repeatedly identify the period of the novel, and the essentially episodic format of the epistolary novel gives the markers of emotion and the expressions of opinion particular weight; in the other, the project of producing the reaction against such emotion occupies center stage as the novel tries to demonstrate its hard-boiledness. For Flaubert, by contrast, the novel is in league with criticism insofar as criticism participates in the process of justification: the novel checks over its own demonstration to see how far it is correct in its deductions. And literature "as we imagine it" would reach its culmination in the moment in which it would become an "occupation for an idiot," "the moment at which one would need as little of a personality or a moral sense or an opinion for writing prose as one did for adding two and two."[19] It is this aspect of Flaubert's project that Baudelaire's essay on *Madame Bovary* captures in basically recapitulating the movements of Poe's "Philosophy of Composition." For if Poe deductively produced an understanding of poetic inevitability—by asking what the most poetic subject would be and what the perfect length for a poem on such a subject would be (instead of choosing to write a sonnet that proceeded from feelings about a particular subject)—then what Baudelaire recognized was that Flaubert had made prose look as though it had all the same deductive inevitability, the same method, that poetry had regularly achieved rather more easily.[20] While the sentimental novelists had found themselves continually producing a punctuation technique and the prose of exclamation in which the characters' emotional judgments tried to capture the process of passing judgment on one's own life, Flaubert had converted prose into a methodical activity in which the actual suffering would take place *in the composition*—not on the page or in the reader—and in which the author necessarily would "enter absolutely minutely into the skin of people who are antipathetic" to him.[21]

Yet to say that Flaubert resisted the sentimental novel for making action look like a simple reflex of the emotions of individual characters is only to begin to see the importance he would attach to the question of identifying and measuring action in the novel. The problem of the measurement of action here revolves, first, around the prominence that the trial attached to Emma's death as evidence that the novel had already completed the process of judgment. (The novel comes to function, in this view, less as an occasion for the reader to exercise judgment—to decide as an individual how he or she feels about Emma Bovary—than as an organized delivery system for a process of judgment that is already contained within the novel.)

In the civil proceeding in which editor, printer, and author were codefendants for having variously participated in the circuit of action that exposed the reading public to *Madame Bovary*, the defendants were all exculpated on the basis of the claim that the novel had left no business undone, no distribution of justice incomplete. Indeed, that claim finds reinforcement in what might otherwise sound like the defense's fairly silly descriptions of Flaubert's hard work on the novel. For it is not simply that the defense was echoing the language that Flaubert (author of many famous laments about his mulelike, slavelike exertions in writing about his Bovary) doubtless supplied to the defense. It is not simply that Sénard described Flaubert's intense labor in the effort to establish his client's good character and his roots in a good family with a good work ethic. It is, instead, that the defense had to insist upon the work that went into the novel, to insist that Flaubert worked to make it complete, and that such completeness made any additional judgment about the business of the novel *de trop*.

I suggest that the debate over whether an individual work of art can be treated as self-judging, whether it constitutes a self-completing and organic whole, is the first way in which action was assessed in the trial. For the purposes of the trial, that debate was resolved by the emphasis on the novel's resemblance to a drama, with drama being seen as particularly important for depicting an action as complete in the purest Aristotelian sense. Yet if it is easy enough to see the point of arguing that the novel is a drama completed by Emma's judgment on herself in committing suicide, the peculiarity of that defense is that Flaubert, while writing, repeatedly complained about the hard time his novel was giving him because it was not a drama. It was, he said, a biography. And it was a biography for the good reason that the novel is centrally concerned with portraying action in a new way. For *Madame Bovary* is, as Flaubert said, a novel with precious little action, if we think of action as involving anything like major events. Indeed, Flaubert spent a great deal of time in his letters worrying "that there is not enough action" and reassuring himself with the thought that "*ideas* are action." On the one hand, he fretted that he now had

fifty pages in a row without a single event. It is an uninterrupted portrayal of a bourgeois existence and of a love that remains inactive—a love all the more difficult to depict because it is timid and deep, but alas! lacking in inner turbulence, because my gentleman has a sober nature. I had something similar in the first part: the husband loves his wife in somewhat the same fashion as her lover. Here are two mediocrities in the same milieu, and I must differentiate between them. If I bring it off it will be a great achievement, I think, for it will be like painting in monotone without contrasts—not easy. But I fear that all these subtleties will be wearisome, and that the reader will long for more movement. But one must be loyal to one's conception. If I tried to insert action I should be following a rule and would spoil everything.[22]

Even as he recognized that he was more than halfway through his writing, he worried that he had

so far 260 pages containing only preparations for action—more or less disguised expositions of character . . . , of landscapes and of places. My conclusion, which will be the account of my little lady's death and funeral and of her husband's grief, will be sixty pages long at least. That leaves, for the body of the action itself, 120 to 160 pages at the most. Isn't this a real defect? What reassures me (though not completely) is that the book is a biography rather than a fully developed story. It is not essentially dramatic; and if the dramatic element is well submerged in the general tone of the book the lack of proportion in the development of the various parts may pass unnoticed.[23]

Now, even though this passage and others with affinities to it are customarily seen as statements about the radical nature of Flaubert's commitment to autonomous art and high modernism, the possibility that Flaubert was more than a little sincere in his anxiety about the story's lack of action is worth noting. (The necessity of Emma's death is perhaps the purest expression of this anxiety; if she had not died, would the novel ever really have seemed to have a shape?) For Flaubert was not content to address the questions that had long preoccupied the novel as it moved from chronicles and diaries to the domestic world; he was not content to suggest that there was more to the stories of daily life than literature—and especially heroic literature—was accustomed to notice. Instead of representing incidents that are public, instead of following the traditional route of the domestic and sentimental novel and representing private incidents, his novel finds its material in the question of when an action is complete. On the one hand, then, he exposed the flaw at the heart of the sentimental novel as Richardson and Rousseau had practiced it—that all action seems to be resolved into the thought of individual characters and that it thus requires an elaborate apparatus of blushes, sighs, and tears to punctuate these thoughts and give them the termination that will enable them to resemble action. On the other hand, he provided a description of how action had changed in his own epoch.

Thus, Flaubert's concern to portray the "existence" of "inactive" love—to portray it in both Emma's husband and in her first lover (Léon of the first part, the lover who loves her so deeply that he can only leave Yonville-l'Abbaye without ever openly declaring his love)—continually insists upon its own peculiar version of the debates over how existence and actions relate to one another. Indeed, it is only when we take into account the significance of the debates over what an action is—and when an action is completed, satisfied, fulfilled—that we can begin to understand the otherwise baffling decision to prosecute the *Revue* for having already removed the most highly suggestive passage, the carriage scene, *before* it published the novel. Only then can we understand why Flaubert could protest the omission of that passage with his defiant remark that "the brutal element [was] basic, not incidental," that it could no more be excised by dropping one passage than "the book's blood could be changed."[24] For the novel essentially absorbs itself with the question of what it means to write a biography—or, indeed, to have a life in a world in which the very notion of action has been made infinitely more complicated than it was for the Don Quixote with whom Emma Bovary is so regularly compared. *Don Quixote* portrays a figure who is so deeply committed to the notion that people once could and did act in substantial ways that he continually refashions the world before him to create occasions for such actions. Emma Bovary resembles the Don in that she, too, is less committed to impossible dreams than to the insistence upon seeing action everywhere, seeing it not as merely possible but as necessary.

From Flaubert's standpoint, the very confidence in the notion of action was the illusion. As he had maintained when his friend Alfred married, "I believe that you are suffering from an illusion, and a big one, as always when one effects an action, whatever it may be."[25] Moreover, the question of measuring and recognizing action was easily more important for him than the question of distinguishing between good and bad action. Indeed, one of the most striking features of the novel is its obsession with formulating action in terms that are more efficient than moral. To be sure, Emma Bovary "falls," as the prosecution puts it, three times. Her lovers Rodolphe and Léon, corrupting and corrupted in their relationships to her, are clearly not candidates for sainthood. Yet people behave rather decorously in the novel, so that the most notoriously bad man—the old nobleman at Vaubyessard who impresses Emma with his glamour (as she learns, he once had affairs with queens)—seems detached from any evil that might seem to infect his entire character. Apart from Homais and his attempts to slander the blind man whom he injured, the novel has far fewer villains than we might expect. It certainly has fewer hypocrites and pious frauds. For if Flaubert relentlessly shows Homais to be as adept at imitating a good man as he is at imitating a certified medical practitioner, he is remarkably unconcerned to show up the characters in the novel. Indeed, this is so notably true that Sénard was able to argue without fear of impeachment that the novel did not disrespect the religion and morals of the nation, that it did not, after the fashion of much other literature, depict corrupt or lascivious priests as Rabelais had. Instead, he justly observed, it depicts priests who never betray their vows—priests (like the curate who tried to teach Latin to the young Charles Bovary) who fall asleep at their work, priests like Abbé Bournisien, who may fail to provide Emma with spiritual comfort in the process of putting duty first and teaching the catechism class to the boys of the parish, and priests (like Abbé Bournisien, again, who administers extreme unction to Emma) who are so ready to perform their duties that they do not stay to ask if the object of their ministrations is worthy of them or not.[26] Epitomized in the person of the verger in the cathedral in Rouen who tried to give Emma and Léon the full tour of the church, such figures might lose their audiences but would never dream of deserting their posts. Flaubert may not describe such characters with admiration, but his descriptions don't express full-blown disrespect, a negative judgment on the very figures whom society cherishes.

Rather, the novel will manage to be stained throughout with a corruption that can't be excised, because the insult will be to describe persons produced through modern techniques with absolute deadpan.[27] If we can imagine the malicious glee he took in making certain characters the victims of their own credulity, it is clear from the letters he wrote during the process of composition that he was sketching Abbé Bournisien as "chaste and dutiful" and that he intended to make Homais evil through an excessive optimism: "What he doesn't realize," Flaubert said of the enlightened pharmacist preparing a salve for the blind man's eyes, "is that the fellow's blindness is incurable."[28] Baudelaire mentioned the critics' objections (such as that of the generally enthusiastic Sainte-Beuve) to the fact that the novel has no "central character who acts as a moral judge" that would stand in for the author.[29] Yet perhaps the most historically significant aspect of this novel is its concern with the fact that French society of the mid-nineteenth century had taken on a "style" and a method that was at least as effective as Flaubert's own highly wrought style.

This is to say that Flaubert's command of *style indirect libre,* his ability to enter the consciousness of his characters or, more accurately, to make his characters say things that they couldn't quite have put their fingers on without him, shares something important with the utilitarian structures of daily life in nineteenth-century France. What they share, however, is not so much ambition or a general commitment to a notion of progress. Rather, it is, first, the sense that an individual can be recognized as performing an action only when it appears in the form of what scientists will come to call work—the output of a system. (Significantly, the novel begins in the classroom, where the students are routinely evaluated both in relation to what they know and in relation to the knowledge of others. The young Charles Bovary is singled out as a country bumpkin, awarded an incomprehension of a world in which gratifications are conspicuously mediated. As the newcomer, he is made the pretext for a detailed inventory of the impressively familiar routines of the organized class. The Charles Bovary who enters the new classroom besotted with love of his cap is an innocent who can't quite conceive that the new group structures that he is entering might interfere with the aesthetic pleasure that he takes so directly.) Second, the novel routinely features one of utilitarianism's great contributions to the theory of action: the reward, which is understood in the novel less as a gift or payment (a way of marking out the exchange value of an action) than as a kind of label that functioned to identify an action as complete. (As Marx understood very clearly, the aim of utilitarian rewards was to isolate the value of actions rather than of property.) For even though utilitarianism has been described as sacrificing the interests of the individual to the interests of the group, one of its major accomplishments was to produce a series of social technologies that demonstrated to individuals that they had been acting. That is, if utilitarianism judged the actions rather than the status of individuals in its efforts to sift its populations for persons of merit rather than persons of birth, this process of judgment develops extraordinary perspicacity in discerning actions. Think, for instance, of the moment in the novel in which "Catherine Nicaise Elizabeth Leroux, of Sassetot-la-Guerrière, for fifty-four years of service at the same farm" is awarded "a silver medal—value, twenty-five francs" (108). She shrinks "within her clothes" as she reluctantly comes forward on the platform to receive her medal, but she shrinks less from modesty or shyness than from a plausible incomprehension—that what she had thought of as daily life is now recognized as a job, that simple duration has been converted into length of service, and that there is a process of entirely secular analysis that effects such conversions. Homais, the representative of bourgeois enlightenment, may disapprove of her "fanaticism" in resolving to give the medal "to our curé at home, to say some masses for me," but her resolve demonstrates her dawning grasp of the new system of singling out actions and making them translatable into other actions (108).

If we think of the highly articulated social structures that come to dominate the classroom, the workhouse, and the prison from the late eighteenth century, their most conspicuous feature is their insistence upon correlating individuals with the groups in which they temporarily participate. In the hands of a figure like Jeremy Bentham, moreover, these social structures were more than techniques for reducing the chaos of large groups to a kind of order. Rather, they carried a series of implicit claims about action. First, their contribution was to morality. They replaced the older catechetical procedures that had coordinated specific hypothetical cases with more general principles. Instead of encouraging people to anticipate, through the lens of a casebook, the different moral dilemmas that might present themselves, these structures minimized the role of forethought in action (on the ground that one would never be prepared simply by forethought for the life one led). Second, their contribution was to politics. They tried to identify merit in a way that would detach it from one's status and, more ingeniously, would detach the process of uncovering merit even from ambition and self-confidence. Individuals in a Benthamite schoolroom (of the kind that Andrew Bell and Joseph Lancaster developed) never needed to know how good they really were, never needed to believe in themselves.[30] For the system related all individual efforts so strongly to their value in the group economy that each individual was continually being told something *new* by the process of being evaluated in relation to the group. Each time the system responded to a student's knowledge not merely with a judgment on its correctness but also with the judgment that the student was first, or seventh, or twenty-sixth, it offered up a perspective on individual action that was quite different from any offered by self-examination. Third, their contribution was to register the impact of one person on another with astonishing rapidity. Insofar as morality can be said to be a concern for the effect one's actions have on other persons, these structures aimed to give morality a concrete instantiation. One could literally see the effects of one's actions in a system in which even one's failure to respond could become apparent as a delinquency alongside the actions of one's companions.

Monitorial systems were among the few joint ventures of the English and the French in the eighteenth century. They were generally inspired by Lockean and Hartleyan associationism and developed as a way of working out the implications of the association of ideas when it was applied to the association of persons. When Elie Halévy describes their intellectual genealogy, moreover, he speaks of the English tradition being transmitted through France; it was, he claims, the French who enabled Bentham to come to recognize the importance of Lockean and Hartleyan empiricism and to think about the weight and force of emotions and ideas for individuals in groups.[31] Indeed, both Napoleonic bureaucracy and Fourierism were, respectively, the more and less practical expressions of the nascent social scientific view that individuals achieve themselves only in cooperation with groups. The science of sociality was to observe how "the various egoisms harmonise of their own accord and automatically bring about the good of the species."[32] It aimed to establish morals as an exact science and to see how the basic feelings of egoism of each individual reconcile themselves with the continuation of the species in demonstrable terms.

In Flaubert's hands, the novel becomes a laboratory for the social scientific depiction of action—what people would do, as opposed to what people have done. The novel distinguishes itself from history because it cares less about past action than about the social sources of individual action. This is to say that Flaubert's famous claims to have put the novel on a "scientific" basis are completely justified.[33] They are, however, justified not because the novel attains what we might think of as the documentary scientism of a realist presentation, but because Flaubert continually deploys a method that is scientific. Moreover, unlike the earlier scientific method, this one does not revolve around observation of phenomena but around the analysis of production, of work seen in terms of outcomes. This is as much as to acknowledge that there is something deeply plausible about all the intuitions that readers have had over the years that Emma would have fared all right "if only she had had a career" or "if only she had been able to live in Paris." Those intuitions simply register the fact that Emma is herself the novel's greatest champion of modern social engineering, that her ability to marvel at Charles's apparent lack of embarrassment in the presence of Hippolyte, the stable boy at the Lion d'Or whose clubfoot Charles so spectacularly failed to correct, is part and parcel of her sense that there is nothing genuinely bad or sad, only misplaced persons, responses calling out for a different context (so that even the desire to die can be subtly transposed into the desire to live in Paris, and so that Emma on her deathbed can bestow a passionate kiss upon the crucifix less because she is embracing an afterlife than because she is persisting in making instantaneous assessments and readaptations of her life).

And if utilitarianism has regularly been represented as largely indifferent to individual emotions (as Martha Nussbaum has recently argued in her *Poetic Justice*), Flaubert's project is to demonstrate how adept it is in engineering them.[34] The part of Emma that might seem most cloyingly sentimental, her sense that she is like someone stranded, an imaginative alien in an all-too-familiar world, is a sentimentality that Flaubert will find at the heart of utilitarian social engineering, with its sense that people can come to have their own efficacy, their own potential goodness demonstrated to them by a context that continually shows them that even their waiting has been an action and that makes life a constant swallowlike migration in search of the place where they "really" belong. Thus, Flaubert's commitment to producing fiction that he suspected would not be appreciated in his lifetime is not simply a dogged commitment to art for art's sake that strikes an amusing contrast with his desire to "live like a bourgeois."[35] It is, instead, the essence of the new bourgeoisie to imagine that no human creation ought to go without a market, a reception that will give it back to itself as good, as validated. Action is always, that is, seen as assisted action, involving not only agents but auxiliaries (assistants who may assist only by being the failed competitors that enabled individuals to come to perceive their own actions as having value).

Now it may seem surprising from today's perspective to claim that Flaubert's novel manages to depict the utilitarian social structures without much obvious contempt for them, but that is, indeed, what I am claiming. The only time that the narrator adopts the first person in the novel is in the opening passage, which recounts that "we" were in the classroom when the young Charles Bovary entered. Homais's boosterism may look contemptible, but Flaubert's depiction of the kind of thing that Homais celebrates is merely matter-of-fact. The agricultural fair—with its modern way of analyzing the diurnal routines of rural life, dividing it into classifications so numerous as to create a nearly infinite number of occasions for distributing prizes and awards, and publicly announcing the victor in each of these contests that are so peaceable that the contestants never encounter one another—merely merits description as well as juxtaposition with Emma and Rodolphe's serious conversation of mutual seduction.

Two questions appear at this point—one about what happens to individuals in this account, the other about why sexual action is singled out. First, why is it difficult for these characters to criticize the utilitarian worldview that they pit themselves against? For although conformism and mediocrity are everywhere the target of Emma's scorn, the novel does not simply point to the impotence of her discontent with the world she lives in by awarding the medal of the Legion of Honor to Homais at its conclusion. The problem is, rather, that Emma is continually trying to combat the elements of the society she loathes by coming up with weapons that regularly turn out to be merely more of the same, aspects of the world she imagines herself breaking free of. That is, the novel repeatedly suggests that a kind of luck inheres in the very rational structure of the artificial classes (the collections of people who fill the classrooms of utilitarian education and the factories of work) that are a regular feature of utilitarian society. In arguing that individuals might really derive different kinds of value from their associations with different kinds of persons, utilitarianism seemed to deprive characters of themselves by making all their actions so reliant upon their connections with other people that they could scarcely recognize themselves as tied to their own actions.

The importance of this detachment from even the actions in which they have most completely participated manifests itself throughout the novel—most notably in the way Flaubert uses *style indirect libre*. Flaubert does more than simply give the narrator privileged access to the thoughts of the characters; he makes it clear that their experience requires as much representation to themselves as it does to other people. The Charles who can see the dress of his first wife immediately after her funeral and say, "She had loved him after all!" is someone who comes at his emotions through a process of representation (14). And the Emma who says to herself, "I have a lover!" is not simply marveling at her situation but is also narrating it to herself and producing the emotions to go with that situation (117).

That feature of the novel—the way that characters are shown describing the effects of their actions and deducing the emotions that they come to have—makes it possible to understand Flaubert's celebrated claim that he *was* Emma Bovary in a slightly different fashion from the one in which it has commonly been understood. For the fact is that lots of people *are* Emma Bovary. Moreover, this identity between the character and the legion of others who *are* Emma does not reflect a similarity of circumstance or a deep psychological identification. It is, rather, an inevitable product of the fact that it is as easy for many to occupy Emma's emotions as it is for her, since others come to her emotions the same way that she does—through deducing them from the effects that she sees around her. Moreover, this point seems to me the essential one to make about the oft-debated and often mistakenly resolved question of whether Flaubert based his novel on an actual case (the story of the second wife of a doctor who had studied medicine under Flaubert's father). Although there is every reason to believe that Flaubert might have read the newspaper accounts of the woman's suicide and might have particularly noticed them on account of the connection between his own family and the principals in this drama, Flaubert repeatedly protested that he had not drawn the novel from that story—or from anything else in life. One could, that is, argue that he might have known every detail of that case without its having much to do with the novel he wrote, because what is important to him—what is scientific—about his novel is that it proceeds from the effect to the causes, from the rewards to the actions, as if it were offering a prize that would then produce prize-winning actions, prize-winning livestock, prize-winning novels. As Baudelaire understood when he described *Madame Bovary* as if he were straightforwardly adapting Poe's "Philosophy of Composition," the point of deductive description is to produce a necessity that will fall with particular intensity upon a certain number of actors who are singled out as if by fate.

I am describing a regular feature of Flaubert's practices of composition and research. For unlike a writer like, say, George Eliot, who worked up a subject and created quarries for her novels out of her research, Flaubert sent out for and ordered up his details. Thus, the process of composition frequently put him in the position of requesting that his correspondents send him not just books but very particular facts that are "pre-tweaked." He wrote to Alfred Baudry, for instance, both that he needed information and exactly what information he would like for it to turn out to be.[36] Moreover, it is this aspect of his work that enabled him to reassure himself that a novel of Champfleury's (*Les Bourgeois de Molinchart*) that was being serialized as he was writing was completely different from his *Bovary*; the two novels might have the same basic story and the same basic setting, but the "conception and the tone" are quite dissimilar.[37] Clearly, they would have to be, because Champfleury read the newspapers, while Flaubert dictated what they should have said and what they will have said (which helps to explain why his letter of response to a young aspiring novelist singles out journalism as a particularly disabling avenue into literary work).[38] Journalism reports what has happened; scientific fiction demands that reality justify itself.

Indeed, this aspect of Flaubert's work marks the opening of *Madame Bovary* and produces such surprising construction that many critics have described it as a lapse—the peculiar opening in which the narrator begins by recalling that "we were in class when the headmaster came in, followed by a new boy," proceeds to produce elaborate details about the boy's family history and about the appearance that he makes with his cap of composite origin, and later announces that "it would now be impossible for any of us to remember any thing about him" (5, 6). This anonymous and transient narrator is, in the manner of anyone reading a newspaper story about someone they once "knew" in the vague way that we feel we know the distant members of our elementary school classes, not so much remembering as producing an account of what they think they ought to remember, a story of what this terrorist bomber or that president was like at that age.

And it is this strange collapse between the inductive and the deductive that continually fuels Flaubert's distinctive use of *style indirect libre,* so that it comes across as a more or less sneering description because it analyzes how things work without any of the emotional enthusiasm and endorsement that usually accompanies such analysis. (Think of how a household advice columnist like Heloise doesn't just provide you with instructions on how to remove a spot in the carpet with soda water but also accompanies the advice with an exclamation. Think of how the crosscut scene at the agricultural fair depends in the first place on having its principals—Rodolphe and Emma, on the one hand, and the mayor, on the other—produce absolutely formulaic speeches for seduction and for morally uplifting public ceremonies. The crosscutting achieves a description of these scenes that eliminates their exclamation points and deprives them of the chance to bask in the success they have so obviously achieved.) Moreover, this way of making individuality look like a mistaken conclusion prompts one of the most famous passages from Flaubert's letters, an account of how he had, a couple of days earlier, discovered

> . . . in a charming spot beside a spring . . . old cigar butts and scraps of paté. People had been picnicking. I described such a scene in *Novembre,* eleven years ago; it was entirely imagined, and the other day it came true. Everything one invents is true, you may be sure. Poetry is as precise as geometry. Induction is as accurate as deduction; and besides, after reaching a certain point one no longer makes any mistake about the things of the soul. My poor Bovary, without a doubt, is suffering and weeping at this very instant in twenty villages of France.[39]

Although critics can say and have said, with Harry Levin, that Flaubert "decid[ed] to portray a particular individual who also happened to be a universal type," it is more to the point to stress that there is nothing universal at all about Flaubert's approach.[40] For Flaubert is stressing an important contribution that utilitarianism makes even to art—the recognition that persons are neither completely internally consistent nor so unique that one can't always see them as tokens of groups of which they are typical. Thus, Emma could easily be shown to have something like twenty lives, and not from any real duplicity but from what is a very familiar pattern in the novel—one in which characters come to do what they should as professionals or as amateurs in a fashion that involves no real commitment of their identities and that has no particularly lasting impact on their future behavior.

The Emma who can go from being completely intrigued by her flirtation with Léon to being conspicuously absorbed in being a good housewife attending to her needlework when Léon comes to tell her that he is leaving Yonville-l'Abbaye is not so much interested in putting on a show as in fulfilling the requirements for showing herself—and anyone else—that she knows how to be a good housewife. Like the promise that Charles's first wife Héloïse extorts from him not to return to the Rouaults' farm, behavior in one place scarcely outlives its immediate occasion. Charles can think "with a kind of naive hypocrisy, that this interdict to see her gave him a sort of right to love her" (13). Once one's actions are seen to be defined by their fulfilling someone else's needs, someone else's desires, success can come with only minimal engagement from those who achieve it. Thus, when Emma requests that Léon write love poems to her, it is predictable that he would respond by copying something from a Keepsake (201). In this chain of persons whose behavior costs them next to no effort, it is not that Emma's treatment of Charles counts as revenge on Charles for his behavior to Héloïse, nor that Léon's treatment of Emma counts as revenge on her for her behavior to Charles. Rather, the utilitarian project of emphasizing outcomes and providing an audience for the slightest gestures has become such a way of life that agents have lost contact with their actions even through a process that was supposed to have made them more conspicuously valuable.

The Emma Bovary who has had something very close to twenty lives is the Emma Bovary whose life could easily be lived by twenty others. While it may seem like a joke on the citizens of Yonville that they move rapidly from gossiping about Emma's gifts to Léon and about his being her lover to praising her exemplary behavior as the manager of her household and her husband's billings, the point of the drastic variation is not to show the crowd's fickleness. The function of publicity in Yonville is to respond instantaneously to any new behavior, to judge it without regard to an individual's previous behavior, to encourage individuals to express their better selves. Thus, although Flaubert depicts them crowding to the windows to get good seats for the theater of life, they are not demonstrating a personal trait like curiosity in this. They are fulfilling what has become an obligation, the commitment to enabling (and requiring) people to be seen, and they are neither immoral nor fickle. Rather, the virtue of this public lies in its willingness never to hold it against Emma the exemplary housewife that they had only recently thought of her as Emma the adulteress. Yet for both Emma and the people of Yonville, this efficiency in updating their views with little interference from even their previous views constitutes a considerable limitation as well. For in this society of the weightless past, Emma can easily lose track of herself.

It thus becomes possible for us to identify with some exactitude why sexual relationships are prominent in the novel. For if Dickens presents his readers with a domestic sphere that is continually invoked as a stay against the confusion of the world outside its borders, Flaubert is interested in analyzing how even marriage is being modernized by the pressure of utilitarian morals. For modern marriage—particularly when one is married to such an inert character as Charles Bovary—is simply not competitive with the efficiency of modern adulterous sexuality. In the recognizably similar but various worlds of Emma's convent school and its prizes and laurel wreaths, the ball at Vaubyessard and its world of recognition and acknowledgment, and the small-town life of Yonville and its ever-renewed assessments of how people are doing, we are presented with situations in which the notions of action and reward for action have been brought into extraordinary proximity.

Now it might seem a flaw in this description of the modern that it appears to apply as well to Charles, that antiquated and bovine figure who is continually represented as ruminating on his own happiness. Charles, on the one hand, approaches the condition of becoming an emblem of happiness, in which satisfaction registers itself organically without his ever needing to refer it to anyone else. He seems like an old-fashioned allegorical cartoon. On the other hand, the novel depicts him as someone who regularly identifies his own happiness and who conspicuously approximates success and reward with his regular consumption of meals (his passing of his medical examination, his wedding, and then his daily life become the occasion for taking meals that are, for him, both simple sustenance and sustenance that bespeaks his complete satisfaction). Yet Charles's happiness is not modern but something that the novel outlines as deeply primitive—a satisfaction in the ordinary rhythms of life that cannot imagine what it would be not to like that life, happiness that feels unmediated and uncompetitive because it never needs to reassure itself that it cannot possibly be misery since it is so conspicuously "happier" than other people's happiness.

This is as much as to say that Charles actually does fail Emma and that he fails her for the very simple reason that he cannot imagine making a judgment on his life that would be different from the direct experience of it. He cannot, in other words, imagine a happiness that can count itself as success only insofar as it travels through someone else. A simpler and better-hearted version of Sade's sexual athletes who are interested in other people as mere occasions for the production of their own individual pleasures, Charles is portrayed in the novel as solitary from the classroom of his youth to the household of his marriage. For Charles's limitation is not simply that he is too innocent to imagine himself sinned against, but that he is unconscious of the possibility that he might be doing something other than succeeding by living his daily life. Emma is driven to distraction by the very husband who is devoted to her—through her life, her death, his discovery of her adultery, and her fury merely registers the fact that he cannot imagine that she is unhappy and that her unhappiness might be a judgment on him.

The novel is nothing if not simultaneously vague and precise about treating the notion of satisfaction in sexual terms. Charles bounds from the marriage bed; Emma develops a sense of uneasiness and melancholy. Her first sexual experience with Rodolphe is clearly marked as the first satisfying sexual experience of her life, and Flaubert presents it in terms that sound the note of the cliché so strongly that there is no temptation to produce a historical genealogy that would identify them as having been fresh once (". . . nothing around them seemed changed; and yet for her something had happened more stupendous than if the mountains had moved in their places" [116]). But it would not be worth remarking on these facts if we were to see them as drawing the moral of the supreme importance of sexuality to individuals and to the marriages and affairs that unite them (and thus as hailing an account of Freud's significance as an interpreter of the fundamentally sexual basis of human identity).

For what is at stake is the discovery of sexual action as a rationalized utilitarian action, complete with the insistence upon the happiness standard and the insistence that it must apply to the greatest number. Sexual action becomes not simply the stuff of advice books but is also discovered as a synchronized success, a feat of timing in which two individuals simultaneously produce the judgment of their own happiness. Sexual experience comes to need to be justified, to meet new standards. For, as Flaubert recognized in his remarks about the development of "love" and Byronic satire's inability to discourage its rise, sex was being made to answer to *bonheur*, so that one's actual experience was continually shadowed with the sense of expectation and disappointment. Its only real alternative, he suggested, was prostitution, which he admired for its professional detachment rather than for its golden-hearted practitioners and for the detachment that it afforded him (a detachment he rather spectacularly displayed in insisting upon keeping a cigar in his mouth while having intercourse at one brothel he frequented with his friends).[41]

What I am arguing here is that Flaubert, in describing utilitarianism's appropriation of and application to sexuality, ceases to need sexual explicitness, because sexuality, in having been socialized, operates according to a logic that plays itself out on a variety of fronts. Thus, though it might be controversial if I were to insist upon the importance of counting Emma's experience of orgasmic sex and were to say that I think that she experienced orgasm exactly once (on the day of the agricultural fair), I think that it's easy to see that a premium attaches to synchronized success and simultaneous happiness, and that this emerges in the language of objects that develops around the gifts that circulate as love tokens in the novel.

Flaubert's depiction of gift exchanges makes them continually bespeak the promise of sexual satisfaction; and this is the case even when they are gifts like the new waistcoat (cut as if for a man) that Emma gives herself. Gifts in the novel are treated as if they were packets of happiness (exactly as they should be, coming from Monsieur Lheureux) and as if they were merely detached material units of the happiness that is frequently rendered in terms of sexual acts. Although "his conviction that he was making her happy looked to [Emma like] a stupid insult," Charles's gifts, like his assessments of happiness, are always oriented toward duration, toward the sense that an object is qualified to be a gift because it has previously been owned, as if the object's being valued by someone else and road tested made its value obvious (77). Thus, this owner of multiply owned volumes of the *Dictionary of Medical Science* ("uncut, but the binding rather the worse for the successive sales through which they had gone") bestows on Emma a "secondhand dogcart" and a horse that someone else has broken in and largely broken down (Monsieur Alexandre's "old filly, still very fine, just a little broken in the knees"), in much the same way that he bestows himself, a secondhand husband whose previous wife's affection ought to count as a good reference, and in much the same way that he takes Héloïse's jealousy of the young Mademoiselle Rouault as confirmation of the appropriateness of his attraction to her (22, 23, 117). He replicates his mother's awareness of the value of what is already established, even if his attentions are broader than the exclusively financial interests that had led to secure for him a widower supposed to have substantial holdings. Like people who don't know what they like until they are told, Charles only knows happiness as confirmed happiness. And he thus cannot imagine that he feels a happiness that might be unshared.[42]

By contrast with Charles's sense that objects have and hold value, Léon and Emma proceed to an exchange of gifts that revolves around staging occasions for experiencing what the other does, as if through their eyes. The two exchange books and romances; he gives her—and himself—matching cactuses; and she installs in his room "a rug in velvet and wool with leaves on a pale ground" (70). They can continue the effects of their initial conversation about the soul-expanding effects of landscapes, music, and poetry by reading the same books, by pricking their fingers (sometimes even simultaneously), and by her gifts of household furnishings that she can deliver to the rooms in which he lives (71). Moreover, they come to share the pleasures of self-renunciation in not proceeding to an affair. Thus, Emma's self-gratulation ("How good I was" [75]) for not having bought anything from Monsieur Lheureux on his first visit is thus simply a version of the process of sharing with Léon a consciousness of love relinquished. It has become possible to take satisfaction in actions that involve inaction. If she takes up her needlework and learns to note her husband's goodness, and if he decides to leave to study in Paris while making enough preparations as if he were going on a trip around the world, the descriptions of each function to indicate that they don't need to exchange actual objects in order to express their sentiments toward one another. They come to give one another the gift of consciousness—here, finally, represented as the refusal of both objects and actions.

Against these two ways of bestowing gifts, we can set the practices that Emma and Rodolphe establish between them, which are remarkable in the first place because Emma's gifts become "an embarrassment" for Rodolphe and "humiliating"—despite the fact that only he and she know of them (137). Emma, that is, produces her gifts to create a private language much like what she had established with Léon before his departure for Paris; and she gives him gifts that also announce their demands on his identity. The riding crop, the signet ring with the motto *Amor nel cor*, the cigar case copied from the one that Emma and Charles had found as they were leaving Vaubyessard create a role for Rodolphe as insistently as Emma's suggestion that Rodolphe might have to have a violent confrontation with Charles. Emma may be desperately in earnest in trying to retain Rodolphe's affections, but only because she creates a completely profligate image of who he is. Thus, when he comes to write his farewell letter to her, the horror of the scene lies not just in the difficulty he has remembering exactly who she is. It is, instead, that his difficulties in picking out which of his memories are memories of her in particular have already been so thoroughly anticipated by the fact that she has been treating him as someone else, the exotic sea captain whom she will later describe to Léon.

Gifts here are as freely given as they might ever be since there is no public decorum to maintain, but Flaubert describes the gifts that Emma gives to Rodolphe as essentially tyrannical. They are tyrannical, moreover, because they so clearly announce a command that Rodolphe think about her. Like her insistence upon creating a miniature private holiday by proclaiming midnight to be a moment out of time when they will turn their thoughts to one another, her giving him various love tokens involves her producing relics designed to prompt him to "recapture something of her presence" (145). These mementos, however, curiously erode the very memory they were supposed to preserve. As Rodolphe tries to remember to whom he is writing so he can style his farewell letter fittingly, he opens the "old Rheims cookie-box, in which he usually kept his love letters":

First he saw a handkerchief stained with pale drops. It was a handkerchief of hers. Once when they were walking her nose had bled; he had forgotten it. Near it, almost too large for the box, was Emma's miniature: her dress seemed pretentious to him, and her languishing look in the worst possible taste. Then, from looking at this image and recalling the memory of the original, Emma's features little by little grew confused in his remembrance, as if the living and the painted face, rubbing one against the other, had erased each other. (145)

Rodolphe's use of his archive makes it clear that he has already replaced memory with history. Recovering the material evidence of his past relationships, he believes that they occurred but can't always connect the evidence with vivid images of exactly who was involved; letters upon letters from various mistresses (with writing and style "as varied as their spelling"), "bouquets, garters, a black mask, pins, and hair ... lots of hair" cause "all these women" to crowd "into his consciousness" and shrink "in size, leveled down by the uniformity of his feeling. A word recalled ... certain gestures, the sound of a voice; sometimes, however, he remembered nothing at all." Given the fact that Rodolphe begins to compose his letter telling Emma he won't run away with her as soon as he arrives at home, that is, *immediately after* having seen her and reassured her that he is "forgetting nothing" (passports, tickets) that they will need for their journey, it's remarkable that Rodolphe has to visit his personal archives "to recapture something of her presence" (144, 145). And it's more remarkable still that it should end by enabling him to forget her almost entirely ("for pleasures, like schoolboys in a school courtyard, had so trampled upon his heart that no green thing was left; whatever entered there, more heedless than children, did not even, like them, leave a name carved upon the wall" [145]). Composing a farewell letter to a woman he has seen within the hour, he can render his own very nearly present experience remote as soon as he begins to speak to himself like his own editorial assistant prodding him to begin writing the right sort of thing: "Come," he said to himself, "let's go" (145).

The key point to be made is that no one—neither novelists nor the characters they might depict—works from life any more because the judgment of happiness is harder to make than the utilitarianism that they live by had quite imagined. For if the distinction between pleasure and pain had anchored the Benthamite project of replacing personal virtue with public behavior, and individual goodness with the capacity to produce good effects, Flaubert wants to say that the difficulty with that project is that is has no clear sense of what it's evaluating. If pleasure and pain had seemed to Bentham to provide good evidence about outcomes, Flaubert suggests, the real question is when an outcome has come out. Does the happiness of a marriage appear on the wedding day, the wedding night, the honeymoon, or a golden anniversary? Does the pleasure of a sexual relationship appear in the anticipation or in the orgasmic conclusion that marks a sex act's success? In a world in which happiness is constantly being checked, the measurement of happiness itself seduces individuals into producing readily identifiable actions, to valuing the techniques of measurement. This is to say that the happiness-measuring system itself promotes both the adultery and the spendthriftiness that lead to Emma's eventual downfall, and that it does so by insistently shortening the unit of action and by insisting on making it ever more insistently perceptible.[43] With the happiness-measuring system, individuals are always on the lookout for occasions in which to demonstrate their happiness to themselves, and sex acts—defined very explicitly as physical pleasures that reach their limit in the satisfaction of orgasm—simply become easier to work with than the notion of a married state that expresses itself in its continuation rather than in its constant production of altered states.

Moreover, acts of purchasing follow this same logic in that value inheres not in the objects that are purchased or passed up but attaches primarily to the transaction itself, the identification of the point of sale. This explains why Flaubert is concerned to depict so many things that get lost. The cap of composite origin that the young student Charles Bovary loses in the impersonal malice of the classroom never turns up again, nor does Emma's greyhound Djali—however this may disappoint the proverbial wisdom one of Emma's fellow passengers on the Hirondelle has produced about dogs seeking out their masters and mistresses after many years and over great distances. The cigar case discovered on the road from the ball at Vaubyessard does not return to its original owner but becomes Emma's possession and the model for the copy that she gives to Rodolphe. But, most importantly, Rodolphe's farewell letter, which Emma drops just before her delirium sets in, completely disappears from her consciousness by the time she rises from her sickbed after forty-three days.

This letter and its eventual discovery, of course, make *Madame Bovary* the novel that it is, and, more importantly, indicate just how disingenuous Flaubert and Sénard were in focusing on Emma's suicide as an act of self-execution that rounded out the novel's circuit of action. For something that Flaubert had observed of Emma—namely, that "she did not believe that things could remain the same in different places"—suggests the problems that will attach to the notion of objects, actions, and selves in the utilitarian scheme as Flaubert represents it (61). For if Emma continually develops so many new versions of her life in her constant production of new avatars for herself that it's unimaginable that she could figure out which one to punish, Flaubert makes it abundantly clear that her work isn't really done at the time of her death. In death, she corrupts the husband who had remained so extraordinarily innocent throughout her life:

> To please her, as if she were still living, he adopted her taste, her ideas; he bought patent leather boots and took to wearing white cravats. He waxed his moustache and, just like her, signed promissory notes. She corrupted him from beyond the grave. (250)

We are told that Charles, having discovered Rodolphe's long-since discarded farewell letter to Emma and a cache of his love letters, accidentally met Rodolphe in the market. "They both turned pale when they caught sight of one another." Then, with the adaptive ingenuity that the novel had given so abundantly to Emma, they sit down to share a bottle of beer. Charles, looking at "the face she had loved," Rodolphe's face, "seemed to find back something of her there." In the place of what might, in another novel set in another world, have been jealousy, Charles expresses a strange wistfulness: "He would have liked to have been this man" (254). The "demoralization" for which the novel was prosecuted is, in this moment, complete. Although the demoralization might have seemed to manifest itself in Charles's having imitated Emma's extravagance, her love of fashionable clothes, her neglect of her daughter, it does not really revolve around these particular instances of flawed behavior. For the demoralization consists less in Charles's behaving badly because he has come to recognize his deception than in his confronting someone whom he takes to have been better at being him than he was himself. It replicates Charles's professional failure by comparison with Monsieur Canivet, the "famous surgeon from Neufchâtel" who is called in after Charles's bungled procedure on Hippolyte (131). It makes competition enter so thoroughly into every aspect of life that there is no refuge. Flaubert's novel, then, inaugurates the novel of modernized "fate," the world in which people come to know their actions so much after the fact and from the evidence of happiness that they come to see themselves less in terms of what they have done than in terms of what they might have done if they had been someone else.

The scandal of *Madame Bovary,* is, in other words, not that it suggests how passionate love or adulterous sexuality gives the lie to modern rationalized structures (or to the "conspiracy of . . ." that Emma and Rodolphe lament in their early conversation), but rather that it depicts the ways in which those structures can betray their most ardent partisans (105). For Emma Bovary, however much face she is given in the novel, is herself on the side of the faceless bureaucrat, the social engineer who is continually casting about to see how life might be different from what it is. Flaubert's novel adapts that bureaucratic vision by making his characters think about nothing except how things might have been different (so that Fate becomes a constant interlocutor in the novel). Sexuality and adultery are not thus the private and subversive alternative to a utilitarian calculation that evaluates actions in terms of their promoting the greatest happiness for the greatest number. They do not offer themselves as a defense of the claims of the individual against a conformist society. Instead, they participate in an analysis of action that leads you to realize that you weren't really happy then, or else, that you—in this case, Charles—were happy as someone else, Rodolphe.

After the publication of *Madame Bovary,* Flaubert received a letter from an unknown admirer, Mademoiselle Leroyer de Chantepie, who became his regular correspondent after she disclosed that she was an old maid twenty-two years his senior and not seeking an amorous relationship. They exchanged letters about his success and her sadness. She identified her sadness with Emma's; he corrected her, saying that Emma is superficial and that Leroyer herself is more like him, that they had both been afflicted with an unhappiness that he took to be wrong: "Life is such a hideous thing that the only way of bearing it is to avoid it."⁴⁴ He advised her to leave off her charitable efforts and to set to work in earnest, by which he meant that she should distance herself from what she had called "les chagrins" and "l'ennui."⁴⁵ And the work he urged on her is reading. This may seem an especially surprising recommendation from a man who had been supplying his other correspondents with detailed quantified reports on how much work he'd been doing: "I've been smoking fifteen pipes a day. I've jerked off three times. I've written eight pages."⁴⁶ But the point of Flaubert's recommendation is to claim that the act of reading involves never feeling that anything is missing. In the world of production, one might need to worry about how much one had done, about when one had finished. And it was for this reason that Flaubert was almost insanely vexed when the *l* was left out of his name in the *Revue*'s announcement of the publication of *Madame Bovary*; he saw it not as a simple printer's error but as a statement that his work wasn't done yet. The novel about nothing was, simply by virtue of its always feeling complete, by virtue of its always being available for a reading that was always synchronized with it, not pornographic but pastoral, not disruptive but therapeutic. It enabled its readers to enter and exit without ever needing to ask themselves if they were happy, and what they had done. Like the inherited money that enabled Flaubert not to work for money, the novel was heritable work that would enable its readers not to work and simply to rest in its completeness.

5

Connie, or The Lawrentian Woman

Lawrence's last novel departs from the other novels in this study in that it does not conspicuously rely on classic utilitarian structures. Instead, while Flaubert describes techniques of objectification that led persons to lose track of themselves in their frenzied effort to keep up with the reports on their actions that came to them from outside, Lawrence addresses the problem of identifying action in a class-based society. His central example is Clifford Chatterley, whose false consciousness emerges clearly in his sense that he might become not just an adoptive but a biological father—in spite of his physical incapacity. What Lawrence describes, I argue, is the way in which Clifford's mistake about biology is an accurate statement about class. Class awards all actions to an aristocratic land- and mine owner like Chatterley, so that he need not have actually done anything in order to be able to congratulate himself on his accomplishments. Against this class-based account, Lawrence sets the relationship of Constance Chatterley and Oliver Mellors as an example of the importance of sex conceived as a series of time-limited acts, to acknowledge the primacy of acts over the individualizing distinctions of aristocratic titles and even proper names.

In 1959 the critic Malcolm Cowley, summoned to appear as an expert witness in the U.S. Post Office trial regarding the ban on *Lady Chatterley's Lover*, explained the value of the book in two at least seemingly contradictory ways. The book expresses, in the first place,

> a consistent social and moral philosophy, which, if you try to sum it up in one word, would call for the word "naturalness." [Lawrence] believes that body and mind should not be separated; that, on a ground partly attributable to the artificial condi-

tions of a mechanical age, we have separated thinking from the body too much, and that a return to the natural human being is essentially a solution....[1]

This formulation, it seems safe to say, emphasizes Lawrence's social and moral commitment to naturalness in a way that suggests at least his opposition to society as he knew it, if not his opposition to the notion of society *tout court.*

Yet, when called upon to explain that "the description of sexual encounters" in the book "is germane to the expression of these ideas," Cowley offered his unqualified assent while altering the terms of the discussion.

It is entirely germane. It is almost at the heart of it, because he is trying to advocate in the book sexual fulfillment in marriage. That is the purpose of the description of the sexual acts throughout.[2]

A position that involves opposition to Lawrence's society requires descriptions of sexual acts, indeed takes such descriptions as intrinsic to its purposes. But these descriptions so intrinsic to the portrayal of a societal error in turn "advocate" a position that was not exactly inimical either to the society that Lawrence knew when he was writing the novel in 1925–26 or to the society in which legal proceedings on the novel took place (1959 in America and 1960 in Britain). The novel could, in other words, criticize society by advocating what society had not, by and large, opposed—the sexual expression of love in marriage.

Lady Chatterley's Lover became, in the account that Cowley and other expert witnesses provided (with some assistance from Lawrence's essay "A Propos of 'Lady Chatterley's Lover'"), a defense neither of adultery nor even of divorce but of married love.[3] In that respect, Cowley claimed, it exactly reflected community values:

I do not find anything in *Lady Chatterley's Lover* that essentially I can't find in *Ladies' Home Journal*. This is in substance, sir. In substance, it is what marriage counselors are telling the counselees five days a week as a result of various forces, including Freudian psychology and great worries about repressions and perversions. This sort of idea of fulfillment in the marriage state has become enormously common.[4]

With Cowley's description of *Lady Chatterley's Lover* as advocacy for "sexual satisfaction in marriage," the use of literary critics as expert witnesses—a controversial practice that had gained favor in the 1930s in America and had been explicitly sanctioned in the Obscene Publications Act of 1959 in

Britain—bore extraordinary fruit.[5] One needed expert witnesses to see the novel correctly, because the experts were testifying about something that was not, strictly speaking, there at all. As Saul J. Mindel, the prosecutor representing the post office in its ban of the novel, was quick to point out, "Not one of the sexual acts in the book involved a lawfully wedded couple."[6] Advocacy of sexual satisfaction in marriage, in other words, found expression precisely in its absence. Cowley therefore found himself explaining that

the whole book is directed toward what doesn't happen in the book, but toward which all the hopes of the characters are directed. The marriage, and the lasting marriage with children, of Lady Chatterley and Oliver Mellors.[7]

He was, as he admitted in his examiner's words, "directing [his] thoughts, then, to something which happens after" one's reading of "350 pages of this book."[8] The battle that had been waged over what unit of a representation should be judged had been answered in a novel way. To judge a work as a whole, instead of judging the potentially offending parts that it included, in fact meant to judge a work as more than a whole.

Cowley's emphasis on the absent marriage was a view with some considerable influence: the defense in the British trial promised the jury, in advance of their own reading of the book, that they would "observe that he [Lawrence] is clearly a very strong supporter of marriage—I mean except in those cases where marriage is obviously perfectly hopeless and for which the law allows divorce," and he likewise recovered the book for the novel-of-marriage tradition by observing that "the book ends with her [Constance Chatterley] and Mellors being about to marry."[9]

I shall later dispute Cowley's specific projection of the novel's tendency in some detail. For the moment, however, I would like to support his representation of literature and of literary criticism. For the importance of Cowley's testimony lies in his exemplifying the practice of literary criticism as the practice of making claims on behalf of what isn't there (and isn't any the less important for it's not being there). Being an expert in literary criticism is from this standpoint not important for involving a highly developed knowledge of popular taste and audience reactions (though Cowley laid claim to such expertise as well). Rather, it is important in much the same way that Freudian psychoanalysis is—for representing the claims of Kantian formal idealism as a version of realism.

Thus, while Cowley's testimony included remarks about public acceptance of certain books and about the currency of certain words in plays, novels, and "the language of co-eds,"[10] he never really faltered either when other readers flatly disagreed with what he saw or when confronted with the fact that other readers absolutely failed to see what he saw. The expertise of literary criticism, as he practiced it, uses a historical account of the development of the novel to suggest the superiority of the expert view over those of people who react to a particular novel in terms of its content and emotional immediacy.

The trials of various books, from *Madame Bovary* to *Ulysses,* had relied on a rather minimal version of formal idealism. They had, that is, played the fact-value distinction for all that it was worth, making it appear that the issue was not whether sexuality was depicted but whether the author portrayed it approvingly or disapprovingly, seductively or "emetically," as Judge Woolsey put it in his brief on *Ulysses.* And the fact-value distinction, or the assertion that one can agree on the facts and disagree about their value, is something like formal idealism in its most minimal and least compelling form. The pornography debate could thus look like an essential agreement over what the book says and an essential disagreement over its importance as long as the argument was one that focused on what keeps, in the debate, being referred to as "realism." Flaubert, Joyce, and Lawrence, according to those attacking their work as pornographic, were "glorifying" immorality. Flaubert, Joyce, and Lawrence, according to those defending their work as nonpornographic, were not approving of the behavior they described; they were merely representing realities, what people actually did, felt, and saw. Wanting to ban pornography or wanting to tolerate it thus looked like a function of one's view toward sex and the extent to which it should be admitted as a reality of life. One should not blame the representation for the reality.

Yet even in the midst of producing the defense-from-realism account of *Lady Chatterley's Lover,* Cowley was entrapped by a clever prosecutor into suggesting a more powerful account of the novel in general and this novel in particular. For, despite the pettifogging moralisms of those who attacked novels like *Madame Bovary, Ulysses,* and *Lady Chatterley's Lover,* one of the basic points that their side had always been able to score was that the existence of reality was never a sufficient explanation for the existence of novels. If they were wrong to circumscribe art to the realm of uplift—what we do not normally see because it is better than reality—they were not wrong to imagine that some version of idealism (formalistic rather than moralistic) was at stake.

It was thus only when Cowley's testimony laid claim to an idealist argument about Lawrence's realism that it started to make sense, for then it began to expose a definitional debate that recurs not only in the discussions of pornography and its censorship but also throughout this particular novel. The debate over whether the novel was a novel of sexual satisfaction in adultery or a novel of sexual satisfaction in marriage is, from my standpoint, less a semantic quibble than one aspect of what I want to call Lawrence's "physical idealism," which occurs in the novel as a persistent pattern of reconfiguring the shapes both of persons and relationships. And it has profound consequences for the very notion of plot, because plot becomes less a chain of events or sequence of occurrences (and the possibility of projecting them beyond where they appear to end in the 300-odd pages of the novel) than just this process of assigning new definitions to what is perceptibly and arguably the same thing. This is, I take it, the most extraordinary achievement of *Lady Chatterley's Lover,* to have converted the education and marriage plots of the novel not so much into an adultery-and-remarriage plot as into the project of reformulating an already formed character.

For Constance Reid had already become Constance Chatterley, Lady Chatterley, before the book's opening. Indeed, the book's announcement of itself as a tragedy revolves around the sense that all bargains have been made, all roles assumed, before the action to be recounted within the novel's pages:

> Ours is essentially a tragic age, so we refuse to take it tragically. The cataclysm has happened, we are among the ruins, we start to build up new little habits, to have new little hopes. . . .
> This was more or less Constance Chatterley's position. (5)

The novel thus proceeds, with extraordinary brisk efficiency in its initial two or three pages, to establish a world in which the whole game seems to be realizing that "les jeux sont faits" and that what will count as success will be bearing that doneness gracefully, taking the facts and lending them value.

In one of the most chillingly rendered examples of free indirect discourse ever written, Lawrence produces the grammar that no one speaks merely by taking the general view, the one that might have been spoken by an omniscient author, and only belatedly putting it in Constance Chatterley's mouth. It is not shocking that there is collective wisdom; it is not shocking that a character might say conventional things; it is only shocking that the "unspeakable sentences"[11] of reported speech and thought should actually be set up as a caption next to the mouth of a character. For anyone remembering Lawrence's views on Jane Austen, his recourse to the Austenian staple of reported speech and thought almost constitutes a statement in itself. Austen represents, for Lawrence, what is wrong with and implicitly pornographic about the nineteenth-century novel, because her writing projects her as "this old maid," who, to his mind, "typifies 'personality' instead of character, the sharp knowing in apartness instead of knowing in togetherness" and who is, to his "feeling, thoroughly unpleasant, English in the bad, mean, snobbish sense of the word, just as Fielding is English in the good, generous sense."[12] If Austen's heroines specialize in "sharp knowing," Constance Chatterley has a corner on blunted, almost insensate, knowing, as if what Lawrence calls "usage" (in connection with Clifford Chatterley),[13] which one might translate as decorous public opinion, were the thing she were most nearly capable of sensing. In a sentence like "His hold on life was marvellous" (5), the closeness of Lawrence's approximation to the rhythms of speech establishes this narrated consciousness as something like the sinkhole of character. The standard story of gossip and collective wisdom is not a paraphrase of Constance's individual story; it is almost a transcript of her story, as if audience reaction were so much taken into account that reception became the only story that she could remember.

Indeed, Constance Reid had, from her youth, an infallible knack for incorporating the talk around her. Her first "tentative love-affair"—undertaken in parallel to her sister's—by the time she was eighteen (5) had itself been a decorous acknowledgment of the enlightened public doctrine of sexual freedom. She had never committed the error that Clifford would later accuse her of—confusing persons and personalities, actual people with their roles (however apparently individualized and specialized those roles may be) (193). Like her relatives—and Clifford's—with their hygienic advice that she have a sexual relationship for the sake of her health, Constance believes for much of the novel that actions always subordinate themselves to one's role, that there is no perceptible form apart from function. She can thus have her affair with Michaelis and have it seem to mean no more (or less) to her marriage than taking a vitamin elixir would. As Clifford will later maintain, in describing himself as a "conservative anarchist," "people can be what they like and feel what they like and do what they like, strictly privately, so long as they keep the *form of life* intact, and the apparatus" (180). He can feel and express rebellion "even against his class," but only when "caught in the general, popular recoil of the young against convention and against any sort of real authority" (10).

Fathers were ridiculous: his own obstinate one supremely so. And Governments were ridiculous: our own wait-and-see sort especially so. . . . Even the war was ridiculous, though it did kill rather a lot of people. (6)

Class in *Lady Chatterley's Lover,* like religious election for Calvinism, is a means of subordinating actions to states. And Clifford's discussion of the apparent oxymoron of "conservative anarchy" merely reveals how little of an oxymoron the phrase represents. Thus, Clifford can, with his siblings, mock their father Sir Geoffrey, but only so long as that mockery is rendered absolutely null by their solicitude for his standing with everyone else in the world. What is perhaps more surprising than the fact that Clifford acts like his class is that he has the marriage of his class. His marriage is of his class not simply because he has married very nearly within it (Constance Chatterley comes from a family that while not aristocratic is still well-to-do intelligentsia). His marriage is more importantly of his class because he, Clifford, continually conceives it as if it operated according to the logic of class.

This class view of marriage involves, at the outset, the view that marriage should involve a kind of spiritual commitment between the two partners. Yet while this view may sound like the harmless enough compensatory program of a sexually incapacitated man, it becomes increasingly an expression of the kind of antinomianism that I have earlier associated with his way of enacting class. What he can or cannot do, he says, is irrelevant to his belief in his marriage. Thus, while many have described Lawrence as "anti-intellectual" because, in part, of his depiction of the "mental-life" arguments of Clifford and his friends, Lawrence's implicit quarrel is less against intellect or abstraction and more against a certain coordination of belief and action that Clifford represents. For although Clifford with his paralysis may represent impotence, his impotence does not translate into a version of what Blake termed "unacted desires" or any inability to live what he feels. What is wrong with Clifford's position, lived as it is, is not its abstraction per se but rather the ways in which a class-defined state or condition operates to vitiate the notion of action, as if character were less an induction from a collection of actions than a classification that rendered actions both invisible and null.

Yet if Clifford's antinomianism involves imagining that one can sustain unacted beliefs (can have a mental marriage that is uncompromised by its lack of physical enactment), it also involves more than the mere possessiveness of his friend Hammond with his "strong property instinct" about his wife (32), his pleasure in seeing "a woman walking around with [his] name-label on her, address and railway station, like a wardrobe trunk" (33). It does not, in short, represent marriage as a husband's property rights in his wife. Yet it is also distinct from the contractual version that imagines two independent entities compromising their independence by incorporating—the small-business version of marriage that Tommy Dukes describes so derisively as "the joint-property, make-a-success-of-it, my husband-my wife sort of love" (39). Clifford's view neither exactly subordinates the wife to the husband nor exactly identifies the individual's interests with the interests of the married pair. Instead, it allows for a curious independence, because it makes belief so primary as to render Connie's actions as irrelevant as his incapacity. Her affair with Michaelis does not, in some very real sense, constitute infidelity. And thus when she says to Michaelis that if Clifford "never knows, never suspects, it hurts nobody" (27), she is not being deceptive. She merely rehearses an article of faith between her and Clifford, that the only "doing" in marriage is the entering into it, the ceremonial act of indicating the change of one's state of belief (thus, Clifford, pressed by his friends for his views of marriage could say, "I suppose marry-and-have-done-with-it would pretty well stand for what I think" [35]).

In the antinomianism of class that sets the terms for Clifford's view of marriage, his physical inaction does not compromise his state, and, moreover, the physical actions of others count as his. Clifford can, with logic on his side, write "his best at this time [when Connie was having her affair with Michaelis]" and be "almost happy in his strange blind way" (30). "He really reaped the fruits of the sensual satisfaction she got out of Michaelis' male passivity erect inside her" (30). This is to say that, in the view represented by Clifford, marriage and class are profoundly linked. For it is not merely that sexual satisfaction between a husband and wife is authorized by marriage, but that all sexual satisfaction becomes authorized by marriage and its benefits transferred to the husband as if it were his profit. It is, likewise, not merely that Clifford represents the coal industry even when he plays the literary lion, but that his personality is that of the capitalist aristocrat no matter what his person does. The most apparently enlightened political and sexual views, in other words, amount to a harmless distraction, the look of anarchy that can superficially attach itself to a position that is ineluctably conservative.

If it sounds as though I have drifted from Constance Chatterley to Clifford, that is because I have. This descriptive elision of Constance into Clifford, or Constance as determined by Clifford, is, it turns out, hard to avoid. This is particularly so with Constance, but it is also true of Clifford, Mellors, and Mrs. Bolton. Being married, however unhappily or remotely, is less a fact about the characters than a part of them; and character becomes one of the most interesting elements of the novel as Lawrence has constructed it because marriage renders character compositely, as a study in the coordination of mutual variation. For character here occurs between persons, as if character were only possible in marriage (if marriage is taken loosely as a relationship between persons).

The English trial of Penguin Books for *Lady Chatterley's Lover* quickly shifted from a trial of the book to a trial of Lady Chatterley the character, as C. H. Rolph, the editor of the trial transcript, observed.[14] And thus elision of the immorality of the book with the immorality of the character was, as naive as it may sound, not really irrelevant. For if the same thing, the same sets of words on the same sets of pages (read by the individual jurors at their own speeds though not in the privacy of their own homes) could look either like literature or pornography, and the same plot could look either like a repudiation of marriage or an affirmation of it, Constance Chatterley herself embodies the very notion of susceptibility that pornography and obscenity statutes were designed to provide armor against. If the words "deprave and corrupt" were taken by the prosecution to mean "raise impure thoughts" and by the defense to mean "effecting a change in character," one can confidently point to at least Constance Chatterley as being "depraved and corrupted" by the novel. Whatever else the prosecution may have felt, it demonstrated a plausible frustration at the fact that it could not save Constance Chatterley from the book. Katherine Anne Porter may not have been deemed an expert on literary value (on the basis of the argument that she—otherwise known at the trial as "the American lady"—wrote short stories and didn't have standing as a critic even though she had reviewed the novel), but her *Encounter* review, cited at length in the trial, made perhaps the shrewdest of all the critical observations entered into testimony:

> ... the real disaster for the lady and the gamekeeper is that they face perpetual exile from their own proper backgrounds and society. Stale, pointless, unhappy as both their lives were before, due to their own deficiencies of character, it would seem, yet now they face, once the sexual furore is past, an utter aimlessness in life shocking to think about.[15]

Porter, making the argument from Clifford's side rather more eloquently than other critics of the novel, notices what she calls Connie's and Mellors's "deficiencies of character" and what I would call their shapelessness of character. For what shocks Porter, the "utter aimlessness in life" that seems to lie in wait for Connie and Mellors, is what seems to me Lawrence's experiment in rendering character in terms of expiration dates or character as a function of plot (rather than plot as revelation of character).

If Porter imagines that "their own proper backgrounds and society" would supply them the look of the character they lack, she is making what I take to be an incorrect point about a very astute observation. For one of the most puzzling things about Constance Chatterley is that her background has so thoroughly failed to "take." She is introduced in the opening pages of the novel as the daughter of a "once well-known" member of the Royal Academy, "old Sir Malcolm Reid" (6), and as someone who has grown up not merely being exposed to intellectual and artistic life but rather being exposed to almost nothing else. And yet she seems curiously untouched by that background. For all her adolescent experience of Germany, for all her association with a university crowd, she has remained a kind of female Caspar Hauser: she "seemed just to have come from her native village" (6). Lawrence describes this naïveté on the one hand as if it were the naïveté of sophistication, the "cosmopolitan provincialism of art that goes with pure social ideals" (6). Yet on the other hand, it is an index to the shapelessness of someone basically unaffected by her own life, as if it were a premonition of the bodily shapelessness that Connie recognizes in her mirrored image (as her body is "going meaningless," becoming "so much insignificant substance," at twenty-seven [70]).

One may wonder, with Porter, what will become of Connie and Mellors, may want to know, with Viscount Hailsham in the House of Lords in 1960, "what sort of parents they became to the child . . . that they were made to launch rather irresponsibly into the world," what "kind of house they proposed to set up together," and "whether they acquired a circle of friends, or, if not, how their relationship survived social isolation."[16] The openness of the question of character at the end of the novel involves asking if the relationship between Connie and Mellors will withstand the test posed by its mere continuation, but the openness of that question at the end of the novel importantly restates the openness of the question of character at its beginning. For if Connie herself constitutes an environment for the talk of Hammond, Dukes, Clifford et al. while she sits as the silent auditor of their talk ("She had to be quiet as a mouse, not to interfere with the immensely important speculations of these highly-mental gentlemen. But she had to be there. They didn't get on so well without her. Their ideas didn't flow so freely" [35]), Constance Chatterley is a character designed to defeat an environmental argument about character formation. She has "no character at all" precisely in having failed to register her environment. What Porter describes as Connie's "stupidity" is a certain imperviousness to environmental imprinting—or, rather, an excessive permeability to one imprint after another. She can seem the country girl while coming from a sophisticated family, the demure and maidenly young matron even as she begins her affairs with Michaelis and Mellors, less because she or appearances are deceiving and more because her experiences have failed to inoculate her enough to give her immunity from other, completely different, kinds of experiences.

Lawrence's name for the kind of character that Constance Chatterley so conspicuously lacks is "personality." By "personality" he means individualism conceived as a combination of inheritance and self-inheritance, as if each new response to one's environment were not merely derived from the environment but were also filtered through one's past responses (developing traits, tics, and characteristic tastes). This account, bowing deferentially toward both heredity and environment, suggests how there can be individual variation in the same general sets of circumstances, and it might sound common enough and compromised enough for it to seem uncontroversial. Yet in "A Propos of 'Lady Chatterley's Lover,'" Lawrence attacks both "personality" and the pooling of personalities that he takes to establish the model of counterfeit marriage:

Modern people are just personalities, and modern marriage takes place when two people are "thrilled" by each other's personality: when they have the same tastes in furniture or books or sport or amusement, when they love "talking" to one another, when they admire one another's "minds."(325)

What is counterfeit about "personality" is not that it is affectless, but rather that it generates affect about tastes, talk, and opinion. Charlie May and Tommy Dukes can agree that "it's an amusing idea . . . that sex is just another form of talk, where you act the words instead of saying them" (33–34), but their agreement represents how the thrill of their friendship rests upon earnest mistakenness, the feeling that one has achieved enlightenment by suggesting that carnal conversations might be, like conversation, just talk. Tommy opines that "you don't talk to a woman unless you have ideas in common: that is you don't talk with any interest," re-urging the view that "sex is a sort of communication like speech" (35), thereby extending the notion of enlightened economic self-interest to sexuality. Lest the desire for candor about sex sound refreshing, let me hasten to say that the notion of candor expressed here is precisely not refreshing. For interests—economic, sexual, and otherwise—emerge here as possessions, emblems of oneself distributed for one's own private and for public consumption; and holding such representations "in common" only gives the notion of property greater freedom without giving persons greater freedom.

For the sexual "personality" that is the imagined product of sexual "communication" here makes not objects but represented objects the only means of access to persons (persons communicate through interests). One can only love, can only marry, in this account that Lawrence takes to be counterfeit, through an annexation of interest to the model of property. Thus, while interests may not literally involve ownership, they, like the real property that was once the primary emblem of legal standing, constitute "personality" by making it visible to other persons.

In sketching out this line of argument, I am subscribing to the frequently held view that Lawrence was attacking a modern tendency. I am, that is, claiming that his attack on modern "personality" is an attack on a distinctly modern possessive individualism, an individualism that discerns itself only insofar as it recognizes itself to possess things, be they as immaterial as interests. Yet while many commentators have seen Lawrence as advocating a return to a pre-industrial society, a state more simply "natural" than the modern state, I would argue that his critique of modernity derives its particularly devastating force from the mere operation of providing such modernity a long genealogy.

This is first of all a genealogy of persons. Thus, the novel continually locates each of its characters in terms of a class identification. (He, Clifford, "was aristocracy. Not the big sort, but still it. His father was a baronet, and his mother had been a viscount's daughter" [10].) Class stratification and the consciousness of it, however, represent only a portion of Lawrence's genealogical move. For he consistently introduces his characters in terms of where they come from, as if the representation of a past were the precondition for the possibility of present action. Mellors thus is described as seeming to have "emerged with such a swift sudden menace . . . , like a sudden rush of a threat out of nowhere" (46) when Clifford and Connie and he initially cross paths, and Clifford's instant reply to Connie's "Where did he come from?" is "Nowhere! He was a Tevershall boy" (48).

Although the town of Tevershall that abuts Wragby, the Chatterley family seat, is almost literally "here," Clifford's infallible class sense enables him to sort "here" and "there" (or even "here" and "here") into "here" and "nowhere." If Connie does the work of sorting people according to classes (registering the menace not only of Mellors as a someone ex nihilo but also suspicion toward the very young girls—the toddler and the five-year-old—and the young mother who appear), Clifford never needs to work at such things. He is Clifford Chatterley, and they're not. Being Clifford Chatterley, as his sister Emma conspicuously demonstrates (with her resentment of Connie for having ousted "her from her unison in consciousness with her brother" [17]), means always bringing forth "something new in the world, that *they*, the Chatterleys, had put there" (17). And although Emma's stake in Clifford's work seems to lie in its being personal, in its not having "organic connection with the thought and expression that had gone before"(17), the trick of this version of personality is that its resemblance to actual persons, living or dead, is incidental.

Indeed, the "something personal" that Emma has in mind, represented by "the Chatterley books," is identical with what seems to be their opposite, what Connie sees as "the curious impersonality" of Clifford's desire for a son (43). And the reconciliation between these apparent opposites of personality and impersonality occurs by means of property. For it is not merely that Clifford as a landholder feels particular protectiveness toward and identification with his land and that he wishes most intensely for a son and heir when he goes to the wood (42–44). It is, rather, that the land on which Clifford's legal personality rests gives Clifford an existence beyond the bounds of actual personal existence. The wood does not merely entitle Clifford; it makes his individual existence seem to extend to the full duration of the title.

Clifford loved the wood; he loved the old oak trees. He felt they were *his own through generations.* He wanted to protect them. He wanted this place inviolate, shut off from the world. (emphasis mine, 42–44)

Property, that is, not only helps to establish legal personality. It even gives actual personality the feeling of impersonality by creating an identification with property (as distinct from a use for property).

Indeed, Clifford's sense of what is "his own through generations" makes him more enraged by the wartime damage to his wood than by the injury to his legs. The "breach in the pure seclusion of the wood" that had been caused by Sir Geoffrey's having had places "cut during the war for trench timber" (42) infuriates him as none of the other depradations of war.

He had been through the war, had seen what it meant. But he didn't get really angry till he saw this bare hill. He was having it re-planted. But it made him hate Sir Geoffrey. (42)

Although it makes sense to see the denuded part in the wood as Clifford's aberrant image of his own physical maiming, although his rage at his father may seem like a standard version of a simple Freudian story that brings everything home to the father, I am more interested here in something other than those versions of substitution. For Clifford's psychology is more than personal as he alternates between an absolute preference for what is his over what is himself, on the one hand, and an inability to distinguish himself from what is his, on the other.

In part, this looks like a subordination of self to tradition: "one is," as Clifford says, "only a link in a chain" (43). But of course the most curious thing about Clifford's desire for an heir is its assimilative capacity. As numerous defenders of Constance Chatterley noted in the trials, Clifford, in the first place, could not fulfill his marital debt to Constance and, in the second place, himself proposed that Constance become pregnant by another man. He could offer up such a proposal while saying that he would not want to know that she was having an affair, because, in his view, another man's child would not really belong to another man. The rearing would make it Clifford's. ("It would almost be a good thing if you had a child by another man.... If we brought it up at Wragby, it would belong to us and to the place.... If we had the child to rear, it would be our own. And it would carry on" [43–44].) Connie imagines herself to be repelled by Clifford's impersonality here, by the way in which "the child, her child, was just an 'it' to him" (44).

Unspoken wrangling over the unborn and indeed as yet unconceived child dominates the Chatterleys' relationship from this stage of the novel. He is, she thinks, impersonal. She is, he thinks, both selfish (in thinking of the child as *her* child) and a Bolshevik. The ease with which Clifford slips between taking Connie to be selfishly possessive and taking her to be a Bolshevik, opposed to all private ownership, helps to delineate his own position. For what looks simultaneously selfishly possessive and Bolshevistic is not an attack on the notion of privacy per se, but an attack on Clifford's inability to register action as having any claim at all. And when, in one of the eeriest moments in the novel, Clifford responds to one of Connie's inquiries about whether he should really like for her to have a child by saying, "Why I might even one day have a child of my own!" (111), he demonstrates knowledge of class rather than ignorance of sex.

Even when he suggests that "it might come back to me one of these days" (111) and she stares at him in amazement, he is not as crazy as he sounds to her ears. For the ability to engage in sexual acts may never come back to him, but, on the other hand, he has never really lost it, in that he can lay claim to the product and evidence of sexual action as his own.

Thus, even when gossip circulates that there may be a Chatterley child someday, Clifford remains strikingly unembarrassed. The rector may ask directly (albeit gently) if "we" may "really hope for an heir to Wragby" (149), and Squire Winter, another holder of a house and lands being mined for coal, may deftly smuggle in his question at the conclusion of an effusive chat about coal ("By the way, dear boy, is there any foundation to the rumor that we may entertain hopes of an heir to Wragby?" [150]). Yet while Connie wonders if such remarks stem from jokes or malice, Clifford can assimilate them to prophecy. So accustomed is he to the impersonal version of personality that he doesn't really have to ask where babies *come from*, because he knows that *where they go* (to "nowhere" or to places like Wragby) constitutes their personalities.

In taking Lawrence's novel as a powerful critique of the notion of personality, I am (as may be obvious by now) suggesting that critics like Kate Millett have misstated Lawrence's position in taking it to involve an enthusiasm for male domination and female subordination. What looks like a plea for naturalness, this argument runs, is in fact a way of returning to a state of nature in which male physical superiority over women can assert itself without encountering any resistance from civilization. Lawrence would, in this account, defeat a lineal hierarchy (subordination and domination based on family) by substituting for it a sexual hierarchy (subordination and domination based on gender).[17] Millett's account applies convincingly to some of Lawrence's critics (anyone who doesn't believe that there is such a thing as misogyny should consult the way in which Graham Hough almost instantaneously combines a complacent dismissal of Katherine Anne Porter and an easy identification of himself with Yeats; indeed, he makes the identification with Yeats the vehicle of his dismissal of Porter), I would argue, however, that *Lady Chatterley's Lover* attempts not merely to replace a lineal hierarchy but also a sexual one. I am also suggesting that Constance Chatterley herself demonstrates the difficulty of avoiding mistakes about what counts as personality.

For few characters in the history of the novel have been as resolutely opposed to what their novelist had in mind for them as Constance Chatterley. Shapeless as she is, she (like Clifford) never lacks for views. And her views continually involve the assimilation of personhood to lineal hierarchy. Though the novel tends to go to generics whenever it registers sexual attractions and sexual acts, its language of "the man" and "the woman," "a man" and "a woman," offends against Connie's sense of herself, because it accords too little respect to individual uniqueness, to the private as opposed to the common. Thus, her first reaction upon seeing Mellors is to remark that "he might almost be a gentleman" (68), and she worries, even after having first made love with him, that "perhaps he wasn't quite individual enough," that "it really wasn't personal," and that "she was only really a female to him" (121). Likewise, his use of dialect has the peculiar effect not of creating a social privacy, the sense of a coterie understanding between persons, but of expressing what feels like impersonality: "His 'tha mun come' seemed not addressed to her, but some common woman" (127).

Connie, that is, imagines sex to be impersonal insofar as sex does not count toward establishing legal personality. Thus, she can respond with ingenuous cruelty to Michaelis's proposal of marriage with "But I'm already married" (52) and can worry about whether she is being seen as special enough by the gamekeeper whom she more than once describes as appearing in "his black oilskin jacket, like a chauffeur," as if to suggest a nagging interchangeability of all members of the servant classes (123). The Connie who has twenty thousand pounds in trust from her mother is accustomed to the personality that gentlemen like Squire Winter accord her: "After all, Mr. Winter, who was really a gentleman and a man of the world, treated her as a person and a discriminating individual. He did not lump her together with all the rest of his female womanhood in his 'thee' and 'tha'" (129).

The acquisition of proper names, individualized names as opposed to the common, generic name, is thus so much at issue in the novel that it is no wonder that Lawrence supplanted the title *Tenderness* first with *John Thomas and Lady Jane* and finally with *Lady Chatterley's Lover*. For if the novel notices with some exactitude where men's titles come from, it wonders even more exactly where women's do. Sir Geoffrey (and then Sir Clifford) may have been born into the aristocracy; Connie's father, Sir Malcolm, may have worked his way into his title by dint of his artistic accomplishment; but the woman who is called "Constance Chatterley" at the opening of the book has her name not by virtue of her mother's having willed her an annuity that would give her independence but by virtue of her marriage. "Constance was," as the narrator quite succinctly puts it, "Lady Chatterley" (5). And if the novel is meticulous in noticing the physical effects of sex on Constance's person, it is equally meticulous in noticing the effects of different persons on her name. Sir Malcolm may have been able to "see plainly that" Connie "had had the love experience" when she came home from her German vacation in her eighteenth year (8); Clifford may, as her affair with Mellors begins, sense "with a sort of second sight" "something new in her" that he ascribes to her preoccupation with having a baby (136). The perceptibility of such apparently private experience may mean that Connie's privacy is less private, less exclusively her own, than she knows. But the local pronunciation of her name could tell her something she does not herself know (and that they do not exactly know either)—that she is the "chattel," the movable possession, of Wragby, and that what she takes to be her distinctiveness (and feels as the restraint and the "denial of the common pulse of humanity" between the village and Wragby Hall [48]) involves her functioning as an infinitely substitutable placeholder. (Indeed, though Connie takes it as a sign of Tevershall's being "hopelessly and offensively nonconformist" [15] that the miners' wives seem to be mocking her station even in the process of acknowledging it, Clifford never has the Chatterley of his name pronounced in the course of the novel.) Thus, when Connie Chatterley stumbles across Mellors and a young girl who turns out to be his daughter, and the young girl turns out to be named "Connie Mellors" (60), it is not really the future marriage between Constance Chatterley and Oliver Mellors that is being adumbrated. Nor is it that all women are the same. Instead, it is that all names must be the same, so that names will not veil the identities that they might be supposed to reveal.

Mellors's child appears only fleetingly in the novel, just long enough to suggest that all women might be called "Connie." That name is itself close enough to sound like the word "cunt" that Connie had apparently never heard before she met Oliver Mellors ("'What is cunt?' she said. 'An doesn't ter know? Cunt! It's thee down theer; an' what I get when I'm i'side thee...'" [177–78]). Yet the interchangeability of women here is less a matter of their being physically and sexually interchangeable than a matter of their appropriability to property. And when, in the scene from which Lawrence took the second title of the novel, *John Thomas and Lady Jane,* Mellors christens his penis and Connie's cunt, the point is not to create a new aristocracy (a sexual or natural aristocracy with a natural marriage that could be represented as a counter to legal marriage) but to make naming and personification rest on nonreplicability. "Thomas" is slang for "male," as "Jane" is slang for "girl," and "John" (as in "little John") is a would-be gentleman. Names of self-modifying gender—Mellors's "gentleman male" to Connie's "lady woman"—they do not ask the question of bawdy: "When Adam delved and Eve span, Who was then the gentleman?" Instead, the penis that Mellors recognizes with the name has a name only by virtue of never coming when he is called. The penis/phallus is the true freeholder, being able to take possession only of bodies—first Mellors's, then Connie's.

Moreover, as if the loss of distinction in names had not been achieved fully enough in "Connie senior" and "Connie junior," Mellors and Connie are here given versions of the same name ("Jane" being the female version of "John"). The commonness of the proper name echoes the commonness of the generic genders, "the man," "the woman." Yet the giving of names to sexual organs, the making of wholes out of parts, involves an account of sexual personification that establishes identity only through a product. For Mellors does not have a phallus, and Connie does not have a cunt. In the material idealism that Lawrence depicts here, personhood rests fundamentally on the commonness of shared property in one another. Whatever the problems of generation may be, sexual acts and conception work in exactly the same way: they produce persons by producing persons out of them. Connie, apparently within minutes of having made love with Mellors under the fir trees, can say to herself, "It feels like a child! . . . it feels like a child in me" (135); and though the novel confirms her diagnosis of her own pregnancy, Lawrence is not so much seeing conception as the sign of sexual satisfaction as suggesting the fundamental resemblance between the two. Both children and sexual organs are personifications that involve defining persons as acts (not as the potentiality for actions, or a state that needs no manifestation in an act). Neither Connie's feeling her cunt or her womb nor Mellors's "addressing his erect penis as if it were another being" (265) represents, in this scheme, any consciousness of self. Rather, they become conscious of body parts becoming persons. Body parts become freestanding sexual entities, just as children figure the continual carving of identity out of masses (the masses of flesh, the masses of persons who make up class and classes). As Connie explains to her friend Duncan, who has agreed to serve as her counterfeit lover for her divorce proceedings, "Perhaps only people who are capable of real togetherness have that look of being alone in the universe. . . . The others have a certain stickiness, they stick to the mass, like Giovanni [the Venetian boatman]" (271).

Personification here, that is, involves deriving individuality not from an opposition to the mass from which it comes but from a transmutation of it. In Mellors's letter to Connie with which Lawrence concludes the book, this transmutation is decked out in Mellors's revisionary Christian language of "my Pentecost, this forked flame between me and you" (300–301). A letter from John Thomas, as a composite figure of the disciple John who witnessed the transfiguration of Christ and the Thomas who had to touch Jesus' wounds before he would believe in the resurrection, it commends its new faith to the other member of the community of believers and gives the hard-bitten Tevershall Methodism of earlier chapters an excuse for its existence.

Yet if Connie Chatterley has been formed by the sexual evangelism that changes bodies and lives, her conversion looks suspiciously like a matter of her being merely duped (with the man who raises bodily hopes looking like the ultimate con artist). One by one, various characters line up to perform an examination of the body (as it were): they meet Oliver Mellors (and discern no miracle). Connie's sister Hilda opines that Mellors is just "acting! Acting!" the part of a simple workingman (243); and Connie's father, Sir Malcolm (in a scene that Graham Hough pronounced "the one utterly, disastrously bad passage" in the book,[18] evidence that Lawrence didn't know or had forgotten how the English upper classes would really talk), gives Mellors credit in a fashion that gives credit a bad name. Sir Malcolm can condone "the intrigue," the notion of a sexual life that derives its sensuality from mere mystery, its simply being kept hidden; and thus he minds only "the scandal," what people will say. ("Think of your stepmother, how she'll take it!" [281].) Mellors can first look to him "like a gold-digger" and Connie like "a pretty easy gold-mine, apparently" (281). But if Sir Malcolm "comes around" on Mellors, he does so by reconverting the scandal into a new version of intrigue—in which he tries to "establish the old free-masonry of male sensuality between" him and Mellors (283), creating the relationship between Connie and Mellors as a private joke between men.

Drinking what Lawrence calls "a fair amount of whisky," becoming "Scotch and lewd," Sir Malcolm makes a string of bad puns: "A gamekeeper, oh, my boy! Bloody good poacher, if you ask me." "So you're a gamekeeper! Oh, you're quite right! That sort of game is worth a man's while, eh, what?" "Gamekeeper! ha-ha, by crickey, I wouldn't trust my game to you!" (283)

But what might seem a drunken old man's tasteless jokes about his daughter's sexuality underscore the importance of Mellors's job for the novel. For Mellors's job is not merely a working-class job, a servant's job (otherwise he could still be a blacksmith as he had been before his army service). Rather, Mellors's job commits him to protecting Clifford's property against the members of his own class, the colliers whose poaching might thin out the ranks of Clifford's game.

Mellors's taking up and taking off with Connie might, according to the logic that immediately suggests itself here, constitute a minor act of class rebellion, with Mellors deciding to leave off doing dirt to his class and to enlist Connie to do dirt to hers. He would, in that account, cease to work to perpetuate the suppression of the colliers' "sporting instincts" (209) and would, instead, see Connie as fair game, what counts as nature rather than property.

Such a reading would converge with a by-now familiar argument, that sex can be politics waged by other means (so that a woman's sexuality counts only as the coin through which a traffic in women can be sustained as an exchange between—or among—men). Yet as plausible and as tempting as that suggestion is, that reading (which is committed to the "lasting marriage with children" not on account of a commitment to marriage but on account of a commitment to class conflict) would leave Lawrence's ending as a plot that had merely broken off with its resolution tantalizingly in view but still unrealized. What Lawrence says in his "A Propos of 'Lady Chatterley's Lover,'" however, indicates something rather different:

If I use the taboo words, there is a reason. We shall never free the phallic reality from the "uplift" taint till we give it its own phallic language, and use the obscene words.... Likewise, if the lady marries the gamekeeper—she hasn't done it yet—it is not class spite, but in spite of class.[19]

Marriage not as "class spite, but in spite of class" means, in one sense, the obstacle that Connie Chatterley and Oliver Mellors have already faced in the mere process of having an affair—imagining that they can relate to one another as if there were not the infinite distances between their classes that Clifford Chatterley consistently sees. In another, however, the difference that class makes is entirely material both to the plot ("she hasn't done it yet") and to an account of who Connie is. For if Sir Malcolm relishes the conceit that Connie is "game" for Mellors the poaching gamekeeper, Clifford has a purer understanding of game. For game, as the movable version of real, that is, immovable property, is not a landholder's because of its emanating from his land. Game, rather, is the landholder's property because it can never escape his claim no matter how far it strays from his land.

As Connie had discussed with Clifford her plans to go to Venice, she had said of his suggestion that there was "something eternal in marriage," "you make eternity sound like a lid or a long, long chain that trailed after one, no matter how far one went" (161). This game-law theory of marriage enables him to maintain his otherwise inexplicably stubborn commitment to having Connie though he can't hold her, to insisting that he will, if she doesn't return now to discuss matters, "consider that you are coming back one day, and act accordingly.... [J]ust go on the same, and wait for you here, if I wait for fifty years" (293). And the problem of Connie's as-yet-unborn child is, from this perspective, less the problem of the child's illegitimacy than that of its legitimacy: "He would not divorce her, and the child would be his, unless she could find some means of establishing its illegitimacy" (293).

The legitimacy of marriage and family is its always coming back. Whether in the form of Bertha Coutts, the estranged wife who returns to Mellors's cottage "a raving, doomed thing in the shape of a woman" (280), or in the form of Wragby, the house that is "a warren," from which "the family never sold anything" (147), marriage and family represent an attachment of name tags even to the most mobile creatures. In the world of legitimacy, that is, people and things may run, but they never escape.

In the park at Wragby, Mellors is trying to reestablish the stock of pheasants that had been killed off during the war when he and Connie first converse alone, but his job as gamekeeper chiefly involves protecting the rabbits from poachers. Newcomers, "riff-raff," come into the area "to poach

Clifford's rabbits among other occupations" (154). The "only thing" Mellors "had to contend with was the colliers setting snares for rabbits," and even they respected "a little" the rabbits' breeding season (143), as if what Hammond had called the "promiscuity of rabbits" were being opposed to the notion of property rights. The state of being property makes Mellors and Connie into Clifford's gamekeeper and Clifford's game; game that fails to acknowledge its owner is promiscuous. The novel's very title lends itself to riddles about possession ("Lady Chatterley's lover is ..."); and both Bertha Coutts and Mrs. Bolton take the physical existence of each of the two lovers as evidence of the existence of the other. Lady Chatterley's lover is Clifford's gamekeeper. Lady Chatterley's lover is the gamekeeper. Lady Chatterley is Clifford's game. It is not, however, that Connie Chatterley is Clifford's game because he possesses her as he does the rabbits or because she is as promiscuous as a rabbit. Instead, it is that in Mellors's dialect her name is rabbit. "Cony" or "coney," the word was "regularly rimed by *honey, money,*" from the sixteenth through the eighteenth centuries. In the nineteenth century the pronunciation with a long "o" "gradually crept in."

> This pronunciation is largely due to the obsolescence of the word in general use, while it occurred in the Bible, and especially in the Psalms, as the name of a foreign animal. . . . It is possible, however, that the desire to avoid certain vulgar association with the word in the *cunny* form, may have contributed to the preference for a different pronunciation in reading the Scriptures. . . .

> As Smart put it in 1836, "it is familiarly pronounced *cunny,* but *cony* is 'proper for a solemn reading.' "[20]

The statutes and the common law alike retain the word "cony" and use it in the place of "rabbit," as does the language of heraldry. But only in Mellors's dialect would the riddle of naming be pronounced. Lady Chatterley's lover is the gamekeeper. The gamekeeper keeps Connie.

Patrick: An Epilogue

When Bret Easton Ellis's novel *American Psycho* appeared in 1991, it met with some critical acclaim and an avalanche of censure, because the book includes descriptions of extreme sexual violence against women—and rich men and the homeless.[1] It has seemed to me that the novel doesn't so much depict sexual violence and recommend it in the process of depicting it as offer a description of the world that makes it seem universally and uniformly pornographic. Some people (such as Catharine MacKinnon, who has given resonance to the notion that our sexual world is a world made by pornography) might treat that as an unequivocally bad thing. I, on the other hand, think that any novel that knows how to present its view as a worldview, that hollows out its central character so as to make it clear that he couldn't have come up with much of anything on his own, that even offers its disclaimer on the opening pages less to people than to products, can't be even close to all bad.

In the mode of novelists ever since the genre began, Ellis opens by offering a defensive protest against the realistic reading that some will give his book:

This is a work of fiction. All of the characters, incidents, and dialogue, except for incidental references to public figures, products, or services, are imaginary and are not intended to refer to any living persons or to disparage any company's products or services.

Were we to take him at his word, we should regard the proper names—of public figures, products, and services—as a simple date stamp for the novel. They establish its setting in the late 1980s, but they aren't, Ellis says, being respected or disrespected by the novel's descriptions. In fact, he seems to believe that they are scarcely being referred to. How can this be?

Ellis's claim that all his references are, strictly speaking, imaginary is at the least suspect. It might seem, moreover, as if some sort of disrespect must be meant by a disclaimer suggesting that products and persons might command equal portions of respect, as if the promiscuous subjectification of products clearly translated itself into the objectification of persons. And there is no doubt that Ellis's protagonist Bateman is not exactly a respecter of persons and their feelings. His various acts of serial sexual murder all devote themselves to a project that has been prominent in pornographic writing from Sade's work on: they do not simply involve a desire for sexual gratification but an assault on the notion of individual psychology per se. Bateman aims, that is, to turn his victims inside out, to convert them and what might be their deep interiors into nothing but surface and the superficial. Indeed, this aspect of his project is so strong that it consumes his approach to a whole host of things that don't seem particularly sexual. When he encounters people, he knows them by their names, but he also knows them by the names of all the elements of their wardrobes—a character appears dressed in Giorgio Armani and A. Testoni and Hugo Boss and Ralph Lauren. A sociobiologist might see Bateman's obsessively deployed sartorial knowledge as essentially Darwinian sexual evaluation and might talk about the ways in which people are drawn to notice one another's appearance for the ultimate purpose of sexual attraction that maximizes reproductive capacity, but Bateman's interest in clothes seems to run another way. For it's not so much that he's briefly interested in the clothes so that he can get past them, but rather that he compulsively treats people's clothes as if they were a new layer of skin. In his relentlessly superficial world, clothes don't make the man; they show that nothing makes a modern man. They are the skin's skin, the attractiveness of appearance with nothing under it. In this reverse striptease, clothes aren't taken off to reveal skin; skin is a sexual organ (in something roughly like the way that Andrea Dworkin describes it in *Pornography: Men Possessing Women*) that becomes more intensely sexualized as it accrues new layers.

The explicit suggestion of *American Psycho* is that pornography is not sexually suggestive, that it does not make explicit something more properly left implicit or private. For in the world of energetic superficiality that Ellis describes in the novel, pornography doesn't appear as a set of objects that one might make judgments about, as if one might answer questions of the form: Does this or that offend public decency? Does this or that show too much skin? Pornography is, instead, a way of life. And this becomes manifest as Ellis accords his characters more and more clothes, because their committed superficiality is clothed nakedness—the commitment to a world that can never be either more implicit or more private because it has no interest in the interior lives of persons. (In that sense, Ellis provides an aggressive backhanded defense of the psychological novel of the eighteenth and nineteenth centuries, as if he were trying to make his readers defend the psychological novel by activating their gag reflexes and prompting them to recognize that there is more in people than they had been imagining.)

In a book full of dialogue, characters speak with fluent idiocy. Vanden rents the video of *High Noon,* thinking it to be a movie about marijuana farmers (20). Over cocktails, Timothy Price airily enjoins his companions to political seriousness: "I mean don't you know anything about Sri Lanka? About how the Sikhs are killing like tons of Israelis there? . . . Doesn't that affect us?" (14) and prompts Bateman to produce a to-do list for the nation and the world: "Well, we have to end apartheid, for one. And slow down the nuclear arms race, stop terrorism and world hunger . . ." (15). Timothy Price would reveal his own ignorance, and not merely expose Vanden's, were there anyone at the dinner party in a position to recognize it. While Bateman's spiel on foreign and domestic policy includes no howlers, it is clearly a piece of ignorant learnedness—a rehearsal of the kind of clichés usually reserved for beauty contestants. It is merely a rehearsal of "good things" so widely circulated as to fit effortlessly into a serial killer's mouth—into anyone's mouth.

In a fictional world in which no one can tell what kind of food they're eating—what kind of animal it comes from—they arrange sushi to spell out the initials of the person who'll eat it. Food is not sustenance but the occasion for another monogram. And when they express anxiety, however fleetingly, they worry that dyslexia is a sexually transmitted disease (5). AIDS doesn't mean either silence or death to them but a reading disorder. Yet to say that a sexually transmitted disease would impair Bateman's reading skills is to say that it would hit him where he lives, where names are more important than the actual existence of the persons to whom they refer and services are more substantial than actions. Bateman, after all, can become apoplectic at people's ability to make mistakes in recognizing Ivana Trump and Brooke Astor. Celebrities, like the clothes that so regularly get recognized and detailed as if their wearers were only so many models, represent the only stability there is to be had in the novel. Bateman can leave a message on an answering machine that says that he has killed scores of people, and the confession will be heard as a joke—one among the numerous dyslexic rather than Freudian puns that associate "mergers and acquisitions" with "mergers and aqua-sessions" and "murders and executions" (202, 206) and confuse "decapitated" with "decaffeinated" (372). In what is perhaps the most frequently recurring gag in a novel full of recurring gags, Bateman continually sees "someone who looks like x [a name that changes from one scene to another]" and is in turn continually hailed with a series of mistaken names: Hamilton (48), McCullough (78), Marcus Halberstam (89, 143, 187), McDonald (111), Taylor (137), Simpson (141), Kevin (162), McCloy (182), Davis (179, 387), Robert Chanc– (222), Ted Owen (262), Saul (262), Henderson (374), Donaldson (388). In this novel of sex, drugs, and rock and roll, Bateman speaks schizophrenically, describing his sexual exploits and murders in lurid detail and also producing weirdly appreciative and rather sentimentally lyric accounts of various albums—as if he were himself not so much inhabiting different roles as adopting different media. He not only wants but needs to have the new Stephen Bishop album "in all three formats" and to buy more copies of magazines that he subscribes to and has already received, because format defines the existence of things for him. The notion that persons and objects might have continuity over time and through formats has ceased to have any significance for him.

Or, rather, it has come to have a kind of negative significance. For the go-go years of the late eighties see the value of packaging and see the profits to be made in the present and the future as involving a repudiation of any continuity with the past and its claim that objects and persons might have properties and characteristics. It is a Teflon era, with Ronald Reagan as its Teflon president. As Bateman puts the matter: "The past isn't real. It's just a dream.... Don't mention the past" (340). For this is a new world of consumption; one in which possession doesn't anchor individualism (as it does in the classic Lockean account). Instead, persons like Bateman start developing different media for themselves so as to become better consumers. They produce themselves in multiple media—the earnest record reviewer, the serial murderer, the expert on the finest points of the appropriateness of clothing; and in the process become improved consumers, people who are such expert consumers that they can imagine needing multiple copies of the same magazines and all the different formats of an album for their various aspects. The various versions of characters like Bateman can't share, because there is, effectively, no connection among them.

The interesting feature of *American Psycho* is that Bateman doesn't just objectify his sexual victims; he also objectifies himself. Relentlessly committed to the world of surfaces without any inegalitarian attachment to himself as an individual, Bateman uses cocaine as if the point were to produce the nosebleeds that would make his interior workings external; makes sex increasingly external to his body (so that it is most intense as an observation of other people); and treats rock albums as if they offered up what would once have been a lifetime's worth of roles for an actor, to produce singers who schizophrenically remake themselves every four minutes (even while working hard to preserve the constancy of the name by producing albums that are "self-titled," as a rhapsodically described Whitney Houston album is).

American Psycho does all this in a fashion that involves a linguistic theory that bears upon the novel's conception of action. In Bateman's world it's significant that his victims are those who are described as having interiors—either the vaginal cavities of the women or the gaping hole of poverty of the homeless, and that these are at the opposite end of the spectrum from the brand name—the proper name that has become capable of applying to both persons and products. In this it sounds as if the novel is just carrying Saul Kripke's account of names to a logical extension that amounts to an ethical position. Kripke's argument in *Naming and Necessity* is that names are inexplicable in descriptive terms, that gold, for instance, would continue to be called gold even if it ceased to look gold (as, of course, it does in "white gold" and "rose gold").[2] The names of things are their names, he insists, because acts of naming involve acts of "primal baptism" that make it possible for one to affirm that the name of something is the name of something simply because that name was and is given to it. Names are, thus, by virtue of the impossibility of resolving them into the kind of "just so" story of genealogical unfolding that Kipling liked to tell, the most profoundly social aspect of language. Names and their recognition mark one as a member of one's community to a degree that the more logical aspects of language don't, because the only way to discover how to use a name is to be a member of the linguistic community that uses it. Neither pointing to the properties of the thing or person named nor explaining the rules of combination (as in grammar) really helps to explain a name.

Kripke calls names "rigid designators," to get at the way in which names themselves carry whatever definition they have within themselves;[3] and it is this kind of rigidity that marks the apotheosis of the brand name in *American Psycho*, the name that connects to a host of different products with a host of different characteristics that are in turn tied together by nothing other than a fashion season and that name. And the force of the brand name is to insist upon the inevitability of a tautology—"It's Giorgio Armani because it's Giorgio Armani"—that is as socialized and, in that sense, as superficial as any linguistic use can be. As Bateman puts it in some of the novel's final pages, "Reflection is useless." For him this means, in part, that "individuality [is] no longer an issue" (375); and what that statement means is there is no available connection between surfaces and internal convictions: "Sex is mathematics.... What does intelligence signify? Define reason. Desire—meaningless. Intellect is not a cure. Justice is dead ..." (375). The Giorgio Armani that might be a tie, a belt, a suit, or a person is not just a name but a name that, in the abundance of its applications, sets itself in opposition to reflection and all its efforts at justification.

The triumph of the name is, in other words, the triumph of a world so socialized that no character has any capacity to produce any reflective resistance to its fast-paced self-reproduction. There is no vision of justice that would provide positive and negative evaluations and incentives for the world that is. One accepts this world—or eliminates parts of it, mutilating a homeless man, a girlfriend, or a woman from an escort service for not being winners in it. For this is a world that encompasses the persons it contains and is not transcended or superintended by them.

What *American Psycho* does is to provide an account of the pornographic as part of a representational strategy. In that respect it is as pornographic when dealing with anodyne material as with sexual material. For the essence of what makes sexual pornography pornographic is, as Sade and especially Flaubert claim, the fact that it subordinates everything in its field to a uniform representational scheme that produces hierarchical evaluations and cannot tolerate the existence of irresolvable conflicts in values. Pornography, in this form, is an example of what Elie Halévy identified as the coercive democratic structures of Benthamite utilitarianism, with its ingenuity in creating bureaucratic techniques that assimilated individuals to them.[4] The essence of these structures is to produce evaluations that can be unequivocal because they focus on one element. They rank individuals on a multitude of consistent scales and configure modern life—so that running the marathon or the 100-meter dash can become the focal point of a lifetime, because the evaluative mechanisms of these events represent such a powerful picture of how actions and value can be represented in our society that a whole life can be made to revolve around the preparation for and the decline from the moment in which one was really capable of acting within them. Like the swaddling clothes that Rousseau recommended for infants in *Emile,* these "events" provide a kind of security and clarity for those who participate in them. Their absence or disappearance represents an unmooring for individuals, but the value of individual action is always meaningful merely as an index of a particular group. It loses its force outside the field of that comparative grouping. Ellis's use of Dostoyevsky's *Notes from Underground*, with its early insistence on what I have earlier called the schizophrenic narrator, seems well chosen to insist upon this point:

Both the author of these *Notes* and the *Notes* themselves are, of course, fictional. Nevertheless, such persons as the composer of these *Notes* not only exist in our society, but indeed must exist, considering the circumstances under which our society has generally been formed.

A character such as the author of the *Notes*, like Patrick Bateman, may be fictional, but not because he doesn't really exist. He is, rather, a virtual character, one that always exists as an instantiation of the "reasons why he appeared and was bound to appear in our midst."[5]

To see the force of this point is to begin to have an explanation for the extraordinary difficulty that has long attached to the prosecution of representations on the grounds that they were pornographic. To feel the force of the pornographic as pornographic is to feel as though one is in its world, not merely viewing it.[6] Pornography is, in that sense, the most immediate literary form. If it doesn't feel contemporaneous, it isn't pornography. Pornography brooks no stance involving historical distance. This is a point made obvious in the way that video stores that specialize in hard-core rentals treat their own stock. Aside from a very small number of "classics," pornography doesn't seem to them worth preserving; the tape is frequently more valuable to them than the images on it, and they substitute new images for old with great alacrity. In that, it seems to me that they are on to something about pornography that scholars like Walter Kendrick miss.[7] When Kendrick talks about a "secret museum" containing historical pornography, he ignores the fact that the difficulty of compiling a museum or archive is not that untold images have been lost under the pressure of censorship. Rather, untold images have been lost because they didn't seem worth saving to some of the very persons who had been their most enthusiastic admirers. Pornographic history is, in other words, the most social of social histories.

A pornographic book or video is pornographic because its audience sees itself as contemporaneous to its representations. Ellis's obsession with writing a book obsessed with the insistent rightness of the immediate fashion system, with what looks good *now*, underscores the importance of this point, but then again so does the reception of the novel. In only a decade, *American Psycho* had ceased to be a book to be denounced; as the movie based on the novel appeared, there was no outcry that visual media are more assaultive than words. Instead, reviewers who had previously criticized the book talked about how they as readers had mellowed, about how it didn't seem so bad now, on reflection.

The books that this study takes as its central cases all look unpornographic now. But that is merely a by-product of the fact that the names that are the names of everyday life, of a world that once made a character like Patrick Bateman an actual or (actually) a virtual person, have themselves disappeared. By the time the novel has been out for a while, the names seem less like the stuff of our world than like the occasion for footnotes (identifying Brooke Astor and Ivana Trump for us; noting that there appears to have been a mistake, because a Rolling Stones song seems to have been attributed to the Beatles, making *American Psycho* look a bit like *The Dunciad,* insofar as it has an insistent topicality that can be translated into footnotes with a certain loss).[8] What was pornographic now seems distant and inoffensive—in short, historical and/or scholarly. The significance of this point is frequently missed—as when people give themselves and their age credit for having become enlightened or tolerant by comparison with their immediate predecessors. However much they congratulate themselves for their tolerance, they haven't gained greater reflective perspective than the preceding generation; they merely have the sense that there are different anxieties that might actually touch them—that AIDS or chainsaw murders of yuppies seem less likely to appear in their actual worlds.

To put it this way, however, is to suggest that pornography may be coercive, but only when it restricts the conditions of the world in general to a palpably articulated restricted environment and has made *this* particular set of circumstances that we happen to be in seem for now like the only possible world. Pornography, as the many exonerations of its putative instances suggest, tends very quickly to lose the capacity to seem like the only possible world. Just as pornography taps into the sense of the ineffable rightness of a particular fashion to a particular place and time, so it is least tolerant toward the subtle changes in haircuts, muscular development, and breast size that make fashion statements involve more than clothing. The extraordinarily high levels of social organization that characterize the pornographic milieux of Sade's work—here represented by *Justine*—are important, then, not just for providing examples of worlds in which there seem to be answers for everything; they are also important for marking the reasons why pornography becomes such a salient issue in the eighteenth century (having effectively ceased to be a workable concept between late Roman antiquity and the time of Restif de la Bretonne and Sade).

What I am arguing, in other words, is that pornography in modern western Europe became significant at the point at which civil societies were developing and trying to identify what difference such societies might make to individuals. It is a crucial literary form for societies that not only allow individuals increased possibilities of education and change but also make individuals educable and malleable. Moreover, the consciousness of society and societies as creating possibilities for actions that are what I call "assisted actions" marks a divide that I would characterize as one between libertarianism and liberalism. Libertarianism, as I have suggested at various points throughout this study, continually allies itself with libertinism in its engagement with an incoherent project—that of affirming the individual's right of choice without recognizing the extent to which clearly identifiable circumstances minimize the significance of that choice, since the individual is seen as only having the capacity to act meaningfully in terms of specific restricted sets of circumstances. As someone like Clifford Chatterley would say, the only important act for individuals in a pornographic world is the entering in—the moment in which one (accidentally, in the manner of Justine, or purposefully, in the manner of a sex worker) becomes part of a group.

And it is on this score that I would take issue with the position of someone like Drucilla Cornell, who draws on John Rawls's liberalism to what I take to be libertarian effect.[9] In my view, Rawls's emphasis on a "whole-life standard" tries to avoid the commitment of some utilitarian schemes to arguing that individuals are plausibly and completely evaluated by their appearance in any given social field. Thus, while I take Cornell to be correct in arguing for zoning that would minimize the degree to which someone might involuntarily be conscripted for images of persons like themselves (women, gays, or transsexuals) that represented them as devalued,[10] I take her to be incorrect in arguing that the way to respect sex "workers' own sense of their worth as persons" is simply to encourage "unionization and self-determination."[11] What seems right about her understanding of zoning is that it reflects the triumph of an account of environment that stems from Benthamite utilitarianism and its carefully articulated social environments (the schoolroom, the prison, and the workhouse): individuals are seen as being reliant on a describable context for both the meaningfulness and the value of their actions and statements. What seems wrong about her understanding of unionization and self-determination is the idea that one could completely resolve self-determination into unionization. For here Cornell is rediscovering the Marxist notion of specialization and the Lévi-Straussian notion of speciation. Marx objects to the kind of specialization that a Benthamite approach encourages by saying it overrestrictively identifies an individual's value with his place in a group. Lévi-Strauss is, on the other hand, more neutral because more interested in the problem of taxonomy, and he merely points to the ways in which speciation provides what we think of as society itself, which it treats as a subset of universal conditions. For Bentham, Marx, and Lévi-Strauss, specialization and speciation help to explain why certain actions and objects can lack universal value but nevertheless have considerable value in a restricted context. Being able to spell "cat," for instance, isn't going to enable most adult English speakers to establish their distinctive value by comparison with other adult English speakers. It can, however, help to distinguish the precocious child in nursery school. Likeness—here, in terms of age—is maximized in order to insist upon the importance of differences in ability. This feature of classic utilitarianism sees social subsets—speciation and specialization—as a means of identifying facts with values. The description that one gives of Susan or Joe is a description that reads like an application for admission to college: it produces facts in terms of percentiles and continually coordinates individuals with the groups in which they appear. It is a fact about Susan or Joe that they were class valedictorians, but it is a fact that does not retain its value outside its relation to the class. Utilitarianism (which I am representing in its most Benthamite form, largely because it is Bentham who is the principal architect of modern Anglo-American law) is principally an analysis of the ways in which societies, groups, and classes enable individuals to achieve perceptible value, not merely to do things but to do things that have a value that can be recognized exclusively through the index that the group provides.[12]

What Bentham scarcely addresses is the insight that Cornell's position is founded on—the fact that individuals are sometimes themselves in a position to choose the groups in which they exist and are evaluated. And what Cornell wants individuals to be able to choose is not exactly the groups with which they associate but the *value* that they have in certain groups rather than others. It seems to me that this view is more nearly libertarian than liberal because it imagines that social groups exist only for the direct promotion of individuals—a view that Bentham himself closely approximated in his conviction that education should be composed of diagnostic groups that enabled each individual to discover what they were themselves uniquely best at: each person should not only be able to be "number one" to themselves but also to find a context or group in which they are "number one."

I have two different objections to this view—first, that it basically sacrifices groups to the notion of personal stardom, the condition in which one's having achieved success and demonstrated one's value in one context is translated into the assumption that one can transport that evaluation to every context; second, that it relies on the ways in which the value an individual develops in a group is extra-individual only long enough for the individual to accrue value, and thus makes it look as though group membership ought to be a matter of individual choice.[13] Both of these objections amount to the same objection—that it is a mistake to see values as capable of being maintained without the conditions in which they could be facts.[14] Moreover, the libertarian character of this claim to take control of one's own value emerges in the moment in which it becomes clear that an account like Cornell's is scanting the capacity of a group to sustain itself over time and exaggerating the extent to which individuals can know enough about their own situations to make choices of their own value. The Hollywood actor who becomes a political pundit exemplifies the first sort of mistake. A New Yorker who keeps being arrested for impersonating a Mass Transit employee exemplifies the second.[15] A vocational autodidact, he imagines that the rules of the job are detachable from the community that employs them. The impersonator of transit employees may know the rules, but what he lacks is a sense of how the rules get continued by being changed, when continuity depends more on reformulations of the rules than on the simple following of them.

This study has aimed to analyze the contributions that pornography, as a genre that concentrates on the relationships between bodies and contexts, and more generally utilitarian social arrangements—as central ways of demonstrating what Foucault calls "bio-power"—make to our understanding of value and the ways in which social groups enable individuals to increase and decline in value.[16] Its central cases are of novels that have run afoul of the law—whether because someone like Sade had to pursue circuitous routes of publication, particularly while he was writing in prison, or because Flaubert's and Lawrence's novels became the occasion for celebrated trials. In all these cases, I argue, the offense of pornography is not its public display of sexually explicit content nor is it the challenge to what we now call "community values." Rather, when pornography really deserves to be called pornography (and very little sexual explicitness does), it is because pornography constitutes not just a message but an environment, a set of circumstances that succeeds in identifying what one is with what one is worth in an inflexible way. It aims to discover the entire value of a person in the process of discovering a local value. Whether in Sade's reinvention of monarchy within the utilitarian terms of Fourier and Loyola or in Flaubert's early depiction of sexual passion as the manic demand for a new narrowly circumscribed world to replace the one in which a person knows only how to be depressed, pornography concerns not just sex and our ideas about it but the values that persons can come to have and our ideas about them.

Notes

Preface

1. Niklas Luhmann, *The Reality of the Mass Media,* trans. Kathleen Cross (Stanford: Stanford University Press, 2000), 59.

2. Raymond Williams, *Culture and Society, 1780–1950* (New York: Columbia University Press, 1958).

3. Catharine A. MacKinnon and Andrea Dworkin, eds., *In Harm's Way: The Pornography Civil Rights Hearings* (Cambridge: Harvard University Press, 1997), 428.

4. Michel Foucault, *Discipline and Punish: The Birth of the Prison,* trans. Alan Sheridan (New York: Pantheon, 1977), esp. 136–38; and "Intellectuals and Power: A Conversation between Michel Foucault and Gilles Deleuze," in *Language, Counter-Memory, Practice: Selected Essays and Interviews,* ed. Donald Bouchard (Ithaca: Cornell University Press, 1977), 205–17.

Introduction

1. Reprinted, with changes, from *Critical Inquiry* 21 (spring 1995): 670–95. See Jeremy Bentham, *Panopticon Writings,* ed. Miran Bozovic (New York: Verso, 1995). Bentham's plan was initially described in *Panopticon; or The Inspection-House: containing the Idea of a New Principle of Construction applicable to any sort of establishment, in which persons of any description are to be kept under instruction; and in particular to penitentiary-houses, prisons, houses of industry, work-houses, poor-houses, manufactories, madhouses, lazarettos, hospitals, and schools: with A Plan of Management adapted to the Principle: in a series of letters written in the year 1787, from Crecheff in White Russia, to a friend in England.* See also his discussion of education, *Chrestomathia,* ed. M. J. Smith and W. H. Burston (Oxford: Clarendon Press, 1984); Andrew Bell, *An Experiment in Education Made at the Male Asylum of Madras* (London, 1797); and Joseph Lancaster, *Improvements in Education* (London: Darton and Harvey, 1798). Michel Foucault focuses on these schemes as examples of "discipline" in *Discipline and Punish: The Birth of the Prison,* trans. Alan Sheridan (New York: Pantheon, 1977).

2. Judith Butler's discussion of the performative proceeds by discussing the performatives in almost exclusively metaphysical terms because her approach involves questioning the possibility of delimited contexts. See her *Excitable Speech: A Politics of the*

Performative (New York: Routledge, 1997). Catharine MacKinnon and Drucilla Cornell have also discussed the Austinian notion of the performative in conjunction with the notion of pornography as a representation with consequences. MacKinnon's use of this notion, which I think is probably implicit in a good deal of her work, appears in *Only Words* (Cambridge: Harvard University Press, 1993), where I think that it suffers from occurring in the form of a claim to be able to provide authoritative empirical judgments. Cornell's appears in *The Imaginary Domain: Abortion, Pornography and Sexual Harassment* (New York: Routledge, 1995), where she appeals to the Rawlsian project of describing humans as having "two basic moral powers—a sense of justice and a capacity for the good" (17) and offers an account of the importance of "symbolically pulling ourselves together" (17) in the process of reviewing MacKinnon's theories of formal and substantive equality (21 ff.).

3. Jeremy Bentham, *A Theory of Fictions*, ed. C. K. Ogden (New York: Harcourt, Brace and Company, 1932). Ogden makes very substantial claims for Bentham's significance as a philosopher, as Miran Bozovic says in his introduction to *The Panopticon Writings*, 20 ff. Many features of Bozovic's introduction are useful, but he ultimately empties out Bentham's notion of fictitious entities when he describes them as "feigned in the imagination" and goes on to say that "although in a strict sense I cannot be said actually to have it, others nevertheless cannot act as if I did not have it" (21). The burden of the discussion should, I think, fall on the implications of the fact that Bentham treats a "fictitious entity" such as a legal right as significant when "others" *do not act* as if one "did not have it" (21). Bentham's anti-metaphysical stance involved him in noticing the behaviors and perceptions that people do not question, rather than in things that they might question but are barred from questioning.

4. Donald Davidson regularly speaks of "sharing, and knowing that one shares, a world, and a way of thinking about the world, with someone else" as crucial to language and thought. See his essay "The Second Person," in which he discusses the point of convergence and divergence between his position and Saul Kripke's position, as represented in his discussion of Wittgenstein. *Subjective, Intersubjective, Objective* (Oxford: Clarendon Press, 2001), esp. 121.

5. Catharine A. MacKinnon, *Feminism Unmodified: Discourses on Life and Law* (Cambridge: Harvard University Press, 1987). See also *In Harm's Way: The Pornography Civil Rights Hearings*, ed. Catharine A. MacKinnon and Andrea Dworkin (Cambridge: Harvard University Press, 1997).

6. Catharine MacKinnon identifies Justice Stewart's remark as an example of the projection of an individual perspective into a universal statement and treats it as an example of a male perspective that imagines that powerful individuals have more authoritative perceptions of the world than the disfranchised do. As will be apparent in a succeeding chapter, I am persuaded by the power of some of MacKinnon's central arguments about pornography—although I see Stewart's remark not as the "empty universalism" that she takes it to be but rather as a strong statement of the importance of a social field. See in particular her discussion of Stewart's remark in *Feminism Unmodified*, 147–48, 266 n. 13. See also Linda Williams's dismissal of Stewart's observation in favor of the saying that "one person's pornography is another person's erotica." Linda Williams, *Hard Core: Power, Pleasure, and the "Frenzy of the Visible"* (Berkeley: University of California Press, 1989), 6.

Williams's project involves extending the Benthamite agnosticism about motives (which does not try to judge motives in advance of the actions that they produce) to a position that comes close to claiming that there is no possibility of judging individual actions that differs from the individual's perspective.

7. The efforts to censor the photographs of Robert Mapplethorpe or the music of 2 Live Crew represent an appeal to "prevailing community standards" that I would take issue with, because those cases revolve around positions that center on content and a community's effort to enforce something that is not really available to it for legislation—a statement of what its own standards are.

8. Bernard Williams, ed. *Obscenity and Film Censorship: An Abridgement of the Williams Report* [Great Britain. Committee on Obscenity and Film Censorship] (Cambridge: Cambridge University Press, 1981), 54.

9. American New Criticism stressed the resistance of poetry—and all other instances of art—to paraphrase, and Archibald MacLeish confirmed this position in his statement that "a Poem should not mean but be." Yet while New Critics like W. K. Wimsatt, Monroe Beardsley, and Cleanth Brooks and writers like MacLeish maintained that literary works are unparaphrasable because they function as wholes that are "apprehended all at once," I think that an account of pornography must differ fundamentally from such descriptions of art, in that a crucial element of the function of pornography is to emphasize that it has no wholeness without a social context.

10. Austin offers one of the best accounts available of the problems associated with the difficulty of treating statements of fact in terms of their verifiability. He pointed, on the one hand, to Kant's having first systematically argued that many "statements" were "strictly nonsense, despite an exceptional grammatical form." On the other, he famously identified "some utterances which can fall into no hitherto recognized *grammatical* category save that of 'statement,' which are not nonsense, and which contain none of those verbal danger-signals which philosophers have by now detected or think they have detected (curious words like 'good' or 'all,' suspect auxiliaries like 'ought' or 'can,' and dubious constructions like the hypothetical). . . ." J. L. Austin, *How to Do Things with Words*, ed. J. O. Urmson and Marina Sbisa (Cambridge: Harvard University Press, 1975), 2–6.

11. Pierre Bourdieu, *Distinction: A Social Critique of the Judgement of Taste,* trans. Richard Nice (Cambridge: Harvard University Press, 1984).

12. See Leo Bersani's work for an account of the importance of sexual experience as a rebuke to the claims of the self. *Baudelaire and Freud* (Berkeley: University of California Press, 1977) offers one particularly lucid example.

13. Foucault, *Discipline and Punish*, 1–7.

14. Bentham, *Chrestomathia*, table I.

15. Ibid., 9.

16. Elie Halévy, *The Growth of Philosophic Radicalism,* trans. Mary Morris (Boston: Beacon Press, 1955), 264.

17. Roland Barthes, *Sade, Fourier, Loyola,* trans. Richard Miller (Berkeley: University of California Press, 1976), 7.

18. Ibid., 80.

19. Charles Rembar, *The End of Obscenity: The Trials of* Lady Chatterley, Tropic of Cancer, *and* Fanny Hill (New York: Harper & Row, 1986). Rembar uses this phrase to des-

ignate the vise of an argument about literary merit and its coming to override the argument that all lustful writing should be treated as obscene and therefore subject to censorship.

20. Ian Watt, *The Rise of the Novel* (Berkeley: University of California Press, 1957). See particularly the chapter called "Private Experience and the Novel," 174–207.

21. Michael McKeon, *The Origins of the English Novel: 1600–1740* (Baltimore: Johns Hopkins University Press, 1987), 3.

22. Ibid., 3, 4.

23. Nancy Armstrong, *Desire and Domestic Fiction: A Political History of the Novel* (New York: Oxford University Press, 1987), 251.

24. Frank Kermode, *The Sense of an Ending: Studies in the Theory of Fiction* (New York: Oxford University Press, 1967).

25. René Girard, *Deceit, Desire, and the Novel: Self and Other in Literary Structure*, trans. Yvonne Freccero (Baltimore: Johns Hopkins University Press, 1965), 148.

26. Michel Foucault, *The History of Sexuality, Volume I: An Introduction*, trans. Robert Hurley (New York: Vintage, 1980), 156–59.

27. D. H. Lawrence, "A Propos of 'Lady Chatterley's Lover,'" in *Lady Chatterley's Lover*, ed. Michael Squires (Cambridge: Cambridge University Press, 1993), 334.

Chapter One

1. Minneapolis Ordinance, 1983, in Catharine A. MacKinnon and Andrea Dworkin, eds., *Harm's Way: The Pornography of Civil Rights Hearings* (Cambridge: Harvard University Press, 1997), 427.

2. Catharine A. MacKinnon, *Only Words* (Cambridge: Harvard University Press, 1993), 54.

3. I tend to leave Andrea Dworkin's work somewhat to the side in this chapter. This is not by any means intended as a gesture of disparagement of Dworkin's work on pornography or of the importance of her collaboration with MacKinnon. It is merely to avoid the awkwardness of continually using both names to refer to a position that I am, in the present chapter, describing almost exclusively through MacKinnon's writing.

4. Catharine A. MacKinnon, "Francis Biddle's Sister: Pornography, Civil Rights, and Speech," in *Feminism Unmodified: Discourses on Law and Life* (Cambridge: Harvard University Press, 1987), 176.

5. This formulation is virtually omnipresent in the work of both Dworkin and MacKinnon. MacKinnon has stated it relatively recently in saying that "the deepest injury of pornography is not what it says, but what it does." See her "Pornography as Defamation and Discrimination," *Boston University Law Review* 71 (1991): 795.

6. MacKinnon, "Francis Biddle's Sister," 176, 177.

7. Richard Posner has reviewed MacKinnon's book *Only Words* in such terms: "The title of Catharine A. MacKinnon's new book is intended as an ironic commentary on the belief that pornography is 'only words' and therefore, unlike sticks and stones, can never hurt anyone. There is a further irony that is unintended: *Only Words* is a rhetorical, rather than an analytical, production; it is only words." Richard A. Posner, "Obsession" [Review of Catharine A. MacKinnon, *Only Words*] *New Republic*, October 18, 1993, 31–36.

8. Robert C. Post has, in a series of articles, provided accounts of the legal traditions governing freedom of expression in Britain and the United States. See "Cultural Heterogeneity and Law: Pornography, Blasphemy, and the First Amendment," *California Law Review* 76 (1988): 297–335; "The Social Foundations of Privacy: Community and Self in the Common Law Tort," *California Law Review* 77 (1989): 957–1010; and "The Constitutional Concept of Public Discourse: Outrageous Opinion, Democratic Deliberation, and *Hustler Magazine v. Falwell*," *Harvard Law Review* 103 (1990): 601–86. In this last in particular, he has emphasized the tradition of separating public discourse from community values and has argued that the difficulty of sustaining such a separation has accounted for the "uneven course of first amendment doctrine" (603), because he conceives of public discourse "as situated in a triangular space" formed by community, "which regulates speech in the interests of civility and dignity"; organization, "which regulates speech in the interests of instrumentally attaining explicit objectives"; and public discourse, "which alone carries within it the freedom of critical interaction that we, in our culturally diverse nation, associate with democratic processes" (685). As will become apparent, I think that this particular division of labor can easily militate against equality interests by minimizing the significance of organization in liberal democracy.

9. Berl Kutchinsky's work on the pattern of sex crimes in Denmark has to many seemed to provide the most reliable information on the effect of pornography on sex crimes, because it has been the only study that has been able to take advantage of a clear shift in the law (as Denmark abolished its prohibition on written pornography in 1967 and its prohibition on obscene pictures in 1969). Yet if Kutchinsky's work was once taken to indicate that the legalization of pornography resulted primarily in a change—a decrease—in sexual crimes against children, it has recently been more strongly challenged. See Bernard Williams, ed., *Report of the Committee on Obscenity and Film Censorship* (Cambridge: Cambridge University Press, 1981), 80–83; and Catherine Itzin, ed., *Pornography: Women, Violence, and Civil Liberties* (Oxford: Oxford University Press, 1992), 248–383.

10. The existence of the feminist anti-censorship position itself amounts to an implicit argument about the inefficiency of pornography as a cause of crimes against women. That is, in addition to making the argument that no causal connections have plausibly been established between pornography and crimes against women, anti-censorship feminists introduce themselves and their own sense of not having been harmed as further evidence that pornography does not regularly result in harm against women. While MacKinnon has frequently argued that women ought to feel more fear than they allow themselves to feel, these writers represent her position as an exercise in the promotion of fear. See Carole S. Vance, ed., *Pleasure and Danger: Exploring Female Sexuality* (Boston: Routledge & Kegan Paul, 1984); Varda Burstyn, ed., *Women against Censorship* (Vancouver: Douglas & McIntyre, 1985); F.A.C.T. Book Committee, eds., *Caught Looking: Feminism, Pornography, and Censorship* (East Haven: Long River Books, 1986); and Katie Roiphe, *The Morning After: Sex, Fear, and Feminism on Campus* (Boston: Little, Brown, 1993).

11. MacKinnon states in *Only Words* that "thirty-eight percent of women are sexually molested as girls; twenty-four percent of us are raped in our marriages. Nearly half are victims of rape or attempted rape at least once in our lives, many more than once, espe-

cially women of color, many involving multiple attackers, mostly men we know. Eighty-five percent of women who work outside the home are sexually harassed at some point by employers." *Only Words*, 7–8.

12. Kant's discussion of the aesthetical normal idea presents one of the most important discussions of the norm or stereotype, and his argument for its insufficiency in accounting for our responses to the things we find beautiful has been important for its emphasis on aesthetical judgments as something other than a response to our composite past experience. See *Critique of Judgment,* trans. J. H. Bernard (New York: Hafner, 1966), 72.

13. Richard Rorty makes a version of this point in testifying that "in our society, straight white males of my generation—even earnestly egalitarian straight white males—cannot easily stop themselves from feeling guilty relief that they were not born women or gay or black, any more than they can stop themselves from being glad that they were not born mentally retarded or schizophrenic." "Feminism and Pragmatism," *Michigan Quarterly Review* 30:2 (spring 1991): 248.

14. Both anti-pornography and anti-censorship feminists agree on this much. Anti-censorship feminists are simply quicker to accept the economy as relatively just for individual women.

15. I am essentially echoing the account that John Rawls gives of libertarianism in *Political Liberalism* (New York: Columbia University Press, 1993).

16. John Rawls's work constitutes the most significant effort to argue for the compatibility between a liberal conception of equality with the diversity of circumstances that actually obtain for individuals. See his *A Theory of Justice* (Cambridge: Harvard University Press, 1971) and *Political Liberalism*.

17. Pierre Bourdieu, *Distinction: A Social Critique of the Judgement of Taste,* trans. Richard Nice (Cambridge: Harvard University Press, 1984), 70. Bourdieu's theme is the transmission of an effective aristocracy even in the absence of explicit ranks and titles.

18. See MacKinnon's discussion of sexual harassment and her view that "to treat [sexual harassment] as a tort is less simply incorrect than inadequate," in *Sexual Harassment of Working Women: A Case of Sex Discrimination* (New Haven: Yale University Press, 1979), 143–213, esp. 171–74.

19. MacKinnon's essay "Francis Biddle's Sister: Pornography, Civil Rights, and Speech" plays upon Virginia Woolf's discussion of "Shakespeare's sister" in "A Room of One's Own" to suggest that there is a positive purpose to be served by implanting artificial histories, in which our current ability to imagine a person in the historical past attempts to capture the same force of recommendation that the actual past might have. See *Feminism Unmodified*, 195–97.

20. See in particular MacKinnon's claim, in the introduction to *Feminism Unmodified*, that "abstract equality undermines substantive inequality, but it reinforces it at the same time" (14).

21. Minneapolis Code of Ordinances Relating to Civil Rights (December 30, 1983). The ordinance was initially passed by the city council, vetoed by the mayor, reintroduced with slight modifications, passed in modified form, and vetoed again in 1984. Excerpts of it are available in Burstyn, *Women against Censorship,* and F.A.C.T. Book Committee, *Caught Looking*. Donald Alexander Downs provides a detailed account of the political

process of the Minneapolis Ordinance in *The New Politics of Pornography* (Chicago: University of Chicago Press, 1989), 34–94.

22. Robin Morgan, "Theory and Practice: Pornography and Rape," in *Take Back the Night: Women on Pornography,* ed. Laura Lederer (New York: William Morrow, 1980), 134–40.

23. "The very power to make the photography (to use the model, to tie her in that way) and the fact of the photograph (the fact that someone did use the model, did tie her in that way, that the photography is published in a magazine and seen by millions of men who buy it specifically to see such photographs) evoke fear in the female observer unless she entirely dissociates herself from the photography.... Terror is finally the content of the photograph, and it is also its effect on the female observer." Andrea Dworkin, *Pornography: Men Possessing Women* (New York: G. P. Putnam, 1981), 27.

24. Sara Diamond, "Pornography: Image and Reality," in *Women against Censorship,* ed. Burstyn, 41; Ann Snitow, "The Politics of the Antipornography Movement," in ibid., 119.

25. Lisa Duggan, Nan Hunter, and Carole S. Vance, "False Promises: Feminist Antipornography Legislation in the U.S.," in *Women against Censorship,* ed. Burstyn, 144–45.

26. See Gayle Rubin, "The Leather Menace: Comments on Politics and S/M," in *Coming to Power: Writing and Graphics on Lesbian S/M: A Form of Eroticism Based on a Consensual Exchange of Power,* ed. SAMOIS (Boston: Alyson, 1981), 194–229; and "Thinking Sex," in *Pleasure and Danger,* ed. Vance, 267–319. See also Linda Williams, *Hard Core: Power, Pleasure, and the "Frenzy of the Visible"* (Berkeley: University of California Press, 1989); and "A Symposium on Pornography," *Threepenny Review* (fall 1993): 8–9.

27. I use "pornography" as an inclusive term incorporating material with both positive and negative effects. In that I am specifically departing from the practice that some antipornography feminists observe in drawing a distinction between "erotica," which, in Gloria Steinem's description, "is about sexuality," and "pornography," which is "about power and sex-as-weapon." "Erotica and Pornography: A Clear and Present Difference," in *Take Back the Night,* ed. Lederer, 35–39.

28. The trial of Penguin Books for its publication of *Lady Chatterley's Lover* in an inexpensive and readily available format has, in line with the translation of access to potentially pornographic images into rights for groups, frequently been presented as upholding the rights of the working man to read literature that is great or pornographic or both. See C. H. Rolph, ed., *The Trial of Lady Chatterley: Regina v. Penguin Books Limited, The Transcript of the Trial* (London: Penguin Books, 1990). In such a line of argument, censorship appears as an attack on the expressive rights of groups, whether defined in terms of social class, sexual minority status, or age. If much lesbian-, bisexual-, and gay-affirmative literature emphasizes how representations that are readily accepted as "decent" and "public"—the figure of the diva, for example, or the opulence of the opera more generally—may be turned to the purpose of a socially stigmatized sexual orientation, the right to have access to a more directly self-expressive pornography comes to be part of what it means to conceive group rights for members of what Gayle Rubin calls "sexual minorities." See Terry Castle, *The Apparitional Lesbian* (New York: Columbia University Press, 1993); and Wayne Koestenbaum, *The Queen's Throat* (New York: Poseidon, 1993).

29. See Rubin, "Thinking Sex"; and Deirdre English, Amber Hollibaugh, and Gayle Ru-

bin, "Talking Sex: A Conversation on Sexuality and Feminism," in *Sexuality: A Reader,* ed. Feminist Review (London: Virago Press, 1987), 63–81, for a discussion of the question of decriminalizing all consensual sexual activity. Rubin's guiding view is that all statutory mechanisms that undermine the authority of individual consent to sex acts ought to be abolished. She thus advocates the elimination of anti-sodomy statutes (which suggest that the sexual consent of homosexuals is somehow deficient by comparison with a normal standard of consent) and, more controversially, the elimination of statutes against sex acts between adults and legal minors.

30. The problems associated with the group or club recur in a variety of discussions of pornography. One view is that memberships in groups or clubs establish willingness to see pornographic images and that this consent to participate in the group or the club makes it ludicrous to enforce obscenity laws, which concern the offensiveness that voluntary participants would never feel. This position is one that rejects the appeal to community norms, on the one hand, and that of the individual at odds with the group, on the other.

31. See her discussion of Linda Marchiano (who appeared in *Deep Throat* under the name Linda Lovelace) in *Feminism Unmodified*:

> But here, put a gun to someone's head and say, act like you're enjoying it. If you have any kind of acting ability, as well as respect for your life, a desire to live, maybe you want to do it well once so you won't have to do a retake—you do it. . . . The fact that Linda was coerced makes the film no less protected as speech, even though the publication of *Ordeal* makes clear that the film documents crimes, acts that violate laws in all fifty states. (129)

32. See Leo Bersani, "Is the Rectum a Grave?" *October* 43 (winter 1987): 197–222, for an account of the misfit between sexuality and the acts that instantiate it.

33. Linda Lovelace, famous as the star of *Deep Throat,* announced herself as Linda Marchiano in her book *Ordeal,* in which she described her pornographic performances as coerced. Linda Lovelace and Michael McGrady, *Ordeal* (New York: Berkeley, 1981); and Linda Lovelace and Mike McGrady, *Out of Bondage* (Secaucus, N.J.: Lyle Stuart, 1986).

34. Williams, *Report of the Committee on Obscenity and Film Censorship,* 139, 138.

35. Susanne Kappeler, *The Pornography of Representation* (Minneapolis: University of Minnesota Press, 1986); and Andrea Dworkin, *Intercourse* (New York: Free Press, 1987).

36. This problem revolves around nothing more than the recognition that being able to describe the actual past easily translates itself into the capacity to manufacture a fiction or a factitious past. See in particular Virginia Woolf's "A Room of One's Own" for an implicit statement of the view that history invites the introduction of artificial epitomes, accounts that can be used as the basis for future behavior by actual persons. Woolf's discussion of "Shakespeare's sister, Judith" provides the model for MacKinnon's discussion of "Francis Biddle's Sister" in *Feminism Unmodified*.

37. "The pimp is an artifact of the illegality of prostitution, and the exploitation of pornographic actresses and models by their employers is parallel to the exploitation of illegal immigrant labor by their employers. These women would be better off if all pornography were legal." Posner, "Obsession," 34.

38. Catharine A. MacKinnon, "The Art of the Impossible," in *Feminism Unmodified,* 15.

39. See Edmund S. Morgan, *American Slavery—American Freedom: The Ordeal of Colonial Virginia* (New York: W. W. Norton, 1975), chap. 18.

40. MacKinnon, "Frances Biddle's Sister," 171.

41. "Bigotry as often produces unconscious lies as knowing ones, indeed often precludes the dominant from seeing the truth of inequality being lived out beneath their station, hence vision." MacKinnon, *Only Words*, 80.

42. Ibid., 67.

43. Ibid., 21.

44. Rorty, "Feminism and Pragmatism," 231–58.

45. MacKinnon, "Francis Biddle's Sister," 173.

46. There is no need to confine the workplace to an actual physical location. As the recent success of upscale strip clubs oriented toward businessmen demonstrates, a movable office—work that can be taken virtually anywhere—provides new opportunities for exclusion. See "Dressing Strip Clubs in a Suit and Tie," *New York Times*, March 26, 1994, 5.

47. Richard A. Posner, *Sex and Reason* (Cambridge: Harvard University Press, 1992), 373.

48. See Jeremy Bentham, "A View of the Hard-Labour Bill" and "Panopticon; or The Inspection-House," in *The Works of Jeremy Bentham*, ed. John Bowring (New York: Russell & Russell, 1962); and *Chrestomathia*, ed. M. J. Smith and W. H. Burston (Oxford: Clarendon Press, 1984).

49. Bentham's commitment to these social structures as promoters of individual rights reaches its apogee when religious belief, for instance, sees itself not simply as religious belief but as religious belief that cannot detach itself from a host of daily routines. Thus, even though Bentham's *Defence of Usury* argues for the positive value of money lending and thereby makes it hard to sustain anti-Semitism as an appropriate judgment on an evil practice, he expresses anxiety about the problems that Jewish dietary laws would present to his proposals for workhouses. If his earlier view allowed room for a connection between one particular kind of action and a group of people and merely urged a revaluation of that action and the group that engaged in it, his later account emphasizes the artificial environment as a means for minimizing such connections. In this regard, I think that Foucault's *Discipline and Punish* while providing an extraordinary account of the behavioral purchase of Bentham's work, tends to use Bentham's Panoptic model in a fashion that threatens to elide Bentham's effort to free individuals from the character of their group and from the sense that individuals have self-consistent characters with the rise of social scientific character types.

50. MacKinnon, "Francis Biddle's Sister," 176.

51. See Post, "Cultural Heterogeneity and Law"; and Posner, "Obsession," 35–36.

52. MacKinnon, *Only Words*, 54. MacKinnon also sometimes includes the family and public spaces in her list of environments to which women are given inadequate access. I single out the points at which she focuses on the school and the workplace because they seem to me to present the clearest model for understanding how artificial groups and environment may foster behavior. I have avoided the question of the family because two quite different sets of issues—the emotional ties between family members and the functioning of the family as an essentially artificial unit in which each member is continually valued in relation to the whole—tend to be elided. I would argue, however, that the cen-

trality that MacKinnon gives to the school and the workplace helps to explain her reaction to some of the negative reviews of her work. Reviews tend to be treated as relatively favorable or unfavorable reactions to a thing that exists, a comparison between it and some imagined standard by which it might be judged good; MacKinnon, I think, would want to advance the argument that some of the negative reviews of her work simply attempt to deny her access to participation in the public sphere.

Chapter Two

Reprinted, with changes, from *Aesthetics and Ideology*, ed. George Levine (New Brunswick, N.J.: Rutgers University Press, 1994): 106–23.

1. I give here only a very abbreviated set of references to indicate something of the extent of the concern with these issues. Some of the most recent relevant discussions appear in works such as John Barrell, *The Political Theory of Painting from Reynolds to Hazlitt: The Body of the Public* (New Haven: Yale University Press, 1986); Terry Eagleton, *The Ideology of the Aesthetic* (Oxford: Basil Blackwell, 1990); my own *Solitude and the Sublime: Romanticism and the Aesthetics of Individuation* (New York: Routledge, 1992); and much of the work of Paul de Man and Fredric Jameson. Both feminist and gay studies have prompted much renewed interest in the development of pornography; and the most influential positions have developed in either sympathetic or hostile response to the work of Michel Foucault, whose emphasis on the discursive structures of sexuality has importantly altered the view that social regulation constantly provides incentives to action by iterating the acceptable and the taboo, and Catharine A. MacKinnon, whose anti-pornography position has drawn considerable fire from anti-censorship feminists as a restraint on freedom of expression.

2. Theodor Adorno speaks of aesthetic autonomy as having involved art's emancipating "itself from cuisine and pornography, an emancipation that has become irrevocable," in *Aesthetic Theory*, trans. C. Lenhardt, ed. Gretel Adorno and Rolf Tiedemann (New York: Routledge and Kegan Paul, 1984), 18.

3. See particularly Leo Bersani and D. A. Miller, *The Novel and the Police* (Berkeley: University of California Press, 1988), for unusually able accounts of an affective position.

4. Roland Barthes has drawn attention to the novel as picaresque in *Sade, Fourier, Loyola*, trans. Richard Miller (Berkeley: University of California Press, 1976), 149.

5. Donatien-Alphonse-François, Marquis de Sade, *Three Complete Novels: Justine, Philosophy in the Bedroom, and Other Writings*, trans. Richard Seaver and Austryn Wainhouse (New York: Grove Press, 1966), 736–37. Until the Pleiade edition of Sade is complete, the best available French text of the novel is *Justine, ou Les Malheurs de la vertu*, vol. 3 of *Oeuvres complètes du Marquis de Sade*, ed. Annie Le Brun and Jean-Jacques Pauvert, 15 vols. (Paris: Pauvert, 1986–91).

6. Charles Secondat, Baron de Montesquieu, *The Spirit of the Laws*, trans. Thomas Nugent (New York: Hafner Press, 1949).

7. Friedrich Nietzsche, *Beyond Good and Evil*, trans. Walter Kaufmann (New York: Random House, 1966), 43–44.

8. See particularly the discussion of "duties to oneself as such" in Immanuel Kant, *The Metaphysics of Morals*, trans. Mary Gregor (Cambridge: Cambridge University Press, 1991), 214 ff.

9. Cesare Beccaria, *On Crimes and Punishments,* trans. David Young (Indianapolis: Hackett Publishing, 1986). Bentham's account of the "principle of utility," however much it has been seen to be committed to crass materialism, is in fact rather a statement of the primacy of consequentialism; see particularly his account of pleasure and pain that transmutes them from individualistic terms into the basic terms for identifying consequences. Jeremy Bentham, *The Principles of Morals and Legislation* (New York: Hafner Press, 1948), pp. 8 ff.

10. Dubois's claim is that "the law's to be blamed for these crimes . . . ; so long as thieves are hanged like murderers, thefts shall never be committed without assassinations. The two misdeeds are punished equally; why then abstain from the second when it may cover up the first?" Sade, *The Complete Justine, Philosophy in the Bedroom, and Other Writings,* 491.

11. Bernard Williams, *Moral Luck: Philosophical Papers 1973–1980* (Cambridge: Cambridge University Press, 1981), 20–39.

12. "Upon the day the surgeon confirms the existence of a pregnancy, one hundred strokes are administered" (581); but we—and Thérèse / Justine—are also told that the detection of contraceptives or abortifacients will provoke Antonin's wrath (586).

13. Jacques Lacan, "Kant with Sade," trans. James Swenson, *October* 51 (winter 1989): 55–75.

14. Michel Foucault, *Discipline and Punish: The Birth of the Prison,* trans. Alan Sheridan (New York: Pantheon, 1977).

15. This has seemed to many of Foucault's ablest commentators to be the crucial message of *Discipline and Punish.* See, for instance, Nancy Armstrong, *Desire and Domestic Fiction: A Political History of the Novel* (New York: Oxford University Press, 1987), where "supervision" seems to constitute an activity much as affect does in affectivist accounts of literature. Thus, she describes the importance of "supervision" in legitimating women's activities:

> Supervision presumably made all the difference between amusements that led to corruption and forms of leisure that occupied a woman constructively. The activities comprising her education could be considered educational only if they were supervised, and by the same token, virtually anything could be considered educational if it provided an occasion for supervision. (100)

16. Ferguson, *Solitude and the Sublime,* esp. 1–36 and 62–96.

Chapter Three

Reprinted, with changes, from *Representations* 36 (fall 1991): 1–21, by permission of the University of California Press. © by The Regents of the University of California.

1. Jeremy Bentham, *Rights, Representation, and Reform: Nonsense upon Stilts and Other Writings on the French Revolution* (London: Oxford University Press, 2002).

2. Sade was first arrested after Rose Keller, in 1768, complained to the authorities that Sade had lured her to his rented cottage, ordered her to undress, threatened her with a knife, flogged her, and locked her in a room. He was later arrested after the "Royal Prosecutor attached to the Seneschal's Court of Marseilles" called for an investigation into Marguerite Coste's complaint that she had been given poisoned sweets by Sade during an orgy with him, his manservant, and three other young women. He was arrested under a

lettre de cachet and imprisoned in the fortress at Vincennes in 1777. For a condensed account, see the chronology in Marquis de Sade, *Three Complete Novels*: Justine, Philosophy in the Bedroom, *and Other Writings*, compiled and translated by Richard Seaver and Austryn Wainhouse (New York: Grove Press, 1966), 79–92.

3. It was Maurice Blanchot who most explicitly identified the co-criminality of Sade and his persecutors: "Now, the strange thing is that it is the guardians of morality who, by condemning Sade to solitary confinement, have thereby made themselves the most faithful accomplices of his immorality." "Sade" in Sade, *Three Complete Novels*, 38. The essay originally appeared in Maurice Blanchot, *Lautreamont et Sade* (Paris: Editions de minuit, 1949).

4. See Robert C. Post, "The Constitutional Concept of Public Discourse: Outrageous Opinion, Democratic Deliberation, and *Hustler Magazine v. Falwell*," *Harvard Law Review* 103 (1990): 601–86. Post offers a wide-ranging analysis of the legal and philosophical tradition of protecting speech that might be personally offensive and of justifying that protection on the basis of a societal claim to a public discourse.

5. In this sense, an argument about the canon (as not only what is taught but as what should be taught) and an argument about censorship converge. The tendency of Carter's discussion is, I think, to suggest that the process of preserving literary works should include not only the reactions of current readers but also a projection of potential future reactions.

6. Angela Carter, *The Sadeian Woman* (New York: Pantheon, 1978), 3–4.

7. Madame de Saint-Ange offers herself in her entirely naked state so that Dolmancé can make his "dissertations upon" her. Sade *Three Complete Novels*, 199. See Marquis de Sade, *Oeuvres complètes du Marquis de Sade*, 15 vols., ed. Annie Le Brun and Jean-Jacques Pauvert (Paris: Pauvert, 1986–91), III:395.

8. Lynn Hunt's Gauss lectures at Princeton in the fall of 1988 addressed the significance of pornographic drawings and writings in the French Revolutionary period. Her emphasis on Sade's materialism seems to me a valuable corrective to Simon Schama's reliance on the symbolic nature of perceptibly human constructions. While Schama is not wrong to stress the public relations aspects of the French Revolution, his account tends to make the symbolic count as both a statement of the problem of modern political thought and an answer to that problem. His engaging account of the theatrical addresses that Sade made to passersby captures Sade's opportunistic self-portrayal as a martyr of the Bastille. What it does not do is to indicate the force of his conclusion that "de Sade had become a revolutionary." Simon Schama, *Citizens: A Chronicle of the French Revolution* (New York: Vintage, 1989), esp. 399.

9. Quoted in Arnold Heumakers, "De Sade, a Pessimistic Libertine," in *From Sappho to De Sade: Moments in the History of Sexuality*, ed. Jan Bremmer (London: Routledge, 1989), 108.

10. Blanchot, "Sade," 37–72.

11. See both Georges Bataille, *Erotism: Death and Sensuality*, trans. Mary Dalwood (San Francisco: City Lights Books, 1986); and idem, "Sade," in *Literature and Evil*, trans. Alastair Hamilton (London: Marion Boyars, 1990).

12. Bataille, *Erotism*, 167.

13. Ibid., 166. Bataille describes Sade's unusually mixed political partisanship in the

following terms: "He worked out his criticism of the past along two lines: in the one he sided with the Revolution and criticised the monarchy, but in the other he exploited the infinite possibilities of literature and propounded to his readers the concept of a sovereign type of humanity whose privileges would not have to be agreed upon by the masses."

14. See the discussion of religion in the pamphlet "Yet Another Effort Frenchmen, if You Would Become Republicans":

As we gradually proceeded to our enlightenment, we came more and more to feel that, motion being inherent in matter, the prime mover existed only as an illusion, and that all that exists essentially having to be in motion, the motor was useless.... (Sade, *Three Complete Novels*, 300)

A mesure que l'on s'est éclairé, on a senti que, le mouvement étant inhérent à la matière, l'agent nécessaire à imprimer ce mouvement devenait un être illusoire et que, tout ce qui existait devant être en mouvement par essence, le moteur était inutile.... (Sade, *Oeuvres complètes*, III:494)

15. See particularly Andrea Dworkin, *Intercourse* (New York: Free Press, 1987); and Catharine A. MacKinnon, *Feminism Unmodified: Discourses on Life and Law* (Cambridge: Harvard University Press, 1987). The essence of their position is that the inequality that obtains in sexual acts between men and women is not a localized phenomenon and that this sexual inequality conditions the very notions of what women "like," "want," and "consent to."

16. Leo Bersani, "Is the Rectum a Grave?" *October* 43 (winter 1987): 197–222.

17. Ibid., 216.

18. Although many different formulations of sexual harassment policies have been produced by individual institutions, the tendency of all such policies is to address educational and workplace inequities in which the power of a superior (a teacher in relation to a student, a supervisor in relation to a supervised employee, etc.) enables him/her to translate that superior position into a more or less explicit demand for sexual relations. The authoritative discussion of sexual harassment is Catharine A. MacKinnon, *Sexual Harassment of Working Women: A Case of Sex Discrimination* (New Haven: Yale University Press, 1979).

19. Sade, *Three Complete Novels*, 295.

Je voudrais savoir si les moeurs sont vraiment nécessaires dans un gouvernment, si leur influence est de quelque poids sur le génie d'une nation. (Sade, *Oeuvres complètes*, III:489)

20. Roland Barthes, *Sade, Fourier, Loyola*, trans. Richard Miller (Berkeley: University of California Press, 1976), 15–37, 123–70, esp. 16.

21. Georges Lefebvre, *The Coming of the French Revolution*, trans. R. R. Palmer (Princeton: Princeton University Press, 1967).

22. Andrea Dworkin, *Pornography: Men Possessing Women* (New York: G. P. Putnam, 1981). Although Dworkin's chapter on Sade seems to me fundamentally misdirected, she is right, I think, to see the force of the notion of pornography as involving writing by means of bodies. The second of her dedications of *Pornography* is to Rose Keller, the first of the women who participated in successful actions to have Sade incarcerated.

23. R. R. Palmer, *The Age of the Democratic Revolution: A Political History of Europe and America, 1760–1800* (Princeton: Princeton University Press, 1959), I:509.

24. Ibid., I:525.

25. I am grateful to Carla Hesse for having suggested that I include an acknowledgment of the shifting importance of property for the franchise in the early 1790s. The Assembly in fact registered a version of Sade's protest against property. In 1793 it voted to end the category of the "active citizen" that had been defined in terms of property rights and instead extended the franchise to all native males at least twenty-one years old who were residents of France (and to "foreigners of the same age who had been domiciled in France for one year; who were in work or lived on private income; who had acquired property; who had married a French woman, adopted a child or old person; or who were naturalised"). The summary I have just cited appears in Colin Jones, *The Longman Companion to the French Revolution* (London: Longman, 1988). See also William Doyle, *The Oxford History of the French Revolution* (New York: Oxford University Press, 1990), 124, 193–94. From my standpoint, however, there is no inconsiderable irony in the conjunction of the elimination of the property requirement for voting eligibility with the nationalization of the debt. These actions occurred within months of one another in 1793.

26. François Furet and Mona Ozouf, *Dictionnaire critique de la Révolution française* (Paris: Flammarion, 1988), 512.

27. William Doyle, *Origins of the French Revolution*, 2nd ed. (New York: Oxford University Press, 1988).

28. Ibid., 159.

29. Ibid., 196.

30. Sade, *Three Complete Novels*, 284.

Cessons d'être la dupe de tout cela: nous ne devons rien à nos parents... pas la moindre chose, Eugénie, et, comme c'est bien moins pour nous que pour eux qu'ils ont travaillé, il nous est permis de les détester, et de nous en défaire même, si leur procédé nous irrite.... (Sade, *Oeuvres complètes*, III:479)

31. Sade, *Three Complete Novels*, 284.

Tant que dure l'acte du coït, je peux, sans doute, avoir besoin de cet objet pour y participer; mais sitôt qu'il est satisfait, que reste-t-il, je vous prie, entre lui et moi? et quelle obligation réelle enchaînera à lui ou à moi les résultats de ce coït? (Sade, *Oeuvres complètes*, III:479)

32. Sade, *Three Complete Novels*, 285.

... parce que les droits de la naissance n'établissent rien, ne fondent rien, et qu'en les scrutant avec sagesse et réflexion, nous n'y trouverons sûrement que des raisons de haine pour ceux qui, ne songeant qu'à leurs plaisirs, ne nous ont donné souvent qu'une existence malheureuse ou malsaine. (Sade, *Oeuvres complètes*, III:479)

33. Sade, *Three Complete Novels*, 284.

Ces derniers liens furent les fruits de la frayeur qu'eurent les parents d'être abandonnés dans leur vieillesse, et les soins intéressés qu'ils ont de nous dans notre enfance ne sont que pour mériter ensuite les mêmes attentions dans leur dernier âge. (Sade, *Oeuvres complètes*, III:479)

34. Sade, *Three Complete Novels*, 206.

Assurément, quoiqu'il soit néanmoins prouvé que ce foetus ne doive son existence qu'au foutre de l'homme; élancé seul, sans mélange avec celui de la femme, il ne réussirait cependant pas; mais celui que nous fournissons ne fait qu'élaborer; il ne crée point, il aide à la création, sans en être la cause. (Sade, *Oeuvres complètes,* III:402)

35. Sade, *Three Complete Novels,* 223.

Premièrement, tant que je couche avec mon mari, tant que sa semence coule au fond de ma matrice, verrais-je dix hommes en même temps que lui, rien ne pourra jamais lui prouver que l'enfant que nâitra ne lui appartienne pas; il peut être à lui comme n'y pas être, et dans le cas de l'incertitude il ne peut ni ne doit jamais (puisqu'il à coopéré à l'existence de cette créature) se faire aucun scrupule d'avouer cette existence. (Sade, *Oeuvres complètes,* III:419–20)

36. Sade, *Three Complete Novels,* 223. "Des qu'elle peut lui appartenir, elle lui appartient..." (Sade, *Oeuvres complètes,* III:420).

37. Sade, *Three Complete Novels,* 237.

Un de mes amis vit habituellement avec la fille qu'il a eue de sa propre mère: il n'y a pas huit jours qu'il dépucela un garçon de treize ans, fruit de son commerce avec cette fille; dans quelques années ce même jeune homme épousera sa mère; ce sont les voeux de mon ami.... (Sade, *Oeuvres complètes,* III:433)

38. Sade, *Three Complete Novels,* 236. "Si l'amour, en un mot, naît de la ressemblance, où peut-elle être plus parfaite qu'entre frère et soeur, qu'entre père et fille?" (Sade, *Oeuvres complètes,* III:432).

39. Jones, *The Longman Companion to the French Revolution,* 33. See also William Doyle, "The Financial Crisis," in *Origins of the French Revolution,* 43–52, for the pre-Revolutionary form of state borrowing.

40. An elegant summary of this view appears in John Scott Keltie, "National Debt," in *Encyclopaedia Britannica,* 11th ed. (1910–11).

41. Sade, *Three Complete Novels,* 319.

S'il devient donc incontestable que nous avons reçu de la nature le droit d'exprimer nos voeux indifféremment à toutes les femmes, il le devient de même que nous avons celui de l'obliger de se soumettre à nos voeux, non pas exclusivement, je me contrarierais, mais momentanément.... (Sade, *Oeuvres complètes,* III:514)

42. See the chronology in Sade, *Three Complete Novels,* 97–104.

Chapter Four

Unless otherwise noted, all translations are my own. Reprinted, with changes, from *Critical Inquiry* 28 (spring 2002): 749–79.

1. A brief description of the trial appears in Gustave Flaubert, *Madame Bovary,* trans. Paul de Man (New York: W. W. Norton, 1965). See also the transcript of the proceedings, "Procès: Le Ministère public contre Gustave Flaubert. Réquisitoire de M. l'Avocat impérial M. Ernest Pinard; Plaidoirie du Défenseur, M. Sénard; Jugenet," in Gustave Flaubert, *Oeuvres,* ed. A. Thibaudet and René Dumesnil, 2 vols. (Paris: Gallimard, 1951), 1:615–83.

2. See Jean-Paul Sartre, *The Family Idiot: Gustave Flaubert 1821–1857,* trans. Carol Cosman, 5 vols. (Chicago: University of Chicago Press, 1981–91), 1:430; and Jonathan Culler, *Flaubert: The Uses of Uncertainty* (Ithaca, N.Y.: Cornell University Press, 1985), 173–74.

3. LaCapra sees the obscenity trial as matter of the "text" coming to "challenge its con-

text and the adequacy of its framing or boundary-marking devices" and goes on to argue that "'crime' of this sort [that is, 'ideological' crime] is not amenable to more or less regular judicial proceedings because it contests the very right of the trial to judge it." Dominick LaCapra, *Madame Bovary on Trial* (Ithaca, N.Y.: Cornell University Press, 1982), 31. The difficulty of this approach is that it suggests that the obscenity trial is unique, when any trial inevitably raises the question of the right of the state to argue that individuals ought to hold views that are different from those they actually have.

4. LaCapra notes that "the difference between the lengths of the [prosecutor's and defense attorney's] speeches is the most obvious one." Ibid., 33.

5. Lamartine's admiration is surprising only because he clearly would have had to struggle to overcome his consciousness of the insult delivered to him by having his name signed to various of Emma's more saccharine musings. See Flaubert, letter to Louise Colet, 19 December 1952, *Correspondance,* ed. Jean Bruneau, 4 vols. (Paris: Gallimard, 1980), 2:211–12; Flaubert, letter to Elisa Schlésinger, 14 January 1857, ibid., 2:665; and Flaubert, letter to his brother Achille, 25 January 1857, ibid., 2:674.

6. Flaubert corresponded with Baudelaire on the occasion of the prosecution of his poetry. See Flaubert, letters to Baudelaire, 14 August 1857 and 23 August 1857, ibid., 2:758, 759.

7. Flaubert, letter to Colet, 29 January 1853, ibid., 2:245.

8. One might also conjecture that Baudelaire's address to his reader aroused new suspicions of the lyric poem and its speaker.

9. "Procès: Le Ministère public contre Gustave Flaubert," *Oeuvres,* 1:683. Sartre describes himself in his preface as attempting to determine "what, at this point in time, can we know about a man?" He goes on to outline this project as one of acknowledging that "man is never an individual" but "a *universal singular.* Summed up and for this reason universalized by his epoch, he in turn resumes it by reproducing himself in it as singularity. Universal by the singular universality of human history, singular by the universalizing singularity of his projects, he requires simultaneous examination from both ends." Sartre, *The Family Idiot,* 1:ix. Because Sartre's account of Flaubert ends before he has reached a full discussion of *Madame Bovary,* we have more information about his views of Gustave in relationship to his family and to his school than to the trial, with its insistence upon giving a reprise of his view of the relationship between the writer in his singularity and the epoch in its universality. See also Pierre Bourdieu, "Flaubert's Point of View," trans. Priscilla Parkhurst Ferguson, *Critical Inquiry* 14 (spring 1988): 539–62.

10. See particularly "Father and Son" in Sartre, *The Family Idiot,* 1:173–438.

11. See Bourdieu, "Flaubert's Point of View."

12. See Flaubert, letter to Frédéric Baudry, 11 February 1857, *Correspondance,* 2:680–81.

13. Charles Augustin Sainte-Beuve, review of *Madame Bovary,* reprinted in Flaubert, *Madame Bovary,* 325.

14. Flaubert, "Procès: Le Ministère public contre Gustave Flaubert," *Oeuvres,* 1:683.

15. In an essay in *Diacritics,* Carla Freccero rehearses the common view that it is repressive even to raise the question of whether a particular book or image might do harm. Thus, she is outraged that Bret Easton Ellis's *American Psycho* was seen by some women as a misogynistic text, and she takes their desire to regulate its distribution as both naive

and contemptible. My own view differs from hers in that I think that the history of the public discussion of novels and images does not suggest that the debate is so rigged that it is necessary to immunize novels from it, even when it occasionally eventuates in trials. See Carla Freccero, "Historical Violence, Censorship, and the Serial Killer: The Case of *American Psycho*," *Diacritics* 27 (summer 1997): 44–58.

16. Flaubert, letter to Colet, 30 September 1853, *Correspondance*, 2:445.

17. See Henry James, "Gustave Flaubert," in *The Future of the Novel*, ed. Leon Edel (New York: Vintage, 1956), 125–61.

18. Flaubert, letter to Colet, 31 March 1853, *Correspondance*, 2:295.

19. Flaubert, letter to Colet, 13 April 1853, ibid., 2:303.

20. Baudelaire, review of *Madame Bovary*, reprinted in Flaubert, *Madame Bovary*, 339. Although Baudelaire does not mention Poe directly, his series of questions and answers ("What is the tritest theme of all . . . ?" "Adultery.") clearly echoes the questions and answers that Poe produced to account for his choices in composing "The Raven." See Edgar Allan Poe, "The Philosophy of Composition," *Essays and Reviews*, ed. G. R. Thompson (New York: Viking, 1984). Baudelaire recurrently refers to Poe as a touchstone. See Baudelaire, *Oeuvres complètes*, ed. Y.-G. Le Dantec and C. Pichois (Paris: Gallimard, 1961), 647–57.

21. Flaubert, letter to Colet, 6 April 1853, *Correspondance*, 2:297.

22. Flaubert, letter to Colet, 15 January 1853, reprinted in *Madame Bovary*, 313, 314.

23. Flaubert, letter to Colet, 25–26 June 1853, ibid., 314–15.

24. Flaubert, letter to Léon Laurent-Pichat, 7 December 1856, *Correspondance*, 2:650.

25. Quoted in Sartre, *The Family Idiot*, 2:426. Although many have offered different conjectures about the identity of the actual person on whom Emma Bovary is supposed to be based (with a young provincial doctor's wife described in the newspapers seeming to be the favorite candidate), I think I am merely anticipating a claim that Sartre did not get around to making (when he left off his writing of *The Family Idiot*) when I say that Flaubert's friend Alfred was the likeliest candidate. Sartre calls attention to Flaubert's conviction of an "intersubjective unity" between him and Alfred that was so intense that they "'mutually forged [their] two handwritings, until one of us by himself could do the school work for both'" (2:431). In Flaubert's account, actions were not so much evidence of individual intentions and predispositions of character; they were, instead, a delusive process of establishing a kind of sham character that will come to antagonize the unacted ideas that Flaubert continually described as more real than any publicly discernible actions.

26. See Flaubert, *Madame Bovary*, 5–6, 79–82, 236–38.

27. This distinction, which is that of the language philosopher W. P. Grice, aims to distinguish between the kind of understanding available on the basis of a simple rehearsal of the words of any utterance and the kind of understanding available on the basis of a recognition of the context of that utterance. See W. P. Grice, "Meaning" in *Philosophical Logic*, ed. P. F. Strawson (Oxford: Oxford University Press, 1967), 39–48.

28. Flaubert, letter to Louis Bouilhet, 16 September 1855, *Correspondance*, 2:593.

29. Baudelaire, review of *Madame Bovary*, reprinted in Flaubert, *Madame Bovary*, 340.

30. See Andrew Bell, *An Experiment in Education Made at the Male Asylum of Madras* (London, 1797); Joseph Lancaster, *Improvements in Education* (London: Darton and Harvey, 1798); and Jeremy Bentham, *Chrestomathia*, ed. M. J. Smith and W. H. Burston (Ox-

ford: Clarendon Press, 1984). Each of these texts present plans for schools on what was called the "monitorial system." They stress the importance of using students themselves as monitors, elements of the school's system of observation. Foucault uses these schools as examples of "discipline" in *Discipline and Punish: The Birth of the Prison,* trans. Alan Sheridan (New York: Pantheon, 1977).

31. See Elie Halévy, *The Growth of Philosophic Radicalism,* trans. Mary Morris (Boston: Beacon Press, 1955), 8–9.

32. Ibid., 15.

33. See Flaubert, letters to Colet, 24 April 1852 and 22 July 1853, *Correspondance,* 2:79, 387–88.

34. Martha C. Nussbaum, *Poetic Justice: The Literary Imagination and Public Life* (Boston: Beacon Press, 1995). See esp. 13–52, 53–78.

35. Flaubert, letter to Colet, 21 August 1853, *Correspondance,* 2:402.

36. See Flaubert, letter to Baudry, February or March 1855, ibid., 2:570–71.

37. Flaubert, letter to Bouilhet, 2 August 1854, ibid., 2:566.

38. Flaubert, letter to Monsieur X***, April 1858, ibid., 2:805–6.

39. Flaubert, letter to Colet, 14 August 1853, reprinted in *Madame Bovary,* 316.

40. Harry Levin, *The Gates of Horn: A Study of Five French Realists* (New York: Oxford University Press, 1963), 255.

41. Flaubert, letter to Colet, 12 April 1854, *Correspondance,* 2:549–50.

42. René Girard's notion of triangulated or mediated desire and Eve Kosofsky Sedgwick's related discussion of male homosocial desire describe what I am identifying in utilitarian terms, but they treat the phenomenon in psychological terms. See René Girard, *Deceit, Desire, and the Novel: Self and Other in Literary Structure,* trans. Yvonne Freccero (Baltimore: Johns Hopkins University Press, 1965); and Eve Kosofsky Sedgwick, *Between Men: English Literature and Male Homosocial Desire* (New York: Columbia University Press, 1985).

43. For Leo Bersani, neither adultery nor its exposure could actually produce either happiness or catastrophe for Emma. The novel needs "the crisis of her debts" (that is, a crisis precipitated by the action of others) since it "dramatizes the anxiety of a consciousness living entirely off itself" and therefore could not possibly depict a solution in the outside world. Bersani's telling observation in support of his view is that Emma is "never more exasperated than during her love affairs." See Leo Bersani, *Balzac to Beckett: Center and Circumference in French Fiction* (New York: Oxford University Press, 1970), 155–59.

44. Flaubert, letter to Leroyer de Chantepie, 18 May 1857, *Correspondance,* 2:717.

45. De Chantepie, letter to Flaubert, 28 March 1857, ibid., 2:690.

46. Flaubert, letter to Bouilhet, 17 August 1854, ibid., 2:567.

Chapter Five

1. See Charles Rembar, *The End of Obscenity: The Trials of* Lady Chatterley, Tropic of Cancer, *and* Fanny Hill (New York: Harper & Row, 1986), 81–82.

2. Quoted in ibid., 82.

3. See D. H. Lawrence, "A Propos of 'Lady Chatterley's Lover,'" in *Lady Chatterley's Lover,* ed. Michael Squires (Cambridge: Cambridge University Press, 1993), 305–35. Future references to *Lady Chatterley's Lover* will be drawn from this edition, which is the

only edition that enables one to track Lawrence's processes of composition and revision, which were unusually complicated, because he usually revised by rewriting from the beginning, as Squires summarizes in his editorial introduction, saying: "All that is known about Lawrence's working practice supports the generalisation that he usually avoided detailed structural revision, and preferred rewriting, something producing draft after draft until he was satisfied" (xxi). There were "three complete and distinct drafts" of *Lady Chatterley's Lover* (xxiv).

4. Quoted in Rembar, *The End of Obscenity*, 83.

5. See the discussion of the problem of trying to judge the relationship among pornography, obscenity, and works of art in Bernard Williams, ed., *Obscenity and Film Censorship: An Abridgement of the Williams Report* [Great Britain. Committee on Obscenity and Film Censorship], (Cambridge: Cambridge University Press, 1981), 103–11.

6. Quoted in Rembar, *The End of Obscenity*, 89.

7. Quoted in ibid.

8. Quoted in ibid., 90.

9. C. H. Rolph, ed., *The Trial of Lady Chatterley: Regina v. Penguin Books Limited, the Transcript of the Trial* (London: Penguin Books, 1990), 29, 31.

10. Quoted in Rembar, *The End of Obscenity*, 92.

11. "Unspeakable sentences" is Ann Banfield's resonant term for reported speech and thought. See her book *Unspeakable Sentences: Narration and Representation in the Language of Fiction* (Boston: Routledge & Kegan Paul, 1982).

12. Lawrence, "A Propos of 'Lady Chatterley's Lover,'" 333.

13. Ibid.

14. Rolph, *The Trial of Lady Chatterley*, ©7–8.

15. Katherine Ann Porter, quoted in ibid., 57.

16. Viscount Hailsham, quoted in *The Trial of Lady Chatterley*, ed. C. H. Rolph (Reading: Cox and Wyman, 1961), 291. While I have earlier cited the 1990 edition, on account of its greater availability, it does not include some of the ancillary material that the 1961 edition does.

17. Kate Millett, *Sexual Politics* (New York: Simon and Schuster, 1990). Millett was, to my knowledge, the first to emphasize the religious terms of Lawrence's descriptions of sexuality: "*Lady Chatterley's Lover* is a quasi-religious tract recounting the salvation of modern woman . . . through the offices of the author's personal cult, 'the mystery of the phallus'" (238). In her view, the moral of Lawrence's tale is that "the world will only be put right when the male reassumes his mastery over the female in that total psychological and sensual domination which alone can offer her the 'fulfillment' of her nature" (242). Millett's analysis is frequently very trenchant, but, for reasons that I outline in my discussion of Lawrence, I think that representing Lawrence in purely doctrinal terms does not register the importance of his exploration of sexuality. Millett understands Lawrence's use of the "natural" as a validation of male domination of women, but I understand his use of the "natural" as an effort to talk about identity that cannot be resolved into propositional statements. Robert M. Polhemus has extended Millett's emphasis on Lawrence's sexual evangelism in his *Erotic Faith: Being in Love from Jane Austen to D. H. Lawrence* (Chicago: University of Chicago Press, 1990), 279–306.

18. Graham Hough, quoted in *The Trial of Lady Chatterley*, ed. Rolph, 50.

19. Lawrence, "A Propos of 'Lady Chatterley's Lover,'" 334.
20. OED.

Epilogue

1. Bret Easton Ellis, *American Psycho* (New York: Vintage, 1991).
2. Saul Kripke, *Naming and Necessity* (Cambridge: Harvard University Press, 1980), 116–19.
3. Ibid., 3.
4. Elie Halévy, *The Growth of Philosophic Radicalism*, trans. Mary Morris (Boston: Beacon Press, 1955), 17–24, 28–34.
5. Ellis uses the passage from Dostoyevsky's *Notes from Underground*, with its brilliant depiction of the voice/voices of a narrator who is a pure utilitarian product of a recognizably Benthamite sort, as his epigraph.
6. The opponents of censorship who argue in terms of "collective fantasy" regularly make a version of this point. For them, being able to take offense is equivalent to feeling the immediacy of a pornographic situation, and the effort to censor is a disingenuous exercise in distancing oneself from something that couldn't be offensive without that felt sense of connection. Fantasy, in this view, is the glue that holds members of a community together and keeps them from being able to separate themselves from one another. What this position fails to take into account is the ways in which modern societies operate to create restricted communities that involve actions, and in which the case of someone like Linda Lovelace/Linda Marchiano would be of particular interest, since she did not claim that she didn't perform the acts that she appears to have performed in her pornographic performances but rather that she was performing them in the context of a community that didn't simply encourage those actions but elicited them as part of a seamless process of interaction.
7. Walter Kendrick, *The Secret Museum: Pornography in Modern Culture* (New York: Viking Penguin, 1987).
8. "Dancing in the Street" by Martha and the Vandellas is attributed to the Shirelles (40); "Cherish" by the Association is said to be a Lovin' Spoonful song (76); and "You Can't Always Get What you Want" by the Rolling Stones is identified as a Beatles song (371).
9. Drucilla Cornell, *The Imaginary Domain: Abortion, Pornography and Sexual Harassment* (New York: Routledge, 1995).
10. Ibid., 103 ff.
11. Ibid., 115 ff.
12. See my "Canons, Poetics, and Social Value: Jeremy Bentham and How to Do Things with People," *MLN* 110 (1995): 1148–64.
13. See Stanley Cavell, *The World Viewed: Reflections on the Ontology of Film* (New York: Viking, 1971), 25–29, for an account of stardom as providing a certain kind of portability for values achieved in a specific context.
14. See John McDowell, "Non-Cognitivism and Rule-Following," *Mind, Value, and Reality* (Cambridge: Harvard University Press, 1998), 198–218.
15. Dean E. Murphy, "Irresistible Lure of Subways Keeps Landing Impostor in Jail," *New York Times*, August 24, 2000.

16. Michel Foucault's *Discipline and Punish: The Birth of the Prison,* trans. Alan Sheridan (New York: Pantheon, 1977), is more crucial to my discussion of pornography than is his *History of Sexuality,* because the former basically describes the rise of the efficacy of utilitarian social structures as ways of shaping individual action while the latter treats the rise of the categorization of behaviors as perversions.

Index

Adorno, Theodor, 58, 166n2
American Psycho (Ellis), 25, 32, 146–56
Armstrong, Nancy, 29–30, 160n2, 167n15
Austen, Jane, 30, 129–30
Austin, J. L., 12, 159n10

Bakhtin, Mikhail, 30
Balzac, Honoré de, 103
Banfield, Ann, 175n11
Barrell, John, 166n1
Barthes, Roland, 22–23, 76, 85, 159nn17–18, 166n4, 169n20
Bataille, Georges, 76, 80, 82–83, 84, 168nn11–13
Baudelaire, Charles, 98, 99, 102, 103–4, 113, 172n8, 173n20, 173n29
Beauvoir, Simone de, 76, 80
Beccaria, Cesare, 64, 167n9
Bell, Andrew, 3, 109, 157n1, 173n30
Bentham, Jeremy, xiv, xv, xvi, 1, 3–5, 12, 13, 15, 17–25, 27, 32, 33, 54–55, 64, 71–72, 75, 109, 110, 151, 154–55, 157n1, 158n3, 159nn14–15, 165nn48–49, 167n1, 167n9, 173n30, 176n5
Bersani, Leo, 80, 83–84, 159n12, 164n32, 166n3, 169n16, 174n43
biopolitics, xiii
bio-power, 15, 156
Blanchot, Maurice, 76, 80, 82, 168n3, 168n10
Bouilhet, Louis, 101
Bourdieu, Pierre, 13, 99–100, 159n11, 162nn15–16, 172n9, 172n11
Bretonne, Restif de la, 14, 153

Burke, Edmund, xii, 86, 91, 93
Burstyn, Varda, 161n10
Butler, Judith, 157n2
Byron, George Gordon, 117

Carter, Angela, 77–78, 168n6
Castle, Terry, 163n28
Cavell, Stanley, 176n13
censorship, 10, 35–36, 42–44, 77
Champfleury (Jules Husson), 113
civil society, 58–59, 71, 80, 87, 94
Cobbett, William, xii
Colet, Louise, 101
comparison, xiv, xv, 16–17, 34
competition, 13, 25, 116, 123
Cornell, Drucilla, 154, 158n2, 176nn9–11
Cowley, Malcolm, 125, 127–29
Culler, Jonathan, 97
culture, xii–xiii, 78, 79, 80, 88, 95
custom, 75, 77, 80, 85, 87, 89, 91, 138

Davidson, Donald, 4, 158n4
Debbie Does Dallas, 11
deconstruction, xiii
Deep Throat, 51
delinquency, 17, 110
de Man, Paul, 166n1
Diamond, Sara, 41, 163n24
Dostoyevsky, Fyodor, 152, 176n5
Downs, Donald Alexander, 162n21
Doyle, William, 89–90, 170n25, 170n27, 171n39
Duggan, Lisa, 41, 163n25

Dworkin, Andrea, xi, xiv, 5, 14, 35, 36, 40, 41, 47, 50, 83, 88, 142, 157n3, 158n5, 163n23, 169n15, 169n22

Eagleton, Terry, 166n1
Eliot, George, 113
elite, xv, 26
Ellis, Bret Easton, 5, 7, 32, 146–56, 172n15; *American Psycho*, 25, 32, 146–56
English, Deirdre, 163n29

Ferguson, Frances, 167n16, 176n12
Fielding, Henry, 60, 130
Flaubert, Gustave, xii, 5, 6, 31–32, 96–124, 128, 156; *Madame Bovary*, 6, 25, 31–32, 96–124
Foucault, Michel, xii, xiii, xv, xvi, 1, 15–20, 22, 32, 62, 71–72, 76, 157n1, 157n4, 159n13, 159n15, 160n26, 165n49, 167n14, 174n30, 177n16
Fourier, Charles, 3, 22–23, 32, 156
Freccero, Carla, 172n15
Freud, Sigmund, xi, xvi, 79, 91, 117, 126, 127, 137, 149
Furet, François, 170n26

Girard, René, 31–32, 160n25, 174n42
Grice, H. P., 173n27

Hailsham, Viscount (Quintin McGarel Hogg), 134, 175n16
Halévy, Elie, 20, 110, 151, 159n16, 174n31, 176n4
Hartley, David, 110
Hollibaugh, Amber, 163n29
Hough, Graham, 142, 175n18
Hunt, Lynn, 168n8
Hunter, Nan, 41, 163n25

incest, 31, 75, 81, 92–93
Itzin, Catherine, 161n9

James, Henry, 102, 173n17
Jameson, Fredric, 166n1
John Thomas and Lady Jane (Lawrence; *Lady Chatterley's Lover*), 140–41
Jones, Colin, 170n25, 171n39

Joyce, James, 128
Justine (Sade), 6, 25, 26, 31, 57–74, 153

Kant, Immanuel, 19, 31, 58, 64, 73–74, 127, 162n12, 166n8, 167n13
Kappeler, Susanne, 47, 164n35
Keltie, John Scott, 171n40
Kendrick, Walter, 152, 176n7
Kermode, Frank, 30, 160n24
Koestenbaum, Wayne, 163n28
Kripke, Saul, 150–51, 158n4, 176nn2–3
Kutchinsky, Berl, 161n9

Lacan, Jacques, xiii, 70, 76, 167n13
LaCapra, Dominick, 97, 171n3, 172n4
Lady Chatterley's Lover (Lawrence), x, 6–7, 32, 125–45
Lamartine, Alphonse de, 97, 103, 172n5
Lancaster, Joseph, 3, 109, 157n1, 173n30
Laurent-Pichat, Léon, 96
Lawrence, D. H., xi, 5, 6–7, 32, 125–45, 156, 160n27; *Lady Chatterley's Lover*, x, 6–7, 32, 125–45
Lefebvre, Georges, 87, 169n21
Levin, Harry, 114, 174n40
Lévi-Strauss, Claude, 154–55
liberalism, xiii, 15, 37–38, 39, 40–45
Locke, John, 90, 110
Lovelace, Linda (Linda Marchiano), xi–xii, 46, 51, 164n31, 164n33, 176n6
Loyola, Saint Ignatius, 22–23, 156
Luhmann, Niklas, x, 157n1

MacKinnon, Catharine, x, xi, xiii, xvi, 1–2, 5, 25, 34–56, 83, 146, 157n3, 158n2, 158n5, 160nn1–7, 161n11, 161n18, 162nn18–20, 164n31, 164n36, 164n38, 165nn40–43, 165n45, 165n50, 165n52, 169n15, 169n18
Madame Bovary (Flaubert), 6, 25, 31–32, 96–124
Mapplethorpe, Robert, 159n7
Marx, Karl, xi, xvi, 5, 38, 108, 154–55
McDowell, John, 176n14
McKeon, Michael, 28–29, 160n21
merit, xv, 3–4, 20, 55, 93, 108, 109
Mill, John Stuart, xiii, 5, 10–11
Miller, D. A., 166n3

Index

Millett, Kate, 139, 175n17
Mindel, Saul J., 127
Minneapolis Ordinance, xiv, 40–41, 44, 160n1, 162n21
Montesquieu, Charles Secondat, Baron de, 61, 166n6
Morgan, Edmund S., 165n39
Morgan, Robin, 41, 163n22
Murphy, Dean E., 176n15

names, 7, 32–33, 86, 124, 124–25, 139–41, 143–47, 150, 151, 153
national debt, 31, 80, 89, 93–94, 171n40
Nietzsche, Friedrich, 63, 166n7
Nussbaum, Martha, 111, 174n34

Obscene Publications Act (1959), 126–27
obscenity, xiv, 27–28, 34
Ozouf, Mona, 170n26

Palmer, R. R., 169n23
Penguin Books, 133
performative, 3, 12, 157n2
Philosophy in the Bedroom (Sade), 6, 25, 75–95
Pillet, Auguste-Alexis, 96
Poe, Edgar Allen, 103, 113, 173n20
Polhemus, Robert M., 175n17
Porter, Katherine Anne, 133, 175n15
Posner, Richard, 48, 54, 160n7, 164n37, 165n47, 168n4
Post, Robert C., 161n8, 165n51

Rabelais, François, 103
Rancière, Jacques, xiii
Rawls, John, xii, 154, 162n16
relative value, xiv, xv, 1–3, 9, 13–15, 17–21, 23, 25, 30–31, 34
Rembar, Charles, 28, 158n2, 159n19, 174nn1–2, 175n4, 175nn6–8, 175n10
Revue de Paris, 96, 97, 106
Richardson, Samuel, 28, 30
Roiphe, Katie, 161n10
Rolph, C. H., 133, 163n28, 175n9, 175n14
Rorty, Richard, 52–54, 162n13, 165n44
Rousseau, Jean-Jacques, 15, 19, 86, 103, 151
Rubin, Gayle, 42, 163n26, 163n29

Sade, Donatien-Alphonse-François, Marquis de: x, xv, xvi, 5, 6, 11, 13, 14, 15, 22–24, 25, 26, 27, 31, 32, 33, 57–74, 75–95, 103, 117, 153, 166n5, 167n2, 167n10, 167n13; *Justine*, 6, 25, 26, 31, 57–74, 153; *Philosophy in the Bedroom*, 6, 25, 75–95
Saint-Beuve, Charles Augustin, 100, 101, 103, 172n13
Sartre, Jean Paul, 97, 98, 99–100, 102, 171n2, 172nn9–10
Schama, Simon, 168n8
Sedgwick, Eve, 174n42
Sénard, Jules, 97, 104, 122
sexual harassment, 34, 49–56, 84
Snitow, Ann, 41, 163n24
social recognition, 2–4, 14–15, 17–19, 24–25, 27
Steinem, Gloria, 163n27
Stewart, Potter, 7–9, 158n6
Stone, Lawrence, 91
style indirect libre, 96, 101, 102, 108, 111–15, 129–30

Tenderness (Lawrence; *Lady Chatterley's Lover*), 140
tort law, 26–27, 38–39, 57–58, 66–69, 71–72

utilitarianism, ix, xiv, xvi–xvii, 1–2, 13–14, 16–27, 29, 32, 34–35, 62, 96, 108–10, 111–12, 115–17, 121–23, 125, 154–55

Vance, Carole, 41, 161n10, 163n25

Watt, Ian, 28–29, 31, 160n20
Weber, Max, 61
Williams, Bernard, 10–11, 67, 159n8, 161n9, 164n34, 167n11, 175n5
Williams, Linda, 42, 158n6, 163n26
Williams, Raymond, xii–xiii; 157n2
Williams Committee on Obscenity and Film Censorship, 46, 159n8, 161n9, 164n34, 175n5
Wittgenstein, Ludwig, xi, 13, 17